To receive more than $1,000 in **FREE BONUSES** from leading Network Marketing experts and trainers (like Dr. Joe Rubino, Jim Rohn, Tom "Big Al" Schreiter, Terry Telford, and many others), please follow the simple three steps below. These **FREE** bonuses are intended to support the success of all network marketers in any company.

1. Purchase your copy of *The Ultimate Guide to Network Marketing* by Dr. Joe Rubino.

2. Visit http://www.thebusinessprofessional.com/bonuses and enter the number on your receipt proving your purchase.

3. You will receive in response an e-mail with complete instructions on how to claim your **FREE BONUSES** with no further obligation.

This is our way of thanking you for your purchase and for making a commitment to your Network Marketing success!

The Ultimate Guide to Network Marketing

37 Top Network Marketing Income-Earners Share Their Most Preciously Guarded Secrets to Building Extreme Wealth

Edited by
Dr. Joe Rubino

WILEY

John Wiley & Sons, Inc.

Published by John Wiley & Sons, Inc., Hoboken, New Jersey.
Published simultaneously in Canada.

For general information on our other products and services or for technical support, please contact our Customer Care Department within the United States at (800) 762-2974, outside the United States at (317) 572-3993 or fax (317) 572-4002.

Designations used by companies to distinguish their products are often claimed by trademarks. In all instances where the author or publisher is aware of a claim, the product names appear in Initial Capital letters. Readers, however, should contact the appropriate companies for more complete information regarding trademarks and registration.

Wiley also publishes its books in a variety of electronic formats. Some content that appears in print may not be available in electronic books. For more information about Wiley products, visit our web site at www.wiley.com.

Library of Congress Cataloging-in-Publication Data:

The ultimate guide to network marketing : 37 top network marketing income-earners share their most preciously guarded secrets to building extreme wealth / [edited by] Joe Rubino.
    p. cm.
  Includes index.
  ISBN-13 978-0-471-71676-1 (pbk)
  ISBN-10 0-471-71676-6 (pbk)
  1. Multilevel marketing. I. Rubino, Joe.
  HF5415.126.U38   2006
  658.8'72—dc22   2005006849

Printed in the United States of America.

10 9 8 7 6 5 4 3 2 1

This book is dedicated to the network marketing leaders, trainers, and experts who generously shared their most preciously guarded secrets and insights into what it takes to reach the top pinnacles of success in the network marketing profession. It is further dedicated to the millions of network marketers whose lives it will impact through those who achieve top levels of success by having utilized any of these principles.

CONTENTS

FOREWORD

Prospecting, following up, and enrolling—these are the three primary behaviors that most would agree support large-scale success in network marketing. But what are the key elements to doing these behaviors in a way that will provide the most productive results? And what of all the other elements necessary to achieve top levels of success in this profession, like effective training, leadership development, and personal growth strategies, to name just a few? Surely there must be thousands of critical topics one could write entire libraries about without totally exhausting the wealth of knowledge available on what is necessary to achieve great things in this industry. And each topic would likewise contain thousands of different approaches proven effective in the hands of different leaders, all intended to achieve the same goal—personal and financial freedom through network marketing.

So, does that mean you'd have to buy and read dozens or perhaps even hundreds of books to glean the wisdom of network marketing's top leaders? Not anymore. The most critical elements distilled from the combined wisdom of some of network marketing's top business builders and trainers are now available in one important book, this one. And who better to put such a book together than Joe Rubino?

Dr. Rubino has spent the past 15 years as a student of the twin disciplines of network marketing and personal development. He knows what works and has learned through actual field experience what does not. Unlike many networkers who subscribe to the philosophy that success comes simply from throwing enough mud against the wall and seeing what sticks, Rubino's approach is one that honors others. In his best-selling books such as *Secrets of Building a Million-Dollar Network Marketing Organization from a Guy Who's Been There Done That and Shows You How You Can Do It, Too* and *The 7-Step System to Building a $1,000,000 Network Marketing Dynasty: How to Achieve Financial Independence through Network Marketing*, you can read about an approach to success that requires building rapport, creating rich value, and looking with prospects to explore how our income opportunity can be a fit by contributing to their lives in some meaningful way. Rubino's way respects that network marketing may not be a fit for everyone. As more and more networkers follow these sound, honoring principles, both those prospects who see a fit for their lives, and more importantly, those who do not will be left feeling good about the experience. No pressure or coercion. No deceptive or dishonoring tactics. No arrogantly self-centered prospecting approaches, but rather listening, contribution, empowerment, and respect instead.

Rubino believes that we must put ourselves into personal development to maximize our effectiveness with others if we wish to see our businesses grow with maximum velocity and if we want all areas of our lives to work optimally. His approach is based on the assumption that our networking businesses will typically grow as rapidly as we do as people.

How do I know so much about Rubino's approach? For the past 15 years, I've worked personally with him, side by side as his business partner in creating a life-impacting network marketing dynasty. I've been a student with him and then a co-teacher, trainer, and success coach in our company, the Center for Personal Reinvention, founded to champion people to be their very best, be most successful in all they do, and live lives without regret.

But let me get back to the question of why Rubino's approach is so important to the future of network marketing and to each of our personal businesses. A business built on manipulation, imbalance, and self-centeredness will be both unlikely to last and unfulfilling at best. After all, isn't fun and fulfillment as important to success as finances?

So why is such awareness so important to the information contained within these pages? Because Rubino hand selected other top networking leaders who share this same respect for others and knowledge of what is needed to be ultra-successful in this business. These leading networkers were asked to take their vast knowledge of the most important factors to reaching the top levels of any company and distill them down to one chapter. Each of this book's contributors has expertise on some aspect crucial to achieving success in this business, and they have agreed to share these precious, guarded secrets with you, the reader, so that you may profit from their experiences.

Some of the contributors are experts at lead generation. That's what they do best. Some talk about values and how values are key to our success and fulfillment. Others offer insights about how to appeal to our prospects' most core values. Some are masters of enrollment, sharing their secrets of how to influence others with integrity. Others are adept at leadership development and share what it takes to champion ordinary people to believe in themselves so that others will believe in them as well and want to follow them. Some have a passion for people and personal development building skills and structures to support productivity and excellence.

In short, each has his or her own strengths and areas of expertise that will support your business-building efforts. None of us are as strong alone as we are by combining our strengths and sharing our insights so that we all may benefit. Just as a chain is only as strong as its weakest link, our networking businesses will be built to last only if all the foundational elements needed for long-term viability are present. This book speaks to each and every critical area necessary for accomplishment and duplication of that accomplishment.

What's more, by covering so many different areas of expertise, the book offers something of value for every reader to take and immediately apply to his or her business. When you consider what one solid tip can mean to your business-building efforts, ponder for a moment what a hundred break-through-generating tips can do.

I suggest you read and reread each chapter. Get clear about the specific ways you can take the pearls offered by each leader and employ them in your own business. Then commit to doing so. No matter how valuable any information or advice is, if not applied and put into action it will be little more than a good idea. Our great vehicle of network marketing has the power to create awesome lives of choice and freedom. Decide to take advantage of its power by devouring each insight offered and applying this wisdom to your business.

To your success,

Dr. Tom Ventullo
President, www.CenterForPersonalReinvention.com

PREFACE

hat are the secrets to building an ultra-successful network marketing business? If you were to ask 30 top distributors and industry leaders, you'd get 30 different answers with many areas of commonality. Each would also possess some totally unique insights into what it takes derived from their own field experiences that would not necessarily be shared by the others.

For more than 50 years, throughout the great profession of network marketing, the gift of a life-changing income, the opportunity to take part in fun and fulfilling work, and the chance to forever impact the lives of countless others has been shared by many top leaders and expert trainers in their own ways. Each of these extraordinary individuals has been successful in conveying the essential principles that have allowed their students (downline) to go out and touch the lives of countless others, creating wealth and with it, personal freedom in the process.

All of these experts, in building their personal fortunes through the vehicle of network marketing, have developed their own insights into what this process requires. And each has acquired some very special success distinctions that have supported their teams to duplicate their achievements to some degree. That is the very special gift that network marketing embodies: Those who reach top levels of accomplishment must have done so by supporting several others to duplicate their success and build networking dynasties of their own. No other profession better rewards its members for the exact levels of success they are able to convey to others. Networkers truly earn what they are worth!

Clearly, each of these networking gurus has much to share, as is evident by the wealth they have championed others to create and the lives they have forever influenced by sharing the awesome gift that networking can be. Many of these experts have written books, recorded tapes, conducted trainings, or otherwise shared their wisdom with others who have benefited from it. So, we asked ourselves the question: How powerful would it be if we could persuade each of these experts to share that one area of expertise they feel most significantly contributed to their own success and to that of their organizations and students? What if we could compile this cumulative wisdom in one book? What if we could share with others those special breakthroughs and closely guarded secrets that resulted in each of these gurus experiencing top-shelf accomplishment levels? Would we not then be able to create a synergistic effect, whereby 2 + 2 does not equal simply 4 but perhaps 40 or even 400?

And that's exactly what we did. As a leading network marketing distributor and trainer, I handpicked those I consider to be the best of the best, the most knowledgeable experts in the network marketing profession. I interviewed hundreds of top distributors, authors, and trainers. From this elite group, I selected these 36 distributors, trainers, and industry leaders and invited them to submit a chapter apiece containing the special wisdom they believe to be responsible for creating their own successful dynasties and those of their students. These leaders were instructed to share actual secrets and tips that they knew would support people to be successful if they utilized this knowledge. No untested or speculative theories, just proven pearls that would have a significant impact on the business-building potential of the book's readers.

The resultant topics you are soon to read about span every aspect necessary to build an ultra-successful network marketing business. They include such critical areas as visioning, prospecting, enrolling, training, building belief, creating personal development structures necessary for top success, and many more. Secrets in the realm of leadership development will be shared, as well as a wide variety of business-building techniques and pathways, from traditional to online building systems, from trade shows to direct mail to party plans. You'll read about the actual tools that these experts shared with their organizations, making them successful in the process. All the key success principles and other areas of focus necessary to build a top network marketing business will be revealed.

The result of this compilation of wisdom from these trainers represents hundreds, perhaps thousands of hours of private training sessions, many to this point shared only within their own companies and personal organizations. The sheer magnitude of the ideas led to this book's title: *The Ultimate Guide to Network Marketing*.

With a few notable exceptions, most network marketing books available today are anecdotal by nature. They share stories of individuals who have achieved success in the network marketing industry. These stories, while interesting and valuable, are no substitution for actual insights into how to build a top organization. To my knowledge, this is the first network marketing book written that gives readers a variety of different informed perspectives around what is necessary to achieve top success. It offers readers a wide variety of proven business-building techniques from many of the most successful network marketing leaders in the industry. It also offers the perspective of a great cross section of well-known top distributors and industry leaders who share the secrets they attribute to creating their own success.

To follow are 37 chapters outlining the core competencies necessary to build wealth while elucidating the leadership concepts that are of critical importance to building an ultimately successful organization.

In Chapter 1, Brian Biro shares how we can all create daily windows of opportunity to transform our lives and businesses. From deciding to live and work from a state of constant gratitude to paying attention to where you focus moment by moment, Biro supports us to pay keen attention to managing our thoughts if we want our businesses to grow and prosper. John Terhune, CEO of Rainmaker Consulting, expands upon this concept as he shares how top success always begins with the proper attitude. He gives step-by-step instructions about how to craft your winning attitude necessary to attract others to you like a magnet. Master motivational speaker Jim Rohn continues on this theme by discussing the qualities he sees as essential to any networker's success. He shares how anyone can start a business with no capital as long as the entrepreneur possesses these critical components.

Cliff Walker, top distributor and industry trainer from England, shares the nine key tasks that make up his winning strategies for duplicating network marketing achievement. See how well you measure up in each of these nine areas by taking Cliff's quiz to clarify where you stand. Shore up any lacking areas, and your business will be back on track. Mark Stevens, CEO of a very successful network marketing company, talks about the power of a great system and why the system is the key factor that can keep distributors on the right track headed toward fulfillment of their dreams. He outlines all the essential components of the system he teaches to his own company's distributors.

Dave Klaybor has been both the CEO of a successful network marketing company and a top distributor. He discusses how our behaviors are shaped by our thoughts and other critical factors. When we are able to recognize what's missing in this critical cycle, we can put it into place to ensure that our behavior will result in the accomplishment of the objects we desire. Glenn and Marian Head of an industry leading magazine, *Networking Times*, outline what the vital signs of a healthy business are. Put your life and business to the test and see how you measure up.

Of course, if you ask any successful networkers, most will tell you that a rock-solid belief level must form the foundation for all accomplishment. Master motivator Steve Siebold discusses the importance of mental toughness. He tells us how we can master our emotions to create a productive business. Art Burleigh tells us why belief is so vital to our businesses and how to build it so that you are unshakable. Top distributor Dan Conlon lists the stages successful entrepreneurs must master if they are to build a business methodically. Learn what the essential components of each stage are and put any missing elements into place for your business.

Tom "Big Al" Schreiter, network marketing CEO, top distributor, best-selling author, and the funniest speaker in the industry, takes a humorous approach to conveying the importance of arming our distributors with the skills they'll need to overcome rejection and make effective presentations. Tom has a unique way of making this business simple and duplicable. Personal development legend Charles E. "Tremendous" Jones shares how we can develop a sense of urgency to move our lives and businesses in the right direction. His seven tremendous laws of leadership will put you on the path to success and fulfillment and have others want to join you in your business.

Master sales expert and motivational speaker Nido Qubein, talks about how anyone can master the art of persuasion. He breaks this skill down into 10 core components while helping you to categorize your prospect into one of eight personality types. Very informative! Speaking of the power of persuasion, network marketing company CEO and industry trainer Kim Klaver discusses the reasons why so many prospects or potential customers get turned off by our approaches. She shares some specific changes you can make to instantly come across as more attractive and authentic when speaking to others. Top distributor and network marketing company founder Kathy Coover outlines how passion must be at the center of our prospecting efforts. She shares how to clarify your passions, what questions to ask to support your prospects to clarify their reasons for joining, and how to apply these insights to create an effective plan of action.

Shannon Anima helps us clarify what our most important values are and then discusses how we can take advantage of these values to come across authentically while powerfully attracting others with the charisma that results from their realization that we are committed to championing their lives. Linda Avery takes this values conversation further, showing us exactly how we can identify what our prospects' most important values are. Linda provides us with an easy way to find a fit for our products or opportunity based on what we discover about others as we ask questions, develop rapport, and contribute value to them.

Brad Hager is a master of recognition. He tells us how and why to include this key tool to build a multimillion dollar business, as he has. Senior vice president Barry Friedman has championed his very successful company's growth by explaining the power of residual income. When your prospects clearly understand this concept as Barry presents it, they will want to join you in your business.

Acclaimed network marketing trainer and author of six books, Randy Gage shares how anyone can create a steady stream of new prospects. Randy reveals how we can support our new distributors to conduct effective, enrolling conversations that get their businesses off to a great start. Follow Randy's direct and indirect prospecting approaches and never experience a shortage of qualified prospects again. Art Jonak, known as the Larry King of network marketing, writes about the importance of creating a simple, effective method of operation to sponsor, train, and duplicate in order to move your business continually in a forward direction. Teach your team these simple, duplicable skills that make the most of company tools, and they will be much more bulletproof and well prepared to succeed in the networking game.

Beatty Carmichael is a master of creating network marketing systems that work. He shares how you can turn any prospect's "no" into the very reason that prospect ends up joining your team. His techniques build belief in even the most skeptical or reluctant prospects. Greg Arnold explains what top network marketing leaders are—and what they are not. See if you fit his definition of a leader. Leading distributor Nick Hetcher teaches us how to generate endless prospects in dozens of creative ways. Follow Nick's advice and you'll find prospects readily available who are qualified to join your business. Continuing on this endless prospects theme, Dr. Tony Alessandra, expert sales trainer and accomplished speaker, explains how to identify and enroll highly qualified sources of prospects. Forgoing the "three-foot rule," Tony shares how to target those centers of influence that can open the door for us to introduce our opportunity to the masses they influence. Romanus Wolter expands upon the art of effective prospecting by revealing how you can utilize "octopus networking" to extend your reach and build your business with velocity. Romanus is adept at showing us just how to create value and reel our prospects in.

But what if you are not interested in (or are incapable of) introducing your friends, family, or those you meet as you go about your day? Amy Posner is an authority when it comes to working the cold market. Amy shares how anyone can work an opportunity-seeker leads program effectively as part of an overall prospecting strategy. She discusses several forms of advertising, the use of scripts, and other components essential to working with strangers who want what you have. Chris Zavadowski is a master Internet marketer. Chris will reveal the seven most profitable Internet prospecting tools you can use to build your business totally online, if you so choose. But I warn you, these are cutting-edge, advanced secrets you won't easily find elsewhere. Great stuff!

Speaking of the Internet, Max Steingart has developed an entire Internet prospecting system using instant messaging. Whether you want to find a soul mate or your next network marketing superstar, Max shares how you can build your business by identifying prospects online and developing cyber-relationships that will lead to golden prospecting opportunities.

If Internet prospecting isn't your style, you may be interested in learning how Dr. Don and Mary Lou Vollmer utilize trade shows, booths, and fairs to introduce their income opportunity and product lines to hundreds or even thousands of qualified targeted prospects over a weekend. The Vollmers share their secrets about what you'll want to do to make this prospecting pathway a successful part of your standard method of operation. They explain how you can reach the top of your company's plan by working just one show a month and following up the interested prospects you generate during the rest of the month.

Still hungry for other ways to easily build your business? Listen to expert author and top distributor Jan Ruhe as she gives you all the details concerning how to build by hosting home parties. Jan shares the secrets that have resulted in her reaching her company's top position, making her one of the most successful women networkers in all of network marketing.

If the Internet, trade shows, and party plans aren't for you, perhaps direct mail may be just the thing. Master mailer Larry Chiappone discusses how he built a direct mail empire and how you can use this strategy to sell your products and find your networking leaders. You'll learn what all the key components to direct mail success are—from ads and headlines that work to mailing lists that put your offer in front of the right people.

No matter what methods you decide to utilize to attract your prospects, all your efforts will be in vain without proper, timely follow-up. Top networking leader Jeff Mack shares step-by-step how to prospect and follow up effectively. Mike Melia takes your business to a higher level by discussing the elements of visionary leadership. Learn the secrets to stepping into effective leadership as you inspire your team to work toward the accomplishment of their visions.

Industry trainer and top distributor Scotty Kufus teaches us the importance of posture in attracting others to us. He also invites us to trust and honor the process while adopting the proper perspective as we expect our impending success and take the actions necessary to realize it.

In any business, there are bound to be challenges that get in the way to impede your success. Top leader Ray Gebauer inspires us with an examination of how to overcome your stops, limitations, and fears that are preventing you from reaching your goals. Take on Ray's approach to problems while working on the areas that will support your personal power and you'll be well prepared to break through whatever obstacles may cross your path.

Finally, in the last chapter, I discuss the one essential component necessary for any distributor to inspire others, lead a team, and realize a shared vision of network marketing success—self-esteem. Learn how to be inspired by a compelling vision that propels you into action. Discover how to diffuse any limiting beliefs and transform negative thoughts instantly. See how acknowledgments and affirmations along with an effective personal development plan can champion your team to achieve new levels of success, fulfillment, peace, and happiness.

Consider this book to be a trusted resource outlining the various unique approaches utilized by top leaders to build their large networking organizations. It serves as a text of knowledge, loaded with wisdom to elucidate the many ways and essential techniques used successfully in building a large business. Due to the variety of ideas shared by the book's many contributors, it encompasses a broadly based perspective written to support entire network marketing organizations or downlines and actual network marketing companies to acquire and pass along sound, duplicable business principles.

You will notice that the book's tone and content stresses an ethical, high-road, honorable, values-based approach. It was compiled to support the network marketing profession in its continuing efforts to transform an often tarnished image due to the unscrupulous practices and policies of some distributors and companies that have opted for the expedient approach over one that is based on honoring others and leaving them with a good feeling about what we do. The book conveys a wide array of styles and business-building techniques, therefore offering something of value that will appeal to every network marketing distributor. In a rapidly changing age, most of the book's content is timeless and of extreme value to today's reader as well as those for decades to come.

Thank you for taking the initiative to learn from the book's masters. As you apply the insights and principles they reveal in these pages, you will be duplicating the components of mastery that will contribute to your business and life success. Enjoy the journey.

Yours in success and partnership,

Joe Rubino

Acknowledgments

Sincere thanks are extended to the following network marketing leaders and teachers for selflessly sharing their wisdom and know-how. Their generous contributions have made this book possible.

Dr. Tony Alessandra
Shannon Anima
Greg Arnold
Linda Avery
Brian Biro
Art Burleigh
Beatty Carmichael
Larry Chiappone
Dan Conlon
Kathy Coover
Barry Friedman
Randy Gage

Ray Gebauer
Brad Hager
Glenn and Marian Head
Nick Hetcher
Art Jonak
Charles E. "Tremendous" Jones
Kim Klaver
Dave Klaybor
Scotty Kufus
Jeff Mack
Mike Melia
Amy Posner

Nido Qubein
Jim Rohn
Jan Ruhe
Tom "Big Al" Schreiter
Steve Siebold
Max Steingart
Mark Stevens
John Terhune
Dr. Don and
    Mary Lou Vollmer
Cliff Walker
Romanus Wolter
Chris Zavadowski

Neither would this book have been possible without the assistance that Matt Holt, Micheline Frederick, Shannon Vargo, and others at Wiley have provided me.

About the Editor

D r. Joe Rubino is an internationally acclaimed network marketing and personal development trainer, a life-changing success coach, and a best-selling author of eight books and two tape sets on such topics as how to achieve top levels of network marketing success, step into personal and leadership development, restore self-esteem, and maximize business productivity. An acclaimed speaker and course leader, he is known worldwide for his work in leadership development; enhancing listening and communication skills; life, business, and network marketing coaching; and team building.

His best-selling books and tapes are currently available in 18 languages and in 47 countries. These include:

- *Secrets of Building a Million-Dollar Network Marketing Organization from a Guy Who's Been There Done That and Shows You How You Can Do It, Too*
- *The 7-Step System to Building a $1,000,000 Network Marketing Dynasty: How to Achieve Financial Independence through Network Marketing*
- *Restore Your Magnificence: A Life-Changing Guide to Reclaiming Your Self-Esteem*
- *The Magic Lantern: A Fable About Leadership, Personal Excellence and Empowerment*
- *The Power to Succeed, Book I: 30 Principles for Maximizing Your Personal Effectiveness*
- *The Power to Succeed, Book II: More Principles for Powerful Living*
- *10 Weeks to Network Marketing Success: The Secrets to Launching Your Very Own Million-Dollar Organization in a 10-Week Business-Building and Personal-Development Self-Study Course*
- "Secret #1: Self-Motivation" affirmations tape set
- *The Legend of the Light-Bearers: A Fable about Personal Reinvention and Global Transformation*

Financially free as a result of creating wealth through network marketing and retired from his very successful dental practice at the age of 37,

Dr. Rubino is the CEO of the Center for Personal Reinvention, www.Center
ForPersonalReinvention.com, an organization committed to the personal excellence and empowerment of all people. In December 1995 Dr. Rubino was
featured on the cover of *Success* magazine and in its cover story, "We Create
Millionaires: How Network Marketing's Entrepreneurial Elite Are Creating
Fortunes at Break-Neck Speed" for his ability to impact people's lives. He is a
certified success coach in life planning technology and the co-developer of the
life-changing course for network marketers, Conversations for Success, a program that provides participants with the tools to maximize their self-esteem,
productivity, and personal effectiveness with others. He is on the faculty of
Networking University, is a guest trainer for MLM Sales University, and provides training and coaching for dozens of leading network marketing companies and their distributors. He is widely published, having written more than
220 articles that have appeared in numerous business and professional publications. His vision is to personally impact the lives of 20 million people to be
their best and to shift the paradigm around resignation—that is, to show that
anyone can effect positive change in their own lives and in the lives of others
if they believe they can.

CHAPTER 1

Carpe WOO!

Brian Biro

Is it possible that your life, business, relationships, energy, health, and balance can flourish as never before, despite even the most difficult of circumstances? Is it possible for you to build supportive, high-performance teams, even with those people you're pretty certain God put on the planet to bug you? Is it really possible for you to have more fun, a greater sense of purpose, and genuine peace of mind in a world accelerating so quickly that there is more computer technology in your children's Christmas toys than in the Apollo spacecraft that went to the moon in 1969? And is it even remotely possible that your family can actually flourish with unstoppable love and connection, despite the seemingly endless distractions of television, the Internet, Madison Avenue, cell phones, traffic, malls, and instant messaging?

The answer to these enormous, vital questions is WOO YES! Stop reading right now and yell out the word "WOO!" Isn't that a *fun* word? Now, if anyone asks you what you've been reading and thinking about, put a big grin on your face, look them right in the eye, and say . . . you've got it! WOO!

WOO stands for something very special. It is the *window of opportunity*, and with every ounce of my heart and soul, I want you to know that we all share the most important, magical, and magnificent of all WOOs right now! Do you know what it is? It is *every precious moment*! Every precious moment is a WOO. What do I mean?

You never know if the next person you meet today may become your lifetime friend, just as you didn't know it when you met your lifetime friends. You never know if the next woman you meet in an elevator may become the most important business builder you've ever recruited! You never know if the next time you talk with your son, daughter, spouse, or friend, something you say in that conversation may be the one crucial thing they could not see without your eyes, and a life that was on its way down is instantly reignited. You never know if the next idea that pops into your head may have the same impact on your own life.

I had a high school counselor named Mr. Anderson who pulled me into his office in the ninth grade, sat me down, and with an intensity that surprised me because he was usually so lighthearted and jovial said, "Brian, a student like you only comes along about once every 10 or 15 years."

At that time, it was pretty likely he meant it in a bad way more than he meant it in a good way! You see, I was at a point in my life where all I really wanted was for everyone to like me. So I was playing the clown, not applying myself anywhere near my potential. But Mr. Anderson saw through all of that. What he really was saying to me in that moment was, "Brian, don't waste the gifts you've been given. Live *fully*. Put your heart into all that you do. When each day is done, know you've given all you had. That's what really matters in life."

And, you know, I *got* it! I would not be a part of this wonderful book right now had Mr. Anderson not seized that WOO so long ago! I never would have earned my way into Stanford University, never would have had my life move in the exciting directions in which it has flowed, and, most of all, would never have come together with my wife and children. The question is not "Is there a WOO?" There is! The real questions are: How many of those WOOs have we missed? And why do we miss them?

This chapter is about "seizing the WOO—*carpe* WOO!" As you learn to make the most of every precious moment, you will discover the secrets that will enable you to answer those enormous questions of life posed at the beginning of this chapter with a triumphant, resounding WOO YES!

CARPE WOO LESSON 1: WHAT YOU FOCUS ON IS WHAT YOU CREATE

Here's a fun little question. What color is a yield sign? When I ask this question in my seminars I always hear the audience call out, "Yellow." But many years ago the United States adopted the International Signage Standards, and the yield signs you and I have seen for all these years are not yellow. They are red and white!

I have a hunch you might be thinking something along the lines of, "Well, maybe they're red and white out there in Asheville, North Carolina, where you live, Brian. But not here!" That's exactly what I thought when I was in the audience at a seminar and was asked the question the first time. My answer was an immediate, "Duh . . . yellow!" But, son of gun, by the time I finished that seminar that day they managed to change every single yield sign I've seen ever since!

The truth is, we've seen thousands of yield signs. We very likely see the same yield signs almost every day when we drive our standard routes to work or school. And yet we haven't seen one of them for what's really there. Why?

The truth is we rarely use our vision to see! Instead we use our memory and our conditioning. The challenge is, when we use our memory to see, we don't see what's here now. We see the past.

Now, I hope you'll chuckle as I do every time I see a yield sign. But there are far more important areas in which to apply this understanding and use our present vision. Where does it really matter to awaken our true vision, and no longer depend on our memory to see?

I believe it's with *people*! Here's an example very close to my heart. My daughter Kelsey is 17 years old and drives her own car. The responsibility of driving has helped her feel more independent, confident, and mature. Yet every so often I treat her like an old yellow yield sign and look at her as if she's still 15. Every time I do, our relationship takes a step backwards and needs rebuilding.

The truth is—what we focus on is what we create! Those yellow yield signs were visual creations far more real to me than the actual metal and paint. The way we see ourselves and others determines the life we create and the messages we send to friends, family, and teammates. As you work with others building businesses with you, remember that one fresh idea, one unusual approach to breaking through a disabling habit, or one small victory can ignite exciting new momentum and results. Look for the best in others and you'll be much more likely to help create it!

CARPE WOO LESSON 2: IF IT'S NOT WORKING, TRY SOMETHING DIFFERENT

You've undoubtedly heard that the definition of insanity is doing the same thing over, and over, and over again—and expecting a different result! Yet how often does that silly definition perfectly describe our actions and choices? What habits do we continue to follow though the results they create are not only ineffective, but even painful, damaging, and self-defeating?

The more closely you look at this principle—if it's not working, try something different—the clearer it becomes that truly living its lesson provides a powerful WOO to ignite momentum where there once was stagnation, to transform adversity into exciting possibilities of benefit.

You need look no further than the light that's illuminating the room you're in right now as you read this book (unless you're outside on a sunny day) for shining proof of the power of this simple principle. The genius who developed the electric light, Thomas Edison, was the king of "if it's not working, try something different." Edison was the Michael Jordan, Tiger Woods, and Wayne Gretzky of innovation all rolled into one, with more than a thousand inventions and patents, more than any other individual in history. You'd think someone who produced such astonishing results must have had a tremendous academic background, yet Thomas Edison had only three months of formal education. In fact, by his late teens, Edison had lost all of his hearing in one ear, with an 80 percent loss in the other. What Edison lacked in formal education and auditory capacity he more than made up for in tenacity, flexibility, and an unstoppable commitment to continually learn and grow. When speaking about the work going on in his laboratory in Menlo Park, New Jersey, he growled, "Hell, there are no rules here—we're trying to *accomplish* something."

When it came to his deafness, he turned that supposed handicap into an important ingredient in his success. He used the silence associated with deafness to sharply enhance his powers of concentration. Edison spent more than four years and experienced some four thousand failed attempts to create a functioning incandescent lightbulb. But after each unsuccessful attempt, he adjusted and tried something different. After more than three years and three thousand failures, one of his top assistants asked the great inventor how he could stand all the failure and lack of results." Edison's reply offers a surefire recipe for a life of wonder, light, growth, and resilience: "Results? Why, man, I have gotten a lot of results. I know several thousand things that won't work."

The most important place to apply this principle is in facing and dealing with fear. Ultimately, all emotions in life fall into one of two foundational categories: love and fear. The instant you choose the loving side, you feel it in every cell of your body. It is unmistakable. Mind, body, and spirit are in harmony. Life, joy, energy, and peace fill you and you know with certainty that the choice you've made is right. The physiological, emotional, and spiritual response when you choose fear is every bit as striking. There is immediate and inescapable dissonance as if the wrong key is struck on the piano. Every single individual who has given up on building a network marketing dream did so because of some form of fear! Your job is to help them break through and move from fear to freedom, from failure to faith!

So remember—if it's not working, try something different! When you live this principle, you live with a constant sense of possibility because you know you can always try a new approach or strategy. Instead of feeling trapped as so many people do, you have a choice in every precious moment.

CARPE WOO LESSON 3: BE A WORLD-CLASS BUDDY THANKER

A great strategy for building an unbeatable team is to become a world-class buddy thanker. When you live with an attitude of gratitude, it becomes natural to catch others doing things right. But let me ask you an eye-opening question. Who are the people in our lives we tend to forget to thank the most?

I've asked this question in every seminar I've ever taught, and have always heard similar responses. The people we most often forget to thank are those to whom we are the closest—our spouse, children, parents, or the people we work beside every day. When triggered by the question, we see how easily we can fall into the habit of taking the people we love most for granted. We can rationalize that we don't need to tell the prized people in our lives how we feel about them because they should already know, but the end result of neglect is decay and diminution. The more we fall into the habit of taking others for granted and withholding our appreciation, the more disconnected we become from the countless blessings in our lives.

How do you reverse this downward cycle and become a world-class buddy thanker? The secret is found in the words *world class*. After all, isn't that the kind of business you'd like to build, one that was viewed as world-class?

Here's a fun and easy way to remember how to become a world-class buddy thanker. When you think of world-class amusement park entertainment, who do you think of? Usually the answer is Disney. When you think of world-class coffeehouses, who do you think of? Sure, Starbucks is at the top of the list. Now, when you think of world-class sports television, who do you think of? That's right, ESPN! How do you become a world-class buddy thanker? Easy . . . just remember ESPN.

The E stands for effort and energy. World-class buddy thankers bring higher levels of effort and energy to the way they express appreciation and praise. They are more heartfelt, creative, and vibrant. They seize the WOO to give third-party compliments that allow other key people to hear of the performance, adding a touch of extraordinary personal attention to the praise that makes it more special and memorable.

But the real key to mastering the E in ESPN is to thank people for their effort and energy, *not* just their results. The truth is, we don't control results. We control the effort, energy, and attitude we apply to work toward results. When you thank others for their effort and energy, guess what? They create more results! Why? Because now they are focusing on what they control rather than what they don't. In 27 years of coaching basketball at UCLA, the greatest coach in history, John Wooden, never used the words *winning* or *losing* with his players. Instead he taught them that success is the peace of mind that comes from knowing you've given the best of which you're capable. In other words, he focused his coaching on his players' effort and energy. That unique focus led to 10 National Collegiate Athletic Association (NCAA) championships. No other men's coach in college history has won as many as four! That same simple principle is here for you right now.

The S in ESPN stands for surprise. This is the least known and one of the most powerful leadership tools you have available to ignite others. Write personal cards to friends, teammates, clients, and family members expressing your gratitude and admiration even when it's not their birthday or anniversary. These expressions will delight the recipients, and they will once again know they are important. E-mail (which stands for energy mail!) and voice mail provide fantastic opportunities to give compliments and to say thanks. Create moments for the special people in your life by giving unexpected gifts, arranging surprise events, or simply holding spontaneous, unexpected award ceremonies. You will light up others and the result will be extraordinary loyalty, commitment, and fun!

The P in ESPN is the most important key to becoming a world-class buddy thanker. In fact, it is the ultimate secret to balance, connection, and trust. The secret centers around a simple, yet immeasurably profound, principle called being fully present.

Perhaps the most powerful way to understand this principle of being present is to look clearly at what it is not. Several years ago, when I was the vice president of a large training company, I became painfully aware of what it means to not be present. At that time, we were a family of three: my wife Carole, me, and our first daughter, Kelsey, who was five years old. Driven by an unrelenting, nearly suffocating feeling of being overwhelmed, I had fallen into the habit of reaching the office by 5:00 A.M. and not returning home until well after 6:00 in the evening. Many weekends I was away, teaching seminars around the country. Not once did I see my daughter get ready for kindergarten. Not once did I surprise her by picking her up from school to spend some special, unexpected moments together. I mistakenly convinced myself that I didn't have time. I had to be at the office first and had to put in more hours than anyone else. After all, I was driving myself for my family, wasn't I?

When I trudged wearily through the door at 6:30 each night, Kelsey ran to me the instant I appeared in the house. She threw her arms around me and told me how much she loved and missed me as she looked into my eyes with pure joy. She then began to tell me all about the wonderful things that happened to her all day—special, magical things that only happen when you are five years old.

And I missed it—I didn't hear a word she said. You see, when I walked in that door, my body showed up. But my mind, my heart, and my spirit were still back at the office. The most important people in my life were right there at home waiting for me, and I never really saw them or heard them when they most needed me because I was not present.

This went on for months until one morning as I drove in to work, I suddenly realized what my lack of presence was communicating to my wife and child. In that excruciating moment, it felt as if someone had bashed me full force in the stomach with a sledge hammer. It's been said, "What you do screams so loudly I can't hear a word you're saying." Nothing screams so loudly as our presence or lack of presence. Every evening when I marched blankly through my front door, my thoughts still focused on the day's events, I expressed to Carole and Kelsey much more clearly than through words that they were not as important as all those other matters. As I continued to drive that morning, all I could see in my mind were Kelsey's shining eyes so filled with love. I was overcome with suffocating feelings of remorse and loss. Sobbing uncontrollably, I finally recognized how many precious moments of connection I had lost with her and Carole by not being present. I understood for the first time that there was nothing more important to me than becoming a master of being fully present for those I love. It was time to make the choice to come home.

By being present, we let others know at a heart level how important they truly are. This is our greatest opportunity as parents, friends, professionals, and caring human beings. When others feel important they begin to live up to their potential. Our presence breathes faith, belief, and positive expectation into their souls. Without this presence, we cannot truly give.

Being present is not something you can fake. It is not a technique. It is a decision. Do you know whether someone is actually fully with you in mind, body, and spirit? Can you even tell over the phone? The answer is clear. We have a definite sense of whether others are right there with us, giving full concentration or drifting off and not truly connected. When we make the conscious and consistent decision to be fully present to the very best of our ability, we open ourselves to more joy than we've ever imagined and create the possibility to make the difference for which we were put on this earth.

Finally, the N in ESPN is simply to do it *now*. The street sign with the words "as soon as" leads directly to an endless loop called "never." Seize the WOO *now*! It is the one sure way to leave regret in the past. You may never pass this way again. If you knew you had only 24 hours left in your life, who are the people you absolutely could not leave before telling them how much you loved them, how much you appreciated them, and how much they mean to you? And my final question: What are you waiting for?

Remember: The past is history,
The future a mystery.
The gift is now—
That's why we call it the *present*!

Brian Biro is one of the nation's foremost speakers and teachers of leadership, possibility thinking, thriving on change, and team building. A major client who has had Brian back to speak several times offered perhaps the most on-target introduction about Brian's impact when he said, "Brian Biro has the energy of a 10-year-old, the enthusiasm of a 20-year-old, and the wisdom of a 70-year-old." He is the author of the internationally acclaimed *Beyond Success*, *The Joyful Spirit*, and *Through the Eyes of a Coach—The New Vision for Parenting, Leading, Loving, and Living*. A former corporate vice president, Brian was rated number one by more than 40 speakers at four consecutive *Inc.* magazine international conferences. With degrees from Stanford University and UCLA, Brian has appeared on *Good Morning America*, CNN's *Business Unusual*, and the Fox News Network. He lives in Asheville, North Carolina with his wife Carole and their beautiful daughters, Kelsey and Jenna.

Visit www.BrianBiro.com to learn about Brian's presentations and seminars and to order his many empowering products. You can reach Brian by phone at (828) 654-8852, by fax at (828) 654-8853, or by e-mail at bbiro@att.net.

CHAPTER 2

Bring the Right Attitude to Your Network Marketing Experience

John Terhune

Having spent a decade of my life in the field building downline organizations, I feel comfortable in telling you that it is impossible to build a successful organization without a consistent, fantastic attitude that inspires others to do what they would not have done without you as an attitude role model. Let's face something right now. Network marketing is more about failure and stumbling than it is about victories and the fast track. Don't be discouraged by that description from a field-tested veteran. Rather, understand that struggle and failure are a part of success in any great endeavor. Don't shy away from that aspect of success. Embrace it and know that the development, maintenance, and protection of a great attitude can dramatically enhance your likelihood of a major life victory in network marketing. Here is why.

One of the most powerful resources available to human beings is their attitude. A person's attitude touches in a positive or negative way every part of one's life. It affects people's relationships, their physical and mental energy, their stamina, their self-image, their work habits, their willingness to try something new and challenging, their ability to deal with stressful situations, their degree of happiness, and of course their ability to achieve beyond their current circumstances. Give me a distributor with average talents and a great attitude any day over the enormously talented person with a bad or even an average attitude. Of all the physical and mental traits possessed by human beings that will separate one person from the next, attitude stands alone as the great divider between average performance and peak performance. Men and women who truly work at creating and then protecting a great attitude will ultimately achieve far more than the person who does not understand the vital nature of this ingredient of success.

So what exactly is a positive attitude? How does one acquire it? Based on both my field and consultant perspective, I would say a positive attitude is a disciplined decision of the mind to maintain a consistently confident expectation of good results. In essence, it is faith in a bright present and a brighter future. It is a decision to believe that God is in your corner desiring to bring about your ultimate well-being even though your current circumstances may not be the best. A positive attitude is not, as some think, psyching yourself up in the hope that your fairy godmother will come to your rescue by dropping the dream downline in your lap. The proper mental outlook is based on faith.

You should regard your attitude as an enormously valuable asset that deserves and demands careful protection. After all, you lock your valuables in a safe at home or you store them in a safe-deposit box at the bank. When you leave your house you probably turn on your alarm system to protect your tangible assets. However, did you ever stop to think that you could acquire them 10 times over if you develop and maintain the right attitude? Just about every network marketer can sustain a positive mind-set when things are going well, and we are all prone to discouragement when things are not going so well. I will share a secret to success in life and especially in your network marketing venture. One of the secrets of being happy is learning how to keep your attitude from being on a constant roller coaster. Anyone can be up when your business is on a roll. How high do you feel when that prospect who you know will go into massive action promoting your opportunity gets in and gets growing? Anyone can be down when adversity strikes. How low do you feel when that person quits two weeks later? The person who survives to achieve success in network marketing is the person who is up when the average person is down.

You must discipline yourself to understand that you are the sole proprietor of your mental outlook. There are innumerable issues that present themselves each and every day that conspire to pollute your positive attitude: difficult family relationships, money troubles, unhappy distributor/associates, rude customers, and the business environment. Have you ever gone through the day suspecting that your world is in a massive conspiracy to steal your attitude? If you allow the circumstances of life or your business to determine your attitude, the circumstances of life or your business *will* determine your attitude. The only thing that separates victory from defeat at these critical moments is a disciplined, positive attitude that has been purposefully developed. A positive attitude is a personal decision to believe the best about you, your organization (both upline and downline) and the potential that your dreams will come true. It is a mental step of faith.

I know that maintaining a positive attitude isn't always easy. It demands continual vigilance. You cannot fly on autopilot here. You have to work on it every day. But there are few things in life that will pay you greater dividends than a fantastic attitude.

Now that we have defined what a great attitude is, let's talk about how to develop one. Allow me to emphasize something right now. I believe that one of the greatest things someone could ever say about me is, "He has a phenomenal attitude." You will get the attention of other human beings, both prospects and distributors, if you exude a great attitude. A great attitude gets noticed in a positive way, just like a negative attitude gets noticed in a negative way. I don't care if it's in your church, in your workplace, during family time or recreation time, or when you are building your network marketing opportunity; you will shine brighter and create far more opportunities in life if you exhibit a great attitude. Keep in mind also that the best way to raise the attitude of the people around you is to exude a great attitude yourself.

One of my goals in interacting with people is that they feel better about themselves and life in general by the time I leave them than when I started out our interaction. That is one of the reasons that I was able to make millions of dollars in network marketing. My attitude constantly acted as a beacon of hope for those around me. People wanted to be around me because I was charging their attitude by my attitude. That is impossible to do without a great attitude that sings out, "I'm happy about who I am, where I'm going, and my expectations of the future."

How do you create this great attitude that will be the foundation for a continuous path to achievement? Work hard at feeling good about yourself. I cannot begin to tell you the impact that how you feel about yourself will have on your attitude. Your view of yourself actually creates the basis for your attitude. If you feel fat, if you don't respect yourself because of your lack of discipline, if you don't have confidence in yourself because of the poor way you handle difficult times that come across your path, if you don't have a sense of worth and believe deeply in your integrity, it is literally impossible to have the type of attitude that will be described as a great or winning attitude. Conversely, if you feel good about the way you look, if you have an inner confidence resulting from the fact that you exercise self-discipline that you know separates you from the next person, if you have a silent but abiding confidence in the way you handle difficult situations, if you know that within you is a reservoir of determination that will get you through any challenge and that you are person of high integrity, then a great attitude is a natural extension of this view of yourself. Every day presents a new opportunity to create a positive experience that merits a deepening sense of self-confidence and thus a great attitude. You have total control from this moment forward to determine the view of yourself. It takes time, but you can establish an entirely new foundation of trusting your instincts for success, making the right decisions, taking chances, preparing, practicing, preserving, and winning—doing whatever it takes for you to develop that unconscious swagger that comes from a solid belief in your own potential. As you can tell, the ability to exhibit a great attitude has an enormous amount to do with your self-image.

What actions can you take to make sure that this building block to a great attitude is in place? First, get on a regular program of exercise and proper diet. The better physical shape you are in, the easier it is to feel good about yourself. I interact with people differently when my waistband feels loose than when it feels tight. Feeling good about yourself physically puts a special bounce in your step and leads to the confident swagger that is a trait gained by every person who has ever succeeded in network marketing. A great attitude is much more likely to grow in the fertile soil of feeling good about your physical presence. Remember, you are not selling a product or a company when you are talking with someone about getting involved in your business; you are selling you.

A regular exercise and eating regimen takes discipline. Anytime you exercise self-discipline you are waging war with the voice inside that wants you to take the path of least resistance and least pain. It is the same voice that opts for the easy way out. We tend to avoid pain and seek instant gratification. The more you wage that battle and the more you win that battle, the better you will feel better about yourself. Personal self-discipline builds character, which leads to a better self-image, which will become a foundation for the creation and maintenance of a great attitude.

The second action you can take is to hang around people who will be a fertile ground for a great attitude. Most of us reflect and adopt the attitudes of those with whom we associate regularly. Bad company corrupts good morals, the proverb reads. In the very same way, associating with people who are consistently negative will corrupt a good attitude. This is especially true when you are seeking to build a successful network marketing organization. The world is full of the negative voices that will spend the day telling you what you cannot do and why you cannot do it. Let's remember our experience as a parent and apply it to our lives as professional networkers.

I happen to be in the wonderful time in life where I have two teenagers at home. I choose to commute to work 100 miles each way each day instead of moving because both of my teenagers have a great circle of friends and associates, in my mind a big reason they are both staying on the straight and narrow. The lesson here is simple. We know the effect that a bad relationship can have on our children's behavior. We guard that aspect of their lives zealously because we know the effect of a good positive relationship versus a bad negative relationship.

I encourage you to be just as zealous in choosing your relationships because they will have a dramatic effect on your attitude. Have you ever been around someone who acted like a drain on your battery because they were always complaining and seeing the negative in everything? When you start your conversation with them your battery is pretty charged, but by the time you leave them it is run down. Conversely, have you ever been around anyone whose positive view of the world and the circumstances of their life just inspire you to the point that they radiate a positive energy? I know you are thinking of people who fit both of these descriptions. You can't afford to be around people who drain your battery and expect to create and maintain a great attitude. You need to associate with people who charge your battery, not drain it. Who you associate with is your choice, set every day. Making good decisions will add another valuable brick in the foundation necessary to exhibit a great attitude.

Write down the names of the five most positive persons you know. These people leave you feeling different—charged, optimistic, and expecting great things. Now let's have you visit the other side of the coin. Write down the names of the five most negative persons you know. These people don't leave you feeling the same, either; they leave you feeling drained. Their very nature leaves you with less air in your balloon than when you first got together. Now write down next to the 10 names how much time you typically spend with each of them. Here is what this exercise is all about. I want you to visually see with whom you are spending your time and with whom you *should* be spending your time. Some of these relationships will by their nature leave less room for your ability to reduce or maximize your interaction. However, keep in mind as you are building your organization, more people quit network marketing in their first month because of the negative naysayer than for any other reason. From this point on I encourage you to maximize the time spent with those persons who charge your battery and minimize the time spent with those persons who drain your battery. You will be pleasantly surprised at the positive effect this will have on your ability to create and maintain a great attitude. Here is a valuable tip, the moment you surrender ownership of your attitude to circumstances or to another person, you compromise its power in your life and you risk its loss.

Third, it is critical for you as a network marketing entrepreneur to read and listen to positive information in an effort to fill your mind with information that lends itself to the creation and maintenance of a great attitude. Develop an insatiable appetite for positive mental nutrition. If you are going to succeed in building an organization, you must set this example. You should view your travel time as attitude maintenance time. Think about the hours you spend every year in your car. What if you made a mental decision to make this personal time, personal growth time, and attitude maintenance time? How many hours did you waste last year listening to some silly radio station that had no impact on the incredible asset called your attitude? Our minds need positive input every bit as much as our bodies do. If we feast on a diet of positive mental food on a daily basis, our minds react favorably and support our cause with a high degree of energy and resilience. And the best thing about this diet is that you don't have to count calories. The more positive mental input you take every day, the better. If you want to have the type of attitude that is the foundation for achievement, make a decision that your mental state of mind is as important as or more important than your physical well-being. Take care of it. Read about inspirational people and the attitudes they exhibited on the way to their great accomplishments. Get into the heads of people who have accomplished what you are seeking to accomplish by listening to CDs, reading books, subscribing to newsletters, going to seminars, whatever it takes to put you in a mode of continuous growth and getting better.

Make a decision that the person you are going to be next month will be better and possess a better attitude than any person that you are this month. The critical part of this habit set is that you are setting an example for the people in your organization. I made a mental decision early in my network marketing experience that I was going to be in a personal growth mode for the rest of my life. I viewed personal growth as a life long journey with no end.

Fourth, dare to dream about a better tomorrow. In other words, live with an attitude of expectation; have a purpose. People who are on a mission and seeking to accomplish great things find having a great attitude much easier because they have a high degree of expectation of tomorrow. That is one of the reasons why you find people in network marketing to be far more positive as a general rule than the people you work with in your job. Most of the people you work with are resigned to the fact that this is as good as it gets. They have no real power in the present because they don't have great hope for the future. If you know that tomorrow is going to be no better than today it's hard to be optimistic and it's hard to have a great attitude about tomorrow.

I meet many people who are trying to achieve goals but face a problem that can be clearly defined: They have not tied the desires of their heart to the activity that they are about to undertake. They just don't have the right mental attitude to be effective. You must maintain a positive perspective by reconnecting to your dreams on a daily basis. Allow your vision of success to act in the same way as a ground wire does for a lightning rod. Think of your mind as the lightning rod. The negative things that inevitably occur in life and business strike at your thoughts just as the lightning strikes the lightning rod. But no matter how powerful the bolt, its force is neutralized because the ground wire carries the negativity away harmlessly. Throughout your life, and particularly in your network marketing experience, bolts of lightning will strike at you. You will experience setbacks and failures. Faced with crushing disappointment, the average person is rocked back on his or her heels. Many never recover. That is why the attrition rate in network marketing is so high. Most people's threshold for total discouragement is low because they don't have the quality of attitude that will sustain them through the tough moments. They quietly sink into the quicksand of despair and ultimate defeat. However, if you have a dream you are pursuing passionately, you will have a far deeper ability to be resilient in your response to situations that would otherwise affect your attitude in a negative way.

Fifth, have a personal mission and values statement that will allow you to reconnect with your vision for your life. I strongly encourage you to create written statements that spell out who you are and what you want your life to become and keep them close at hand for regular review. When setbacks have left you momentarily disheartened, pull out your written statements and remind yourself of the person you are and of the emotionally compelling vision you are working to achieve. This will help you refocus on your ultimate destination and reconnect with your passion. My heart goes out to those people who get up in the morning with no vision for their lives. There is such an incredibly powerful energy available to those who see a golden vision of what they want their lives to be. They spring out of bed in the morning and they renew the quest to make that dream a reality. This again is a key area where you must set an example for the organization that you are building. Don't expect your people to take the time to commit their vision to writing or to create a compelling values and mission statement if you don't take the time to do so.

Sixth, live life with passion. People follow people, not companies, and ultimately people follow passionate people. I have lived a life passionately of the pursuit of my dreams. I've also known a life in the pursuit of a paycheck. I would choose to passionately pursue my dreams any day because that is when I am most alive and when I exhibit most consistently a great attitude. I've been blessed with the exhilarating feeling of waking up in the morning, every morning, with an exciting vision of a greater day. I briefly lost that sensation near the end of my law career, and that's when I knew it was time to move on to something else. When you have crafted a compelling dream and you are engaged in the passionate pursuit of that dream, you glow with purposefulness. It is rare that the pack will exhibit passion or dream to a greater extent than its leader. Dream big and chase your dream with extreme passion. You will be duplicated.

Finally, develop an attitude that makes you unstoppable. Can you imagine waking in the morning knowing in your heart and in your soul that if you decide to put your mind to a task it is all but done? You talk about a swagger. When you have an attitude that you are unstoppable, you *can't* be stopped. I have had the great fortune to have that attitude since I've been a very young man. When I decided I was going to go to law school and become a trial lawyer and when I decided to win the national trial competition, I was unstoppable. Nothing was going to get in my way. When I became a trial lawyer and I decided to win cases, 232 times out of 241 times I was unstoppable. Despite the fact that I lost 9 of the 241 cases that I tried, I went into every single one of them with the attitude that I knew where I was going and by golly I was going to get there. When I involved myself in the network marketing sector and decided to develop an organization that would create sufficient residual income to be financially independent, I was unstoppable. It simply did not matter if the next person said yes or no or if the next person engaged as a business builder. I had a mission that I was going to accomplish. A very wise person once stated, "Don't ever get in the way of a man or a woman who desires something with all of their heart that they have decided they will have, whatever it takes . . . because they will run you over like a blade of grass." Being unstoppable is an attitude.

The quality of your life will be measured by your attitude. The degree of success that you enjoy in this wonderful business sport called network marketing will have everything to do with the attitude that you bring to your network marketing experience. Decide that your mission every day is to be in a constant state of developing, maintaining, and protecting one of the truly great assets of your life—your attitude.

To learn about further products or services offered by John Terhune or his company, Rainmaker Consulting Services, visit the web sites www.attitudepump.com, www.rainmakerconsultingservices.com, or www.thetrueentrepreneur.com, or e-mail Mr. Terhune at jterhune@rainmakermail.com.

CHAPTER 3

Nine Things More Important Than Capital for Achieving Network Marketing Success

Jim Rohn

Capital in your network marketing business isn't what matters. It isn't the money that buys you a future; it's your skills that buy you a future. Money and no skills, I'm telling you, you are still poor. Money and no ambition, where are you? Money and no courage, you're broke. A little bit of money and a whole lot of courage is all we need.

When looking for people, don't always look for the ones with money. Money doesn't matter. What matters is somebody's willingness, somebody's ingenuity, somebody's willingness to try. If they have a dollar to invest, that's plenty for me. A dollar and some ambition and I can show you how to get rich, and it will be one of the classic stories of the company. When I was recruiting somebody and they would say, "I don't have any money," I'd say, "I've been looking for you for six months! Let me show you how to do it without any money."

Because here are the rules of capitalism: You can either buy and sell or, if you are in certain circumstances, you can sell and buy. That is, if you've got ambition. Now, if you haven't got ambition we can't cure that, and money can't cure lack of ambition, either. But if you have a dollar and some ambition I will show you how to get rich. Even if you don't have a dollar I will show you how to get rich, because you can sell and buy. Somebody says, "As soon as the product arrives I'll sell it." No, no, you don't understand. You don't understand the magic of fortune if you say I have to wait till the product gets here. And you probably don't understand the value of your own story.

By selling and buying you are simply sharing from your own excitement and belief about the product and the opportunity. Once the customer says yes, ask for the money and then go get the product. After doing this three or four times, you will be able to buy and sell, but never let money keep you from an opportunity when you have in its place true ambition, faith, and courage.

So, let's recap and break it down a bit further. When starting any enterprise or business, whether it is full-time or part-time, we all know the value of having plenty of capital (money). But I bet we both know or at least have heard of people who started with no capital who went on to make fortunes. This is particularly true in the network marketing profession. I believe there are actually some things that are more valuable than capital that can lead to your entrepreneurial success in building a thriving network marketing business. Let me give you the list.

1. *Time*. Time is more valuable than capital. The time you set aside not to be wasted, not to be given away. Time you set aside to be invested in an enterprise that brings value to the marketplace with the hope of making a profit. Now we have capital time.

   How valuable is time? Time properly invested is worth a fortune. Time wasted can be devastation. Time invested can perform miracles, so you invest your time.

2. *Desperation*. I have a friend named Lydia whose first major investment in her new network marketing business was desperation. She said, "My kids are hungry, I've got to make this work. If this doesn't work, what will I do?" So she invested $1 in her enterprise selling a product she believed in. The $1 was to buy a few flyers so she could make a sale at retail, collect the money, and then buy the product wholesale to deliver back to the customer.

   My friend Bill Bailey went to Chicago as a teenager after he got out of high school. And the first job he got was as a night janitor. Someone said, "Bill, why would you settle for a night janitor job?" He said, "Malnutrition." You work at whatever job you can possibly get when you are hungry. You go to work at something—night janitor, it doesn't matter what it is. Years later, Bill is a recipient of the Horatio Alger award. He's now rich and powerful and one of the great examples of lifestyle that I know. But his first job—night janitor. Desperation can be a powerful incentive when you say, "I must."

3. *Determination*. Determination says "I will." First Lydia said, "I must find a customer." Desperation. Second, she said, "I will find someone before this first day is over." Sure enough, she found someone. She said, "If it works once, it will work again." But then the next person said no. Now what must you invest?

4. *Courage*. Courage is more valuable than capital. If you've got only $1 and a lot of courage, I'm telling you, you've got a good future ahead of you. Courage in spite of the circumstances. Humans can do the most incredible things no matter what happens. Haven't we heard the stories? There are some recent ones from Afghanistan and Iraq that are

some of the most classic, unbelievable stories of being in the depths of hell and finally making it out. You can't sell humans short. Courage in spite of, not because of, but in spite of. Now once Lydia has made three or four sales and gotten going, here's what now takes over.

5. *Ambition.* "Wow! If I can sell 3, I can sell 33. If I can sell 33, I can sell 103." Wow. Lydia is now dazzled by her own dreams of the future.

6. *Faith.* Now she begins to believe she has got a good product. This is probably a good company. And she then starts to believe in herself. Lydia, single mother, two kids, no job. "My gosh, I'm going to pull it off!" Her self-esteem starts to soar. These are investments that are unmatched. Money can't touch it. What if you had a million dollars and no faith? You'd be poor; you wouldn't be rich. Now here is the next one, the reason why she's a millionaire today.

7. *Ingenuity.* Put your brains to work. Probably up until now, you've put about one-tenth of your brainpower to work. What if you employed the other nine-tenths? You wouldn't believe what can happen. Humans can come up with the most intriguing things to do. Ingenuity. What's ingenuity worth? A fortune. It is more valuable than money. All you need is a $1 and plenty of ingenuity. Figuring out a way to make it work, make it work, make it work.

8. *Heart and soul.* What is a substitute for heart and soul? It's not money. Money can't buy heart and soul. Heart and soul are more valuable than a million dollars. A million dollars without heart and soul, you have no life. You are ineffective. But heart and soul are like the unseen magic that moves people, moves people to buy, moves people to make decisions, moves people to act, moves people to respond.

9. *Personality.* You've just got to spruce up and sharpen up your own personality. You've got plenty of personality. Just get it developed to where it is effective every day no matter who you talk to—whether it is a child or a businessperson, whether it is a rich person or a poor person. A unique personality that is at home anywhere. My mentor Bill Bailey taught me, "You've got to learn to be just as comfortable, Mr. Rohn, whether it is in a little shack in Kentucky having a beer and watching the fights with Winfred, my old friend, or in a Georgian mansion in Washington, D.C., as a senator's guest." Move with ease whether it is with the rich or with the poor. And it makes no difference to you who is rich or who is poor. Each offers a chance to have a unique relationship with whomever. Develop the kind of personality that's comfortable, the kind of personality that's not bent out of shape. And lastly, let's not forget charisma and sophistication. Charisma with a touch of humility.

This entire list is more valuable than money. With $1 and the list I just gave you, you can harness the power inherent in the vehicle of network marketing and the world is yours. It belongs to you, whatever piece of it you desire, whatever development you wish for your life. I've given you the secret. Capital. The kind of capital that is more valuable than money and that can secure your future and fortune. Remember that you lack not the resources.

Jim Rohn is the 1985 recipient of the coveted Council of Peers Award for Excellence (CPAE) in speaking as well as the 2004 recipient of the Masters of Influence Award from the National Speakers Association and is the author of more than 25 books, audiotapes, and video programs.

Jim has been hailed over the years as one of the most influential thinkers of our time. He has helped to motivate and train an entire generation of personal development trainers as well as hundreds of executives from America's top corporations. Jim has been described as everything from a master motivator by Mark Victor Hansen; a national treasure by Vic Conant; one of the most profound thinkers and mind-expanding individuals of our time by Les Brown; one of the most articulate, powerful, thought-provoking speakers ever seen by Harvey Mackay; an extraordinary human being and mentor by Anthony Robbins; all the way to a modern-day Will Rogers by Tom Hopkins and a legend by Nido R. Qubein.

To subscribe to the free Jim Rohn's Weekly E-Zine go to www.jimrohn.com and also receive 20 to 60 percent off on all books and tapes.

CHAPTER 4

Creating a Winning Strategy for Your Network Marketing Business

Cliff Walker

n the excitement to launch a potentially lucrative business, the temptation is to take a "fire, ready, aim!" approach and dive right in. But if you don't take a good look first and account for what lies below the surface, you could be setting yourself up for a painful experience.

One of the wonderful things about network marketing is that the most important factor in the success equation is the person running the business—you. You don't need a lot of money or fancy office space or great connections to make a go of it. What you do need, however, is a plan that enables you to make the most of the resources in your possession.

There is no magic formula or instructions carved in stone for putting together a strategy. The major task of a strategy, however, is to establish a clear purpose and direction for your business. In this chapter we will learn about the nine key tasks that need to be completed in order to construct and customize your own strategy. The nine key tasks fall into nine areas and are:

1. *Life priorities.* Clearly state the priorities that are important to you as you look to the future.

2. *Purpose.* Clearly state your reasons for building the business, your overall purpose, and what you are striving to achieve.

3. *Vision.* Create a vision of what you want your future to be and communicate it to everyone associated with your business.

4. *Core values.* Identify your core values and use them to drive behavior and as the criteria for decision making.

5. *Core skills.* Identify your core skills and the skills that are required for success. Leverage these skills to establish competitive advantage in the marketplace.

6. *Marketplace*. Examine the marketplace in which you operate, determine the threats and opportunities, and then select target markets to capitalize on. Be clear about how you intend to penetrate your chosen markets.

7. *System*. Ensure the provision of a system that meets the needs of your team in the markets where you will be required to support the implementation of your business strategy.

8. *Key interfaces*. Identify key internal and external interfaces, assess their impact on your business, and develop effective strategies to determine and address their needs and interests.

9. *Key resources*. Identify the tangible and intangible resources that are key to your business, and ensure an adequate supply of them.

Individuals vary in how far along they are in the development of the key areas. Most of us like to focus on what we're best at and maybe take care of the rest as we go along. We should, in fact, pay the closest attention to the areas where we are weakest; for it is here that our strategy is in the most danger of coming apart.

The questionnaire that follows is designed to help you assess where you are in the different areas needed for a coherent strategy and identify just where it is you need to focus. Once the questionnaire is completed and you have a good general picture of where you are, the rest of the chapter will address each of the nine key tasks in turn.

STRATEGY QUESTIONNAIRE

This simple questionnaire is designed to help you assess how far along you are in the development of a complete strategy for your network marketing business. The score you give yourself after completing it does not reflect how well or how poorly you are doing. Indeed, it is possible to be very successful with no strategy at all in place (though rare). The intent is to help you get started in the process, or flesh out what you have already done, and call attention to the areas you can key in on in order to make your business more successful.

Be sure to respond to every statement and be completely honest in your answers. Remember, the aim here is not to grade you, but to assist you in reaching your goals. Beginning with the first two questions, each pair of questions corresponds to one of the nine areas listed earlier, in the order given.

Instructions

Read each statement carefully, then circle a number below it according to how much you agree or disagree. 1 = Disagree completely, 2 = Disagree somewhat, 3 = Neither agree nor disagree, 4 = Agree somewhat, 5 = Agree completely. After you have completed the questionnaire, follow the directions at the end of it for scoring.

1. I have clearly identified my life priorities.

   1 2 3 4 5

2. I use these life priorities to set my direction and guide my decision making.

   1 2 3 4 5

3. I have a clearly articulated purpose that provides focus and direction for my network marketing business.

   1 2 3 4 5

4. My purpose is in line with my life priorities and is an accurate description of who I am and what I am about.

   1 2 3 4 5

5. I have a very clear vision of where I will be in three to five years and have put it in writing.

   1 2 3 4 5

6. My vision is an energizing force that provides powerful incentives for everybody on my team.

   1 2 3 4 5

7. I know what my core values are and why I have them.

   1 2 3 4 5

8. These same core values drive the decision making in my business.

   1 2 3 4 5

9. I understand the core skills that are required to succeed in network marketing and constantly work to develop and improve them.

   1 2 3 4 5

10. I know how to leverage core skills into new areas of opportunity.

    1 2 3 4 5

11. I am clear about where I wish to build my business and have an effective system in place for generating and attracting new prospects in my chosen markets.

    1 2 3 4 5

12. I have an excellent knowledge of the network marketing industry and am constantly on the lookout for opportunities and threats that will affect my business so I can evaluate them and take appropriate action.

    1   2   3   4   5

13. I have a system that allows me to establish significant market share in the markets where I wish to operate and create effective duplication.

    1   2   3   4   5

14. I am able to develop the supports necessary to service the needs of my team and the markets they operate in.

    1   2   3   4   5

15. I am familiar with the groups and individuals who are affected by the way I run my business and am able to get consistent buy-in to my strategy from all these parties.

    1   2   3   4   5

16. I am constantly working to develop true win-win relationships with everybody affected by my business.

    1   2   3   4   5

17. I have clearly identified the resources required to run my business and achieve my business strategy.

    1   2   3   4   5

18. I have ensured that these key resources support the focus of my business and that I have a regular supply of them.

    1   2   3   4   5

To score the questionnaire: Add up the numbers you gave the individual statements, divide the total by 90, then multiply this answer by 100 to get a percentage that reflects how thorough your strategy is.

Remember, there is no such thing as failure here, so make sure your score is accurate. The closer you are to 100 percent, the more thoroughly you have covered the elements of a successful strategy. The further away from 100 percent you are, the more ground you need to cover in the quest to build a strong strategy. The good news is that anybody reading this is perfectly capable of getting an "A" with some thought and a little work, so, starting with the first area, let's dive right in!

Life Priorities

Clearly state the priorities that are important to you as you look to the future.

1. I have clearly identified my life priorities.

    1   2   3   4   5

2. I use these life priorities to set my direction and guide my decision making.

    1   2   3   4   5

Before you launch your network marketing business it is important to make sure that this endeavor is in tune with your life priorities. At this point, you may not even be clear on what they are. However, if you do not define them, there will be no synergy between your life and business, which leaves you off balance and reduces your chances of being successful. Here is an example that illustrates the kind of strife that may follow:

> *When Joe began his network marketing business, he was full of enthusiasm and envisioned a bright future. He and Liz had two young daughters, ages 5 and 7, whom he loved spending time with. The flexibility network marketing offers appealed to him greatly. Joe was working this new venture only part-time on top of his regular job, and success did not come easily. He had to put in a lot of hours, often working late into the night and through the weekends. Pretty soon, he wasn't spending much time with his family at all.*
>
> *All the hours Joe was spending on network marketing created increasing tension with his wife. Eventually she gave him an ultimatum: the business or his family. The choice was clear, and Joe's promising career in network marketing came to an abrupt halt.*

Giving up his business could have been avoided if Joe had thought through his priorities in the beginning and structured his business strategy accordingly. He would have put less overall time into it, of course, and taken longer to reap the rewards, but he would still have had a growing business and the benefits that come along with it. The problem was that Joe launched his network marketing enterprise without first making sure it was in harmony with his family life, his number one priority.

Life priorities are as diverse as the people who enter network marketing. For some, there is a single guiding priority, for others a mix of them. Here are some of the key life areas where priorities may be set:

- Family
- Spiritual and personal growth
- Financial security
- Career satisfaction
- Health and well-being
- Relationships
- Recreation
- Community service

Whatever your life priorities are, you must identify each clearly and rank them according to their importance before striking out. Your business should be something that helps you achieve what is important to you, a force for transforming these priorities from goals on paper or in your head to a reality that you live.

When the sacrifices of time and effort necessary to succeed in network marketing clash with your life priorities, as in Joe's case, the fit is wrong and your strategy becomes unworkable. Either you make adjustments or you risk not just losing your network marketing business, but also doing harm to what matters most to you.

Of course, success calls for sacrifice. Without investing the necessary resources of time and effort, there will be no rewards in the future. The key is in striking a balance between what kind of resources you devote to your business and what you need to devote to other things. In Joe's case, if he had taken the time to perform a realistic assessment of his priorities at the beginning, he could have scheduled time away from his family in a way where the sacrifices were acceptable. It might have taken him longer to achieve his business goals as a result, but he would have gotten there in harmony with his priorities, instead of being derailed along the way.

Julie loved her job. It brought her into contact with many financially successful people, and she wanted the same kind of success for herself. By chance, she was introduced to network marketing and, after overcoming her skepticism, became convinced it was the right vehicle for achieving the lifestyle she desired.

From the start, she identified her life priority as "financial success" and threw herself into her new business. Before long, however, she discovered that devoting herself to one priority was interfering with another, her social life, which was very important to her. While she was at home working in the evening, her friends were out having fun.

Julie reevaluated her priorities. Though financial success remained the most important, she realized there needed to be room for others, too. She reduced her evening work hours enough to give her some social "breathing room" while still devoting enough time to her business to make it work. With her life priorities and business aspirations in balance, Julie went on to become one of the most successful distributors in her company.

Julie's example makes a number of important points. Our priorities are not set in stone. They change over time and, very often, we are not even aware something is as important a priority until after our business is up and running. Suddenly something we used to do or be involved with has been set aside, and only then do we realize how significant it is. There's no crisis here, especially when you consider that one of the big reasons for going into network marketing, to begin with, is the flexibility. Making adjustments is not a problem. The problems arise when we fail to adjust.

In terms of creating a strategy for success, failing to adequately define and account for our life priorities can undermine the entire process and leave us with no workable strategy at all. Understanding our priorities, however, and building a business around them, has a multiplier effect. Our business supports what matters most to us, and, with these priorities nurtured by our efforts, the business itself is a harmonious part of who we are and has an excellent chance of flourishing as a result.

Purpose

Clearly state your reasons for building your business, your overall purpose, and what you are striving to achieve.

3. I have a clearly articulated purpose that provides focus and direction for my network marketing business.

    1   2   3   4   5

4. My purpose is in line with my life priorities and is an accurate description of who I am and what I am about.

    1   2   3   4   5

It is critical to define a purpose for your business that is in line with both your priorities and how you conduct your life in general. A good way to clarify this purpose is by writing out a mission statement. It does not have to be long or complicated, but it does need to be clear on your reasons for doing what you are doing. After all, these are what get you up and moving every day.

If your life priority is to provide financial security for your family, for example, then the mission of your business could be to generate the kind of steady, ongoing cash flows that make that possible. If your life priority is to constantly challenge yourself by doing new things, your mission might be to succeed in an area where change is constant and security is secondary.

Your purpose is not something that needs to be written in stone for all time. It can change, just as your priorities do. When your purpose changes, it is time to write up a new mission statement to reflect it. Otherwise, you are in danger of ending up with a business that functions at odds with what you want to accomplish. Here is an example of a network marketer who defined a specific mission that was a direct outgrowth of his purpose:

> Jerry was a successful financial consultant who made plenty of money but had little control over his time. The business was running him instead of him running it. His wife's job was demanding, too, and it seemed as though they hardly saw each other. For Jerry, network marketing offered him an opportunity to regain control of his time.
>
> The purpose of Jerry's business was clear: to free his wife from having to work. His mission, then, followed naturally, and was simply to earn enough money to match their combined income. With clarity on what he was playing for, Jerry was focused and willing to pay the price necessary to achieve his goals. Nothing came easy, but a clear sense of mission kept him motivated. He marked the accomplishment of his mission by walking into the hospital where his wife worked and carrying her out triumphantly.
>
> Jerry went on to become a legend in the industry, and now his mission has changed—to helping others achieve their own success.

Having an ongoing mission to keep you on track is the thing that will keep you going when others hit the tough times and give up. You have a light at the end of the tunnel to move toward. Those without a mission get lost in the dark.

Vision

Create a vision of what you want your future to be and communicate it to everyone associated with your business.

5. I have a very clear vision of where I will be in three to five years and have put it in writing.

1   2   3   4   5

6. My vision is an energizing force that provides powerful incentives for everybody on my team.

1   2   3   4   5

Great leaders have vision. They know where they are going and how to get others to come aboard for the journey. An important key to your own success is having the same kind of vision for your own future. This means a vision that is compelling and inspiring, and that is a constant source of motivation for you and your team, not just in the present, but in the weeks, months, and years ahead.

A wonderful thing about vision is that, although you cannot change the past, you can create your future. So how is a vision developed? A good way to start is by projecting yourself five years into a future you would like to see come to pass and imagining that it is the present. Paint a mental picture of it. Where are you living, who are you with, what are you doing, what is a typical day like, how much are you earning, what are your pastimes? And the list can be as detailed as you want it to be; your aim is to develop a clear mental picture that helps you settle what is best for you.

Once your vision is in place, you should put it into words and generate a plan for making it happen. Your goal here is to take a great vision for the future and take the actions necessary to make it come true. Remember, this vision is yours. Make it reflect where you want to go, not somebody else's destination. Maybe you'll come up with something similar to the example here:

> It is five years from today and I'm lying on the beach in the sunshine, surrounded by palm trees. We're staying at a beautiful villa in an exclusive resort. As I lie here, I reflect on the success we have achieved so far.
>
> We are earning a residual income of $200,000 per month and have $5 million in the bank. We have developed 1,000 leaders, and our team now totals 150,000 affiliates spread throughout the many countries we operate in. We have created financial security for many of our team members. We own a beautiful home as our primary residence and have two vacation residences. Never have we looked so good or been so healthy.
>
> Grateful for what we have, we are now able to contribute significantly to a variety of children's charities. I've been able to write books and develop training programs that help other people become successful in network marketing. As a result, our great industry is now seen as a viable career option for people from all walks of life.

When you read over your vision, you should be encouraged, motivated, and excited by it. Just think, this is where you could be in five years! Done properly, the detailing of your vision will be an empowering experience because it shows you just how much you are capable of.

Core Values

Identify your core values and use them to drive behavior and as the criteria for decision making.

7. I know what my core values are and why I have them.

    1 2 3 4 5

8. These same core values drive the decision making in my business.

    1 2 3 4 5

Top performers in any field know what they stand for and they stand by their values. Success is much more likely when your business is in line with your personal values. After all, our values determine who we are and guide our decisions. If you are involved in a pursuit that is not in line with your values, you will always be at odds with yourself, and your performance will suffer.

To help clarify your values, ask yourself the following questions:

- What do I believe in?
- What is important to me?
- What do I stand for?
- What drives me?
- What are my criteria for decision making?

As you answer these questions, a number of values will emerge. Some examples of these might be: integrity, honesty, excellence, hard work, happiness, creativity, compassion, and loyalty.

An Exercise in Values Clarity

After giving it an appropriate amount of thought, list three to six of the values that best represent what you stand for. Then ask others, such as your spouse, co-workers, or friends, to list the three to six values they think you stand for. Compare the lists. The closer they are, the more apparent you have made them in the conduct of your life. The further apart they are, the more work you need to do in focusing on your values and making them obvious in how you work and live. A major benefit of this exercise is that it helps you identify like-minded people to work with!

With your values defined and clear to yourself and those you come in contact with, your actions will reflect what you are about and your business will be consistent with you as a human being. Not only will your decision making and general operations become more effective, but you will be amazed at how you attract both the kinds of customers you want to serve and the kinds of team members with whom you want to work.

What follows is a case study that demonstrates how values clarification can ignite your business:

Though Susan had started her network marketing business a few years earlier, she had never really applied herself to it. This fact was reflected by the small income she generated. Everything changed, however, when her full-time job was eliminated. All of a sudden her steady income was gone, and, as a 44-year-old woman with little formal education, her future looked bleak.

To Susan, her best opportunity lay in developing her business. In order to do this, though, she had to bring in new people and start building a team. Susan decided that defining her core values would help her establish guidelines for running an expanding business. Paramount among these values was integrity, something Susan saw as vital to all aspects of her life, both personal and business.

When she got down to really growing her business, Susan made sure to enroll quality people whose values were in line with her own. Her income began to grow, and over time she emerged as one of the company's most successful and respected leaders. In fact, Susan was so dedicated to integrity that she passed up on an opportunity to significantly increase her income by allowing another woman, Jenny (who was in a different line of sponsorship), to work with her. Why did she decline? Because Susan knew that taking someone from somebody else's business just wasn't in line with her core value of integrity. However, this didn't stop Susan from helping Jenny. With no thought of gain for herself, she supported Jenny and helped her achieve the top position in her company.

It wasn't long, of course, before Susan hit the same mark in her own company. In fact, the integrity she displayed in her dealings with Jenny, her customers, and those who worked with her has continued to pay dividends.

Though they do not appear as a specific entry in a balance sheet or income statement, your values have a lot to do with your performance, especially in a field like network marketing, where personal contact is so important. Customers and team members alike are not buying into just your products. They are buying into your core values, too. In effect, it is your own values and how you express them that determine who you are surrounded with. So, choose wisely!

Core Skills

Identify your core skills and the skills that are required for success. Leverage these skills to establish competitive advantage in the marketplace.

9. I understand the core skills that are required to succeed in network marketing and constantly work to develop and improve them.

1   2   3   4   5

10. I know how to leverage core skills into new areas of opportunity.

1   2   3   4   5

Why do so many talented people fail in business? Of course, the reasons are many. However, a big one that does not get nearly enough attention lies in the difference between what they are good at and what they need to be good at. In network marketing, as in any other area, acquiring and developing the right set of core skills is critical to succeeding.

A good way to get a picture of where you stand in relation to the essential core skills necessary for your own business is to conduct a personal audit. The first step is to make a list of skills that are crucial to your operation, such as leadership, coaching, presenting information, listening, and enrolling. Next, make an honest assessment of yourself and evaluate how the skills you have compare to those you need.

Just because you may be weak in a few areas, or even completely lack skill in some, does not have to be the death knell of your business. True, there are some skills you absolutely must have yourself. But there are plenty that can be brought in from the outside or developed in members of your team. Rare is the person who is good at everything. And even if you are good at everything, there simply won't be time to cover it all.

Once you know which skills need to be brought in or further developed, you have to set priorities so that the most important can be addressed first. Ask yourself, "What one skill would make the most dramatic impact on my business?" Become great at that skill, or bring in somebody who is, and you will witness quick gains in your business.

Another thing to pay close attention to is how existing skills you or your team members have can be leveraged. Bear in mind that the skills people possess are our most important assets. If you can tap into abilities left dormant in the past, you will have made a very cost-effective investment that can pay wonderful dividends in the future.

After spending many years in the personal development and consultancy field, Dave was anxious to succeed at network marketing. As part of putting together his business strategy, he decided to do a personal skills audit. He began by listing his key skills according to his level of competence in each. They included listening, building relationships, teaching others, presenting to groups, and decision making. Next, he identified the additional core skills necessary to succeed in his new part-time career. These included prospecting, enrolling others, making telephone calls, coaching, leading, and a number of others.

The next step was to compare the two lists and make a plan for bridging any gaps. Dave saw that he was not good at time management or using computer technology. He addressed this by hiring a part-time assistant who instituted efficient protocols for handling these areas. For example, scheduling phone calls and handling e-mails both improved how the business functioned and freed Dave up to focus on what he was best at.

An interesting result of Dave's approach in this case study is that by identifying core skills he was weak in, he was then able to take action that turned these things into strengths! Further, with these functioning smoothly, Dave got more out of the core skills he was strong in. It is easy to focus only on what you are good at. But if you ignore critical areas of your business that cry out for more specialized attention, you may sabotage your own best assets.

Marketplace

Examine the marketplace in which you operate, determine the threats and opportunities, and then select target markets to capitalize on. Be clear about how you intend to penetrate your chosen markets.

11. I am clear about where I wish to build my business and have an effective system in place for generating and attracting new prospects in my chosen markets.

1 2 3 4 5

12. I have an excellent knowledge of the network marketing industry and am constantly on the lookout for opportunities and threats that will affect my business so I can evaluate them and take appropriate action.

1   2   3   4   5

To achieve real success in network marketing, you must become a scholar of the industry. Study everything you can about your industry, the markets you operate in, and especially the people who have achieved success in them.

The development of a successful business strategy calls for you to identify just who your customers are and what markets to target. Where are your best opportunities? A good way to clarify this is to ask these key questions:

- Who are my customers (including those who may be interested in my business opportunity)?
- What is my customer proposition?
- What do my ideal customers look for? What is important to them?
- Who are my competitors?
- Why should my customers do business with me?
- How can I add value for my potential customers?
- What niche markets can I penetrate?

When considering a market niche, perform a SWOT analysis to determine if it is a good one for you to enter. A SWOT analysis includes the following:

Strengths: Identify and define your strengths.

Weaknesses: Identify your weaknesses and how they might affect you if you entered this market.

Opportunities: Identify and learn about the opportunities that exist.

Threats: Identify and analyze threats to you in this market, such as competitors.

The case study of Don, seen next, provides a good example of what it means to get acquainted with one's market:

After 15 years as a computer consultant, Don understood the industry and the challenges faced by people who worked in it.

Though he did not wish to work directly in the industry any longer, he felt that his knowledge and experience of this market would serve him well in attracting others from the industry to join his network marketing business. Not willing to just "trust his gut," he performed a SWOT analysis to get a better understanding of the potential opportunities.

Don started by developing a questionnaire and interviewing people he knew in the industry, and focused on items of particular importance to him, such as what motivated the respondents, how they felt about their futures, and their openness to alternative income options.

The only threat he saw was from other computer companies, and it wasn't significant enough to deter him. So Don, based on his SWOT analysis, decided to enter the market and used the information he had gained to develop a strategy specific to his market. As a result, he was able to attract plenty of qualified people. He went on to develop a team of several hundred distributors.

System

Ensure the provision of a system that meets the needs of your team in the markets where you will be required to support the implementation of your business strategy.

13. I have a system that allows me to establish significant market share in the markets where I wish to operate and create effective duplication.

1 2 3 4 5

14. I am able to develop the supports necessary to service the needs of my team and the markets they operate in.

1 2 3 4 5

One of the many things that makes network marketing unique is that those who buy the company's products aren't your only customers; members of your team are your customers, too. This means that you need to add value to your team so that they succeed along with you. Remember, those who join your team will be looking to you for leadership, as you set an example of how to conduct the business.

A very important thing to provide members of your team is a system for them to build their businesses. Having a system that works and can be duplicated can lead to great success for everyone involved. So, make sure it is clearly understood by everybody. There are three critical elements of any network marketing system:

1. Bringing people into the business.
2. Keeping people in the business.
3. Developing competent people into leaders.

If no system is in place, or you need a better one, the best thing to do is study existing systems that are successful and adapt them, or portions of them, to your own venture.

Why is it so important to have a strong system in place? It is your system that allows you to develop true residual income. You should not be the focal point of income generation. Instead, you need a system that guarantees continued growth without you! Here is a case study that shows you how it can be done:

Steve had been working his network marketing business for six months. Although his own individual performance was strong, he was having trouble getting new people he brought in to duplicate it. So he decided to create a system that could be used to enroll people, and then, in turn, be duplicated by them. Steve developed a five-step process:

1. *Get started properly.*
2. *Generate potential business partners.*
3. *Prospect and invite.*
4. *Present the business.*
5. *Follow up.*

Steve recognized that keeping people in was at least as important as bringing them in. Therefore, he established a business planning process that kept them engaged in building their businesses for at least 12 months. He made sure that support materials were developed, and initiated Internet-based training, as well as event scheduling and conference calling to provide further support. His masterstroke was to provide a coaching system and institute a program for developing leaders.

As you read Steve's case study, you might have been struck by the amount of work and time it took before the system was in place. But it paid off handsomely and resulted in Steve becoming the most successful distributor in his company.

Key Interfaces

Identify key internal and external interfaces, assess their impact on your business, and develop effective strategies to determine and address their needs and interests.

15. I am familiar with the groups and individuals who are affected by the way I run my business and am able to get consistent buy-in to my strategy from all these parties.

1 2 3 4 5

16. I am constantly working to develop true win-win relationships with everybody affected by my business.

1 2 3 4 5

So much time is spent in strategic development on how to operate our own businesses most effectively that it is easy to lose sight of the other parties who are affected by it. To do so is a mistake. Not only are they affected by our decisions, but the actions they in turn take affect us. Your key interfaces may include any of the following, and more:

- Family
- Bankers
- Accountant
- Lawyer
- Customers
- Team members
- Key leaders
- Company management
- Local communities

No matter who your key interfaces are, it is important to develop a plan for each one that promotes a true win-win relationship. You need these people to be on your side! Here is a simple exercise designed to assist you in making the most of them:

Interface Exercise

Make a list of all the people who are, or will be, affected by your business. Next, go back through the list and identify with a "+" all those who are invested in your success that you have win-win relationships with, then put a "−" by the names of the people you do not have this kind of relationship with—yet. For each person with a "–" by their name, develop a specific, realistic plan to get them to buy into your strategy. Implement your plan and keep a close watch on the results.

When you develop plans for instituting win-win relationships, bear in mind that when you follow through with them, you are reinforcing a positive relationship and making it stronger, and thus more beneficial to everybody involved. But if you do not institute a plan when needed, or you ignore the follow-through, then you reinforce a negative relationship. Because your key interfaces are often people with the power to have a significant impact on your business, for better or worse, be sure to tend to them diligently.

Key Resources

Identify the tangible and intangible resources that are key to your business, and ensure an adequate supply of them.

17. I have clearly identified the resources required to run my business and achieve my business strategy.

1   2   3   4   5

18. I have ensured that these key resources support the focus of my business and that I have a regular supply of them.

1   2   3   4   5

The establishment of a successful business calls for the investment of a variety of resources whose mix will be different according to the area of endeavor and what the operators bring to the table. In network marketing, necessary resources will include time, money, people, equipment, space, expertise, and many other things. Rare is the business that opens up shop feeling that every one of the necessary resources are present in adequate amounts. For most of us, the reality is that we focus on the most important resources first, then acquire and develop the others as we go along.

It took Joan three months of struggling with her new network marketing business before she realized that she needed to reevaluate her approach to it completely. She had no clear direction for the business and was experiencing only limited success. Chief among the resources she saw the need for was somebody to help her set goals and hold her accountable for accomplishing them.

Joan sought out a business coach and committed to a 12-month program. Together, they developed realistic goals for Joan and set up a program of regular communication so that her coach could keep tabs on her progress and provide assistance in generating new ideas and dealing with the challenges that came along. Before long, Joan felt that she was moving forward with real purpose and velocity.

Like a recipe with key ingredients, adding the right resource can make the whole dish come alive. It does not have to be anything expensive or fancy; it just has to be right.

PUTTING IT ALL TOGETHER

Congratulations! You have completed all nine key tasks and are ready to put together a strong, clear strategy for success that allows you to fully leverage the considerable assets at your disposal. As you probably noticed, just going through the nine tasks gives you a well-organized body of material. All that needs to be done now is adapt it to your particular network marketing business.

One last thing: Do not let your time spent with the nine tasks end here; they always remain important, no matter how successful you are or how long you are in business. Come back often for checkups. Generate some new thinking for a tune-up, and always make sure your network marketing business is the best possible reflection of who you are and what you are capable of.

Cliff Walker has over 20 years of experience working in large organizations, including senior management positions. For the past 15 years, Cliff has dedicated himself to improving the performance of individuals and helping them reach their full potential. He has worked in the United States, Canada, Australia, Japan, Hong Kong, and throughout Europe.

He discovered network marketing as a result of researching the industry on behalf of a major international company and immediately recognized the potential. Cliff is now recognized as one of the top network marketing professionals in Europe. After less than four years building a serious network marketing business, Cliff's team numbers more than 70,000 distributors and 350,000 customers, spanning the United Kingdom, Ireland, Belgium, and the Netherlands.

He was instrumental in taking the company he partnered with to over $150 million in sales after just three years in business, generating income in excess of $3 million. Cliff is now CEO of Success Systems International, which is committed to providing support, training, and a professional environment that will enable fulfillment of individual goals and long-term success.

Success Systems International is committed to forging new and exciting partnerships to further spread the message of Cliff's proven principles and methodologies of training, communication, marketing, and success throughout the world. For more information, visit www.cliffwalker.co.uk.

CHAPTER 5

The Power of a Great System

Mark Stevens

Most people fail in network marketing because they are not given a clear road map, a system, to follow. Without this type of well-defined system, many new independent representatives can quickly become discouraged. They do not experience the success that first enticed them to become involved in our industry and quickly lose passion, excitement, and commitment.

Did you know that, according to industry averages, 8 out of 10 people who sign up with a direct-sales/network marketing company stay less than one year? Most people would agree that they work too hard recruiting to experience that level of loss and frustration. An effective system can be instrumental in addressing two essential areas—first, it will help equip new enrollees to achieve quick and consistent success, and second, it sets the stage for long-term retention. As all network marketers know, the more positive and rewarding the experience, the longer people will remain active in the opportunity.

Statistics show that the new enrollee's first 90 days are absolutely vital. To really drive home how important these first 90 days are, consider statistics showing that of those 8 out of 10 people who stay less than a year, most companies lose 40 percent to 60 percent of them in the first 90 days. So, doing the right things as an enroller begins when you first introduce the business to your friends. A well-planned, easy-to-follow system creates a partnership between the company and you to help ensure that new enrollees have early, essential success experiences. This system must be simple and duplicable, and never overwhelming. The emphasis should always be that anyone willing to be persistent and consistent can do it if they just follow the clearly defined steps.

It is vital that people realize the power of following a system that includes a fast way to get started. A great example of this power is the McDonald's franchise chain. Whether you order a Big Mac in New York, Hong Kong, or anywhere in between, you will get the very same taste, same ingredients, and same packaging. You see, Ray Kroc realized a very important principle in successful business, and that is the power of an easily and consistently followed system. When a new McDonald's franchise owner opens the doors of a new restaurant, you can be assured that the owner and the employees have been given extensive and specific training on how to successfully operate that franchise. The key to their success is plugging into and following the proven McDonald's system. The same holds true in network marketing. If new enrollees are left to their own devices, their business is doomed to failure from the very start. However, if those new team members are given a step-by-step, very clear system to follow, they are much more likely to experience success from the very beginning.

Always help people realize that they are starting an actual business. Help them understand that they are not just buying product; they are the CEO of their own national or worldwide business. Build up the integrity of the business they are involved in as well as the network marketing industry, and the vast potential of both their business and this industry. The network marketing industry has created more millionaires than any other industry, including real estate, and has attained a high level of respect as a very viable and legitimate industry. Additionally, this exciting industry offers individuals an opportunity to create very formidable businesses with incomes rivaling or exceeding those of highly paid executives.

There are four initial activities you want a new enrollee to do, and these should be accomplished either with the help of the person who brought the enrollee into the business or by a qualified team leader.

ESTABLISH GOALS

The first thing a new enrollee should do is establish goals—the "why" for building his or her network marketing business. This is an exciting time as people are encouraged to take all the limitations off of their circumstances and to actually begin to consider their real potential. Many times, the process of setting goals and attaching them to dreams and desires can be absolutely explosive. There is a great deal of emotion connected to setting goals, because we all have dreams of glorious accomplishments and we all want to create an impressive legacy. These goals cannot be about just money, although money usually funds a goal. The goal must be a tangible, material accomplishment, such as college funding for a child, support for a ministry or charity, a new home, or the financial freedom of being debt free. The more emotion that is attached to a goal, the stronger the drive is within an individual to accomplish that goal. You become unswervingly committed to achieving the goal.

This is also the time when a new enrollee should be encouraged to plug into the company's recognition program. Many times, specific actions tied to a recognition program actually fuel team growth and increased income. As new enrollees begin to build their businesses by following a proven system, they also begin to realize success in achieving daily goals. These daily goals build into life-changing goals, and soon what was only a dream becomes a reality. Many top producers will confirm that as team members earn recognition awards, excitement and momentum will build within an organization. This type of momentum causes a business to experience explosive growth and success.

Do not just set business goals, though. Be sure that this process of goal setting also includes personal goals and personal growth. Everyone, regardless of their dream or vocation, should establish short-term goals for the next six months and the next year, as well as long-term goals for the next three years. Write these goals down. Read them often to help stay focused on your own personal "why."

MAKE A COMMITMENT

The next activity important in a new enrollee's success is to make a commitment to the business. What amount of time, resources, and effort is the person willing to devote to developing the new business? Is this level of commitment sufficient to help these goals become a reality? The level of commitment must match the size of the goals, or the goals must be adjusted to the level of commitment your new enrollee is willing to make.

Remember, honesty is crucial. Be honest with your new enrollee so his or her goals are realistic. For example, you must be sure he understands that he cannot just work his new business four hours a week and expect to make $10,000 in a short period of time. The familiar saying that you can work a network marketing business part-time but not in your spare time is very true. Today, it seems that no one has spare time. So treat your business as a business, not an occasional diversion, and encourage your team members to have that same mind-set. It is only logical to realize that in order to generate income and business-building activity, one must commit to talking to a certain number of people each day, each week, each month. Set aside specific hours each week for your new business, and commit to work your business during those hours. Do not give in to excuses or procrastination.

It is essential that people commit to educating themselves about the incredible business we are in. Network marketing, or direct sales, truly offers the kind of independence and prosperity that our country's founders envisioned and longed for. This industry is one of the few areas where a level playing field is available to anyone, regardless of age, gender, education, or social station.

The network marketing industry offers some absolutely marvelous resources to further personal development, and every member of this amazing industry should commit to taking advantage of these resources. There is a wealth of phenomenal trainers, life-changing books, and information-packed audios at our fingertips in the direct-sales arena. Set aside a specific time, whether daily or weekly, to plug into some of these resources. Other important resources are both corporate events and local team events. Commit to attending these events, and you will not only glean important personal development information, but you will also develop wonderful relationships with other members of your team.

DEVELOP A PROSPECT LIST

Now we are up to the third activity on our list of the four things a new enrollee should do for fast success. It is important for new team members to immediately make a list of as many people as possible to whom they can present their business. This list may include 100 to 200 names, and it should always be a work in progress. Always add to your prospect list. As your new business is developed, you will continually meet new people and come in contact with prior acquaintances. Add these contacts to your prospect list and follow up with them.

One common downfall for many people as they develop prospect lists is that they first identify the poorest, most down-and-out people they can think of. They instead should be looking for the busiest, most industrious people they know! These are the people to partner with in this business. The beauty of network marketing is that you can choose with whom you work, unlike a traditional job where you simply do not have that luxury.

Other important qualities to look for when developing a prospect list are a positive, upbeat personality and the desire for more from life—more money, more time, more freedom. These are personality traits that attract people and that cause people to look beyond their current limitations into the big, bright world of possibility.

GET BUSY!

Finally, I cannot stress enough just how important it is to get new team members actively approaching the people on their prospect list—again, looking for busy people, positive people, people who are hungry for more out of life. Identifying five or six people who would be the very best candidates and approaching them first can be a great way to get someone off to a fast start.

It is so important for a new person to understand that in approaching people, the initial goal is only to connect a prospect with a team leader so the leader can make the presentation. A problem that has torpedoed many new network marketing business owners is that, because they are so very excited, they go out and immediately begin talking to people, giving incorrect information or, even worse, too much information. The ensuing rejection is usually inevitable.

So how should you approach people? The purpose of approaching people is to uncover the needs in their lives that your opportunity can fill. A technique that has been used with great success by many people in the network marketing industry is the FORM method (family, occupation, recreation, message). Now, the only way this method works is if the individual employing it disciplines himself to always keep the conversation on the prospect. Keep the main focus of the conversation on the prospect. The FORM method asks questions about the prospect's family, occupation, and favorite recreation. As the conversation unfolds, you will uncover needs in the prospect's life, whether it is a working mother who yearns to be home with her children but needs an income or a highly paid executive who has sold all his time to earn the kind of income that his career provides. Once you uncover the need, you are able to connect that need to the message of your opportunity.

Remember, the less you talk when utilizing this prospecting method, the more successful you will be. For example, if you are talking with Pam, who is a working mom, once you uncover her need, you might say:

"Pam, I'm involved with a company that has helped moms just like you to be with their children and still earn a very nice income. I'd like to connect you with a business associate of mine so you can look into this opportunity. I can't make any guarantees, but I know it would be worth your time to explore the possibilities."

If the prospect asks for more information, just explain that you are new and would not want to give her any wrong information, and that your associate is very experienced and successful. Your sole concern is that she gets all the information she needs to make an educated decision.

The four actions we have discussed so far should be completed by a new enrollee within 24 to 72 hours after joining your team. It is important to note that new enrollees are most excited when they first come into a business. So the sooner you propel people toward activities that will begin developing their successful business, the more activity they will produce in your organization.

THE SYSTEM AS AN OPPORTUNITY TOOL

As a new team member is learning the business, building one's own team is essential to encouraging commitment and ongoing activity. A great system provides team members with a variety of tools to make professional opportunity presentations. These tools can include live opportunity conference calls, three-way conference calls, opportunity meetings, company literature, an opportunity DVD, and Web-based presentations.

WHAT ELSE?

Other integral facets of a fast-start system must include product training and business development training, in addition to the personal development discussed earlier. These activities must be made available in various, multiple mediums to make the information accessible to all new enrollees. Consider utilizing Web-based resources, fax on demand, voice on demand, conference calls, and printed materials.

Strive to build rapport among team members and leaders in your organization as well as the corporation itself, building both relationships and belief. As you increase the belief level in new enrollees, their belief in their abilities, their team, and the company they are associated with will rise accordingly. This is accomplished by introducing them to any conference calls hosted by the company, whether the calls are training or opportunity calls. Local events, meetings, and training sessions are also important, as well as regional or national corporate events. I believe, though, that the most powerful way to establish and elevate your new team member's belief level is by generating income checks as quickly as possible. By simply receiving that first check, a person realizes that the system works and that where that first check came from, there are thousands more just waiting to be earned.

Perhaps the most important element in getting a new enrollee off to a great start is to meet him or her at their level of need and expectation. Never force your new enrollees into a particular goal or level of achievement, but rather reinforce the validity of their own goals. This will always generate a much more enthusiastic, committed team. Perhaps your new team member only wants to use your company's products—do not exert pressure to be more than that or you may end up losing a great product user. Your new team member may have a goal of earning just a few hundred dollars a month, or a few thousand, while others may see your opportunity as a way to earn tens of thousands of dollars each month. The important thing is to discover where a person wants to go and then help him or her get there. And, remember, once your team members achieve milestone goals be sure to celebrate their success.

CELEBRATE!

So many times, celebration is reserved for only an organization's top earners, when in reality celebration is for everyone at their individual level of accomplishment. When team members are approached this way, you will motivate them to continue to push toward increased success. So celebrate the little successes as well as the monumental successes in each person's life.

An effective system must also tie into a company's recognition program. Everyone wants to be recognized for accomplishments in their lives, and no other industry celebrates recognition like the network marketing industry.

The final and perhaps most important part of a great system is constant communication with new enrollees, particularly during the first 90 days. Make a personal commitment to help your new enrollees stay on track with their goals and commitments. Reinforce the knowledge that they are in business for themselves, but not by themselves. You are there to support them, and the company is there to support them. When you invest yourself in building relationships with your team members, you will find that you gain much more than a stellar income. You will also enjoy a high level of trust, loyalty, and lifelong friendships. This type of relationship building reinforces the knowledge that regardless of any bumps in the road to success that your organization faces, it can weather the storm.

Perhaps the most appealing and unique aspect of network marketing is that, in an age of faceless, cold electronic business transactions, relationship building—actually getting to know people and valuing them as individuals—is the bedrock of a successful business. Relationships intertwined with a powerful business system form an unbreakable cord, and together, any challenges you and your team may encounter on the journey toward unlimited success can be overcome.

Mark Stevens is the CEO and president of Vision for Life International, a seven-year-old nutritional supplement network marketing company that enjoys a significant presence in the United States, Philippines, Nigeria, Hong Kong, and Canada. After becoming the president of a multimillion-dollar worldwide company at the age of just 16, Mr. Stevens has successfully built multimillion-dollar companies as well as successful network marketing organizations of thousands.

He is listed in *Who's Who in Corporate America*, has served on a national industry board of directors, and is quickly becoming recognized as a gifted and effective motivational speaker.

As the driving force of Vision for Life International, Mr. Stevens has developed a system that has allowed thousands of people to create spectacular incomes—many of which are six-figure and more. This system equips people with the skills and tools necessary to realize quicker and more successful results as they step out and begin living the American dream, which is, of course, to become an independent business owner.

Mr. Stevens has traveled worldwide speaking on living a life filled with freedom, and has touched the hearts and minds of many thousands with his message of hope, freedom, and life without limits.

Chapter 6

Behave Your Way to a Six-Figure Income

Captain Dave Klaybor

I like the way my pastor puts it. He says, "You are what you have been becoming." This is so true. You are today the product of your collective decisions. *You* ultimately create the world you live in. Your business environment is the product of all your habits, behavior, programming, and conditioning. So, reflect for a moment on the person you really are right now and what you have become, especially with regard to your network marketing business.

I learned a great lesson from my dad. He told me many times, "A small error in judgment, compounded over time, can be devastating to your business, family, health, and life." And conversely, he stressed, "Good decisions, compounded over time, will become amazingly positive to all aspects of your life."

Our thoughts influence our emotions and feelings. These influence our attitudes, which impact our programming and conditioning. Pretty soon, we've established our habits, which continue to dictate our actions and become our behavior patterns. And our behavior loops right back around into re-creating another either positive or negative thought. This brain function is all a part of our human nature. Be careful what you think, because these positive or negative thoughts all revolve around over and over in a continual loop that is hard to break. Learn to control your thoughts so they do not detract from your overall business success.

This is important when it comes to your businesses because network marketing is a state of mind. Your mind-set directs your actions and generates results. This is why it is so important to maintain a proactive, positive, optimistic attitude about where your networking business is headed.

The good news is it's never too late to become the person you wanted to be with respect to all aspects of your business. If you recruited only one or two solid business builders, you could likely reach many of your goals. So it's time to assume a leadership role and design your business deliberately, starting today.

Every decision we make, behavior we undertake, habit we form, and action we take has a positive or negative impact on our businesses. So let's begin by identifying where our thoughts have contributed to business decisions that have not supported our success. Where have these actions become habits, and what patterns have you created that are undermining what you want to achieve? What skill sets are missing to take you to the top of your company? And what unproductive actions do you find yourself repeating on a regular basis?

Consider these questions:

- Have you studied the methods of operation of top network marketing leaders?
- Are your work habits in line with the level of achievement you wish to attain?
- What skills will you need to master to enhance your effectiveness in enrollment and training?
- Are you building your business from a solid commitment to do what it takes to achieve success, or do you do it only when it is convenient?

When you are able to identify and duplicate the habit patterns of those who are successful in this business and learn a few more skills that may currently be missing, you'll also have the tools to become a six-figure-income earner. Acquire and then use the proven success systems that have already been developed and organized for you to implement. Learn how to take the correct action steps that produce results consistent with those you desire. This is the behavior that will virtually guarantee your business success.

Your network marketing success will be determined by your state of mind. If you are not achieving the success you seek, then perhaps your mindset is a little off-center. All you need to do to get back on track is to positively enhance your attitude. And your attitude is directly influenced by your habit patterns, skill sets, programming, and conditioning.

Many will not possess the unshakable commitment to do the things required to make it in network marketing. Some are not ready to employ themselves and run their own businesses in a self-directed, effective manner. However, for those who do possess the will to make the long-term commitment necessary to overcome the obstacles and become a leader in this industry and are teachable and can learn all the skills required, network marketing offers an unequaled, potentially life-changing opportunity.

Those who take the time and put out the effort to accomplish this mission will enjoy the satisfaction that comes from seeing the big picture. Clarity never comes all at once. It comes slowly as more and more pieces are laid out in front of you (with the help of others on your team). And little by little, the confounding pieces of the jigsaw puzzle slowly convert from a mess on the table into smaller visions of what the industry is all about. The clarity of what network marketing is all about will unfold if you have the patience to stick to putting the puzzle together. If you quit too soon, you'll never see or understand what the game truly is.

The foundation for your success is already in place inside the essence of your being. You have what it takes to put a jigsaw puzzle together. Your success will result from your decision to do whatever it takes to make it happen.

The benefits of doing all the hard work necessary to succeed include retiring in the next few years with a handsome income, driving the vehicle you want, living in your dream house, becoming a public speaker, winning free vacations, giving your family everything they could wish for, and so on. All of this is waiting for those who decide to reprogram their habits for success.

One of my mentors used to say, "To know, and not to do . . . is not to know!" At first I did not quite understand this personal development message. But if you reread the phrase a few times, it becomes crystal clear. We know that we shouldn't procrastinate, lie, smoke, get angry at others, speed, or eat junk food, but we often do. We know poor eating habits will make us fat, clog our arteries, and expose us to greater disease risks. Yet we find ourselves doing things that hold us back from achieving our true potential. Most people fail to implement the information that they think they know.

We become what we eat. We get stressed out and our blood pressure soars due to all the insignificant work-related projects we perform that produce little financial gain. Then we get angry because we think we're failing, while others on our team become angry with us for the lack of results we produce.

Rather than despair over mistakes made, commit now to learn from these errors in order to move your business and life in a forward direction. We have it that our failures are bad, but we forget that it is through these challenges that we learn our greatest life lessons. Most self-help books, tapes, and seminars were born from the trials and errors of others. Take advantage of these lessons learned and shared by others and eliminate the stress of needing to learn them the hard way. It's not the number of errors one makes but how fast one gets back on track. If you fall a couple of feet, the ground isn't so hard; but if you fall a couple of stories, then the fall is very harmful indeed. The earlier you catch yourself off-track, the sooner you will be able to adjust your course. Get in the habit of looking for the signs of going in the wrong direction and you will save yourself lots of money, lost time, embarrassment, and stress. You will gain respect from your peers, and people will be more inclined to want to follow you. That's what leadership is all about: having the courage to inspire others with your vision and actions, admit when you make mistakes, clean up the mess, and commit to doing better next time. The sooner you are able to recognize when you make bad decisions and do what is necessary to correct your misjudgments, the sooner you will inspire more confidence in your ability to lead.

Let's map this principle onto your network marketing business. Once you realize you've erred by working your business the wrong way, simply do what it takes to get back on course. Getting angry, stressed out, depressed, or even quitting is entirely optional. Learn to reverse your negative state immediately, like flipping a light switch, and turn your plight into proactive actions to get yourself back in the game.

Admission of a wrongdoing is key to network marketing business success. John Lennon said, "How can we go forward when we don't know which way we're facing?" Become fully aware of your strengths and weaknesses as soon as you can. Identify your positive qualities first. Some examples of your positive traits might be confidence, loyalty, being hardworking, having a positive outlook, being ambitious, proactive, motivational, enthusiastic, or insightful, and being a team player. In contrast, perhaps your business-building weaknesses may lie in your skill sets (e.g., poor organization, weak follow-up, poor time management, inconsistent prospecting, weak sales phraseology, ineffective communication, weak event management, inability to create rich value for your prospects, poor use of three-way or conference-calling technologies, weak use of computer tools, poor teaching skills, etc.). Knowing what may be missing is the first step toward implementing a plan to put these necessary elements in place. In network marketing, we truly get paid what we are worth. So if you are not earning the sort of income you desire, ask yourself, "What may be missing that if put into place would dramatically impact my business-building results?" To get on track, all you need to do is address the areas holding you back from success.

Learn how to tap into the resources that you already possess internally, and you will realize the success you desire.

It all comes down to the choices we make. We can decide whether to take the hard or the smart path. If you are not realizing the level of success you desire, it may be necessary to admit that you do not have all the answers. Study the books, tapes, and trainings of those who have reached top levels of success. Become a perpetual student of the network marketing profession. But remember that it isn't enough to simply study what to do. It is essential to take action in order to really learn the success distinctions necessary for top-level field accomplishment.

Since my youth, I had been taught lots of vital information over time from many credible sources. However, most of these insider secrets just didn't sink in because I didn't really listen. I did not internalize the powerful data others were sharing. And I did not act upon the knowledge I received. Contrary to popular belief, knowledge alone is not power. Rather, effective actions based on sound principles generate powerful results.

How does one change old habits and reprogram and recondition oneself to achieve the goal of building a large network marketing organization? First, find a success coach—and then become a success coach to others in your group. A network marketing success coach is a person who can champion you to create an effective action plan and then hold you accountable to your commitment to follow through on the actions necessary to achieve it. A coach isn't there to make you do something you don't want to do. Rather, a coach is a person who can support you in analyzing whether your actions are consistent with the results you desire. Network marketing coaches can't force you to take action. They can only return you to your commitment to act when you stray from it. They act much like a coach acts on a sports team. They are there to teach, guide, challenge, and champion your success. Good coaches are rigorous when they need to be to return you to your commitments, should you forget and prefer to act out of convenience instead.

Every decision you make regarding your network marketing business will have either positive or negative consequences on the growth of your check. Remember that thoughts create emotions, which determine attitudes. Our attitudes influence our behaviors. These behaviors, often repeated, become habits. These habits influence our actions. And our actions determine the outcomes of our lives and the ultimate success of our network marketing businesses.

Your mind can hold only one thought at any moment. It can be a proactive, positive, or optimistic thought or a stressful, nonproductive, negative thought. You get to decide which it will be, moment by moment. Decide now to monitor your thoughts and actions to impact the cycle in a way that will support you in being the person you want to be while realizing the success possible through network marketing.

Captain Dave Klaybor is president of www.PowerLineSystems.ws, a 15-year-old world-class training and consulting firm noted for offering a fine network marketing business-planning system. Dave has been on the covers of many business publications and five books. His cash-flow-producing tools are sold in industry catalogs. Dave is a record-breaking veteran builder, author, columnist, and speaker. He has won top awards for his training programs, which are celebrity endorsed, and for product excellence. Dave is available to train and inspire network marketing organizations by conference call. E-mail Dave at CaptainDave@PowerLineSystems.ws to request his free tape on how to make $100,000 per year in network marketing.

CHAPTER 7

VITAL Signs of a Healthy Business

Glenn and Marian Head

Like a healthy person, a healthy business reflects a strong body, mind, and spirit. In business, this translates to continuous action (physical aspect), positive attitude (mental aspect), and compelling purpose (spiritual aspect). The acronym VITAL can guide you to create a healthy business that will serve you, your team, and your customers for many high-quality years to come.

Visualize your vision.

Ignite your intention.

Train your team.

Act authentically.

Love your life.

VISUALIZE YOUR VISION

Cherish your vision and your dreams as they are the children of your soul, the blueprints of your ultimate achievements.

—Napoleon Hill

This foundational step gives you the "why" behind every other step you take in business. It is the driving force, the light at the end of the tunnel that attracts you to move toward your heart's desire. Envisioning life at its best gives you the courage to step out of your comfort zone and learn new skills in order to make a difference in your life and in the lives of others.

Lack of vision is the reason most people and businesses fail. Obstacles inevitably crop up in our journey toward success; our vision gives us a compelling reason to remove them. Without a compelling vision, it becomes too easy to give up and give in to the mediocrity that binds us to an ordinary life, rather than an extraordinary one.

Thus, the first step when entering this or any profession is to ask yourself, "Why am I doing this? What would my ideal life look like? What would I have, do, and be if the resources of time, money, and health were bountiful in my life?" Then have fun writing down your answers.

Use your imagination and creativity. In his book *Mach II Starring You*, network marketing CEO Richard Brooke takes you on a joyful, inspiring journey that illuminates your personal vision by guiding you to direct and star in a movie of your life. It's a great way to visualize your vision.

Another is to use VisionWorks: Setting Your Sights on Success, a program we used with huge success in the 1980s with corporate clients. We have modified it for the network marketing profession. Grab your hat and let's go for a ride! The following is a quick vision process to get you started.

Ask a friend or associate to assist you in creating a personal vision. Find a quiet, relaxing place away from your office; play soft instrumental music. Ask your friend to slowly read the following to you, pausing to allow you ample time to envision the answers to each question. You may want to close your eyes so that you can eliminate visual distractions and use your mind's eye. Take a few slow, deep breaths just before you begin.

Have a journal close at hand to capture your vision and anchor it in writing. If you are doing this exercise on your own without someone reading it to you, get into a comfortable, quiet space with your journal and write as you visualize the following:

Imagine that it's five years from now and you have just awakened to a perfect day. Your life is great! You feel energized and excited. Look around your perfect bedroom. What do you see around you?

Leaving the comfort of your bed, you delight in the beauty of your home. You notice any sounds—from nature outside your window or perhaps music playing—that comfort you and enhance your sense of well-being. As you walk through your home, what colors do you see? Is the temperature just right—not too hot or cold? What smells do you notice?

Sitting down in one of your favorite chairs, you enjoy a beverage of your choice and contemplate your day. What do you look forward to? What gives you the greatest pleasure? How will your work play a role in your day? What company do you represent? What products or services do you offer? How do you feel about them?

As you walk into your office, you notice a letter on your desk from the most prestigious international journal in the networking profession. You smile as you recall opening that letter yesterday when you learned you had been recognized for creating one of the most outstanding organizations of professional networkers in the entire world!

You are being honored by this journal as one of the highest achievers and outstanding leaders of the profession. They've invited you to share your secrets of success at a gala awards celebration. As you consider your presentation, you think about the road you traveled to this ideal life you now enjoy. What are some of the things you accomplished over the past years that have led to your outstanding success? What kept you going when obstacles entered your path? Who have you and your team helped with your products or services? In what ways have those lives benefited? How does that make you feel? What will you tell your audience about the leaders who have emerged in your organization? What are your leaders' lives like?

What can you share with your audience about the rewards of achieving your dreams through network marketing? How will you describe your life at this perfect time? What do you have that you've always wanted? What are you doing that gives you great joy? Who have you become?

You stretch your arms up, reaching high to the ceiling and then relaxing into a fulfilled state of gratitude. How exciting and energizing life is!

Now stop and really stretch slowly as you open your eyes and return to the present. Write as much as you can in your journal about what you visualized. Capture the sounds, colors, feelings, images, and thoughts you experienced as you imagined your ideal morning. Take all the time you would like.

The moment you write your vision down, it begins to become reality. Robert Fritz describes this phenomenon in his book *The Path of Least Resistance*. See yourself stretching a rubber band between your two hands. One end of the rubber band represents your current reality, the other your vision. When you are aware of your current condition and have clarified your vision by writing it down, the forces of nature begin working for you immediately, moving you toward that vision. Fritz calls this natural phenomenon "structural tension," reminding us that all tension seeks resolution.

Don't delay. Start moving toward your vision today. Allow masters like Richard Brooke to guide you to visualize your ideal life's journey. Or take 20 minutes now to allow VisionWorks to guide you so that you're ready to ignite your intention!

IGNITE YOUR INTENTION

Our intention creates our reality.

—Wayne Dyer

Read over your vision. See if you can distill the essence of what gives you joy. Step into your vision by laser focusing it into an intention statement such as the following:

> I am committed to being a devoted wife, mother, and friend who blesses family, friends, and people I meet with a plan to assist them in growing older with grace, hope, and financial health.

My intention is to have fun coaching others to build successful businesses for themselves, ensuring both them and myself a lifetime of financial freedom to live the lifestyles we desire.

I attract people whom I can best serve with my products and with whom I will have fun helping to build huge networking organizations! I am surrounded by smart, fun businesspeople who are committed to being physically, emotionally, spiritually, and financially healthy.

These intention statements are more than just words; they are deep commitments. They clarify our most important values and instill a profound knowing that this is what we choose for our life.

Read your vision. Explore your deepest desires. How does your business fit into your picture of an ideal life? Capture this in writing; then read your intention aloud daily, both when you arise and before you go to bed. When you speak these words with conviction, they become *you*.

The fuel that keeps your intention ignited is your beliefs. First and foremost is your belief that you are worthy of your vision and intention. Personal development programs, audios, and books can help you to strengthen the belief that you deserve what you desire in your life. Allow Les Brown, Wayne Dyer, Joe Rubino, Napoleon Hill, Lynne Grabhorn, Jim Rohn, and other print and audio authors to guide you in your growth.

Closely tied to believing that you deserve the best in life is your belief in your ability to create that success. Lack of this belief is one of the key objections to becoming involved in our profession. After all, who wouldn't want financial freedom—if they thought it was actually in their power to create it?

Steep yourself in stories of others' success. Before we have our own success, these stories of others who have already succeeded inspire and teach us the skills we need to grow our business. In addition to the wealth of stories you'll hear from your upline, *Networking Times*, our profession's leading journal, is loaded with great stories and resources to build your belief. Reading the success stories of ordinary people creating extraordinary lives through network marketing is invaluable in strengthening belief in our own potential.

By surrounding yourself with success stories and learning the basic skills to build a successful business, you have begun strengthening the next necessary step: your belief in the network marketing profession. Some of our favorite tools for doing so include Tim Sales's *Brilliant Compensation* video and Richard Poe's book, *Wave 3: A New Era in Network Marketing*.

Next comes building your belief in your company and its products or services. Two concurrent paths will take you to the end goal: being a "product of the product" by personally using your company's products/services, and hearing the positive experiences others have had with them. Your company's audios and videos, conferences and trainings are all keys to strengthening this belief!

One way to gauge the VITAL signs of your business is to notice if your TV is playing videos rather than sitcoms, and if your car stereo is playing inspiring or training audios rather than talk shows. When your beliefs are strong enough in these three critical areas—personal worthiness and ability, the network marketing profession, and your company and its products/services—then you're ready to build and train your team! (See Figure 7.1.)

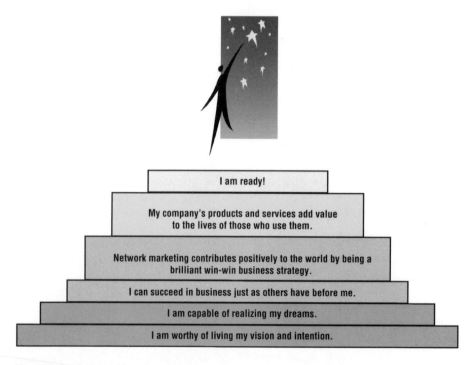

Figure 7.1   Building Your Foundation of Beliefs

TRAIN YOUR TEAM

What we have to learn to do, we learn by doing.

—Aristotle

Your team members may arise out of your existing customer base or from your inviting others to look at your business opportunity. Regardless of what brought them here, for your distributors to build successful businesses, they must be trained, mentored, and coached by you.

After guiding your new distributor through the VITAL whys of visualizing his (or her) vision and igniting his intention, it's time to teach the how-tos. The most mutually satisfying way to train a new distributor is to engage with him in building his business. Teaming up with your distributor allows you to apply your experience with his contacts to demonstrate your company's or upline's system together.

The best format for training is for you to first demonstrate, then ask your associate to practice, and, finally, give him feedback. This three-step training process works regardless of your chosen method for initial contact, follow-up, and presentation. Whether you use home parties, hotel meetings, three-way calls, PowerPoint presentations, or other techniques, by working together you can guide, demonstrate, evaluate, and refine the process to suit your distributor's personality, style, and schedule.

Success breeds success. Working closely with your distributors helps them experience success early on. The more they can practice under your experienced watch, the more quickly they will build the confidence and competence needed to train their own team members.

Help your teammates set realistic action goals tailored to the intended result. An action goal to build momentum might include, for example, speaking with 10 people daily for the next 10 days about the opportunity, and then following up. An action goal to maintain steady growth might be a simple 3-2-1 plan: Daily, talk with three new contacts about the products, follow up with two prior contacts, and offer one team member a good idea.

Action goals, as distinguished from specific results (such as "five new customers per week") are always under our control. As Stephen Covey says in *7 Habits of Highly Successful People*, "While we are free to choose our actions, we are not free to choose the consequences of those actions." Based on the results your team members get, you can help them to adjust their action goals to increase the potential for achieving their vision.

In addition to your company's and upline's how-to trainings, you and your team also have access to ever-expanding resources. Among our favorites are Networking University's "webinars," and step-by-step guides by masters such as Bob Burg, Jerry Clark, Randy Gage, Joe Rubino, Tom Schreiter, Mark Yarnell, and all of the faculty of Networking University. Learn more at www.networkinguniversity.net.

ACT AUTHENTICALLY

The prime source of nourishing interaction
is authentic, intimate relating.

—Jerry Greenwald

This VITAL sign promotes two key ideas for a healthy business: action and authenticity.

Too many new distributors start this business and then go into an extended period of analysis paralysis: reading e-mails, researching their products, reading network marketing books, filing, organizing—planning to get ready. While all of this does play a role in your business, only action (backed by belief) will give you results.

The Pareto Principle is important to learn early on: 20 percent of what you do will give you 80 percent of the return on your invested energy. If you did 10 business-related things every day and two of those (20 percent) were critical to your success, what would they likely be? (1) Contacting potential customers/team members and (2) following up with them!

During your initial contact and in all of your interactions with potential customers and team members, keep in mind this VITAL sign: act authentically. In a world where selling has gotten a bad name from those who exaggerate or downright lie in order to convince a prospective customer to buy, we have a duty and an obligation to act ethically and authentically.

Networking University has developed the following Code of Ethics setting forth fair and ethical principles and practices to guide our profession. Networking University certified professionals agree to adhere to these ethics in the conduct of their business, and thus join us in representing our industry as one committed to honesty, integrity, and opportunity for all. (This code is based in part on the Code of Ethics of the Direct Selling Association.)

A University Certified Networker shall:

1. Represent yourself, your company, its products, and services truthfully and with integrity.
2. Carefully consider the prospect's best interests. Never encourage prospects to purchase products or make commitments that you believe might have an adverse effect on their health or financial stability.

3. Truthfully identify yourself, your company, your products, and the purposes of your solicitation to any prospective customer or associate. Answer questions directly and honestly.

4. Represent realistic income projections that are in alignment with your company's reported sales, profits, and individual average earnings.

5. Tell prospects that their financial results will be directly related to their marketing and leadership skills and their own personal efforts—not a get-rich-quick opportunity.

6. Give information, not advice.

7. Support our profession by never discrediting any networking company or associate.

8. Support and encourage other networkers to be successful in the company they are in versus luring them into your company. Never knowingly initiate recruitment of an active associate from another company or from another line of sponsorship within your own company. (Should an associate initiate contact with you, then you may provide information related to their request. Should they decide to move their position to your organization, confirm that all required requests and notifications necessary or ethically desired within their organization regarding such a transfer have been completed.)

9. Not engage in illegal pyramid or endless chain schemes, the use of spamming via the Internet, sending unsolicited fax materials, or holding "ambush marketing" meetings.

10. Represent the benefits of your products only as suggested in your company's marketing materials and from your personal experience.

11. Maintain the continuing education required for professional certification.

12. Be a leader. The Networkers Team Agreements can guide you in building a high-integrity organization.

Authenticity builds trust. As Tom Schreiter relates so eloquently: "There are three reasons why people buy from you. Most of us think it's because of (1) our company (yet how well do you know its financial statement?), (2) our products/services (when was the last time you did a market study to compare similar products?), or (3) the comp plan (can you even explain it?). No, here are the three real reasons: People buy from you because (1) they know you, (2) they like you, and (3) they trust you."

If your products are excellent, your customers will use them for a long, long time. If they are not, you don't have a residual business. Therefore, if you have excellent products, why exaggerate? Acting authentically will gain you the trust necessary for new customers to say yes and for your business to be built on a solid foundation of confidence in you.

Another way to think about how we offer our products and business opportunities in an authentic way is to consider prospects as friends. A good friend listens to the other and offers ideas when asked. The adage, "People don't care how much you know until they know how much you care," plays a huge role in network marketing success. Be a friend, act authentically, and share your products, services, and opportunities from your heart. The rest will take care of itself.

LOVE YOUR LIFE

The love of life is necessary to the
vigorous prosecution of any undertaking.

—Samuel Johnson

The last—and certainly not least—VITAL sign of a healthy business is how much you enjoy your work and your life. We are in a relationship business. In addition to our products and services, we sell the potential for financial and time freedom. Are you attracted to working with someone who is over-whelmed and stressed out or exudes a poverty mentality? Or are you more excited about working with someone who is joyful and excited about life and has an attitude of abundance?

The law of attraction plays a key role in magnetizing customers and team members to our networking businesses. It must not be underestimated! One way to ignite the law of attraction is to begin living your vision *today*. While some details may not be possible to implement immediately, the feel-ings you would derive from living that vision are available to you anytime. Look deeply into your vision and intention statements: What would give you the greatest joy if your vision were to be true today? How can you have the essence of your vision today, in this very moment, so you can feel the fullness of what you desire in your life every day, beginning now?

One of our favorite resources for living a life of freedom and joy—even before having financial freedom—is Marian's book, *Revolutionary Agree-ments: Twelve Ways to Transform Stress and Struggle into Freedom and Joy*. In this book are guidelines for living an authentic life that honors and cele-brates the best in each of us.

Follow these VITAL signs of a healthy business to success in networking and life. See you at the top!

Glenn and Marian Head have been engaged in network marketing since 1995. Glenn combines his degrees in business management and educational psychology with his 11 years as president of a training design company to serve the networking community as founding dean of Networking University. Marian quickly achieved top leadership status in her networking company and then served its associates by writing for the company's newsletter, recording 24/7 training calls, facilitating weekly worldwide live conference calls, and co-designing her company's first standardized field training program. Marian and Glenn were elected by their leader-peers to Mannatech Inc.'s Associate Advisory Council, and Marian was subsequently elected by the Council to serve as its first woman chairperson.

Prior to network marketing, Glenn and Marian offered team-building and organizational development processes to companies from small start-ups to Fortune 100 firms. They designed processes and facilitated meetings from corporate boardrooms across the United States to their ropes course program in the foothills of the Rockies to international venues that hosted thousands of diverse participants in problem solving for mutual benefit. One such conference series was for the Global Forum of Spiritual and Parliamentary Leaders, which included such luminaries as Mother Teresa, the Dalai Lama, Al Gore, and Mikhail Gorbachev.

Glenn is the award-winning author of *Training Cost Analysis: A Practical Guide*. Marian is a contributing writer/editor to *Networking Times* and author of *Revolutionary Agreements: Twelve Ways to Transform Stress and Struggle into Freedom and Joy* (www.revolutionaryagreements.com). They can be reached at (303) 485-8561, glenn@mesanetworks.net, and marian@revolutionary agreements.com.

Glenn and Marian enjoy living in Colorado and Kauai with their son, Michael, and golden retriever, Boomer.

Books and audios mentioned in this chapter are available from the industry's largest supplier of network marketing resources: www.networkingtimes.com.

CHAPTER
8

The Most Critical Skill Every Network Marketing Professional Must Possess

Steve Siebold

Many people would say that recruiting is the most important skill in network marketing. Others would say contacting and inviting. Even more would argue it's learning to be effective on the phone. I disagree with all of these answers. All are important, but not *most* important. Before any of these skills contribute to building your network marketing empire, you're going to have to be mentally tough. In other words, you're going to have to learn to become a master of your emotions. This means learning how to control your thoughts, feelings, and attitudes—especially under pressure.

Why is this the single most critical skill? Because without it you will fail. Period. The rejection you face on a daily basis in this business will wipe you out, just as it has wiped out millions of other sharp, ambitious, well-educated people. The masses don't understand network marketing, and their ignorance often takes the form of ridicule. If you are mentally tough enough to keep bouncing back while growing stronger with each attack, you have a legitimate shot at living your dream in this business. There are no guarantees, but you have a shot.

The majority of people are addicted to the approval of others. Most of us are taught from an early age to place a high value on what other people think of us. We're told to obey the rules, respect our elders, and comply with society's value structure. When we stray from these commands, we are punished. Network marketing demands that you abandon this philosophy and dive into the mix. In other words, make a decision to place your highest value on your approval of yourself. This is a decision to lead rather than follow. The Gallup Organization tells us there are approximately 10 million leaders in the world leading approximately 6 billion people. Your ability to break any addiction you might have to acquiring the approval of others will determine which group you fall into.

The masses are not engaged in critical thinking. The average prospect you're contacting is more concerned about what television program they're going to watch tonight than they are about securing their future. By middle age, most people have given up hope of converting their dreams into reality and subsequently seek solace in activities where effort is minimal and pleasure is king. According to *USA Today*, the average American watches 1,669 hours of television per year. My point is that the average person's criticism of your opportunity shouldn't carry much weight if you're a true leader. I'm not putting anyone down; I'm simply suggesting the next time you experience a harsh rejection to consider the source. On the other end of the spectrum, most successful people are slow to ridicule something they don't understand. These people are accustomed to using their critical thinking skills on a daily basis and tend to carefully consider and weigh all options before reaching a conclusion.

How mentally tough are you? Mental toughness means controlling your emotions in performance situations, and people who are mentally tough develop thick skin when it comes to rejection. Mental toughness in network marketing is developed by getting in front of a predetermined number of prospects every day, either on the phone or face-to-face. The people who join you won't make you mentally tough. The people who decline but are positive about the business won't make you tough, either. It's the people that laugh at you and the whole concept of network marketing that will temper the steel inside your psyche. They will facilitate your emotional growth or they will blow you out of the business. It depends on how tough you are when the rejection hits.

The secret to survival is mental preparation. Many of the network marketing leaders I've encountered over the past 20 years spend a substantial amount of time trying to persuade their prospects and distributors how easy it is to build a successful network marketing business, while behind the scenes working 12-to-15-hour days. The average leader in this profession spends a lot of time trying to control attrition and sponsor new people. The yearly attrition rate in network marketing is well over 90 percent, and the reason is lack of mental preparation. Instead of telling people how easy it is to build a million-dollar business, do the direct opposite. Tell them it's going to be difficult. Prepare them for the onslaught of rejection headed their way. Give them examples. Role-play with them. Let them experience the emotional assault that awaits them in the field. This doesn't guarantee their success, but it gives them a fighting chance to survive their first year in the business.

Take a tip from trial lawyers. Go for the throat during role-play. If you've ever observed a trial lawyer preparing a client or witness to be cross-examined, you have the blueprint to effective role-play for mental toughness. The lawyer's job is to simulate the attack the client is about to encounter, especially during emotionally charged questions and accusations. The goal is to get under the client's skin and tap the anger, frustration, and guilt before the opposing lawyer has a chance to do the same thing in court in front of the jury. At first, the witness is shocked by the attack. But after a while he becomes desensitized to the emotionally charged language and begins to emotionally separate himself.

Spaced repetition is the secret. The emotional toughening process works best through spaced repetition. I would recommend at least four training sessions in the first 30 days after the new distributor signs up. The key is to keep him or her out of the field before this training is completed. The old strategy of throwing a new person out in the field before arming him or her with the mental tools necessary to survive is unfair at best, and malpractice at worst. Your job as a leader is to help prepare your charge for what lies ahead on the battlefield. Be responsible and do it right. Competent coaching means investing the necessary time to do the job properly.

Start with the premise of the problem. Excited new network marketers can't understand why the entire world doesn't get it. They often go out in the field for the first time with the expectation that everyone is going to see the opportunity like they do. When people don't respond, they are incredulous. It just doesn't make sense to them. They were so sure everyone would see it the way they do. Your job as a leader/coach is to help them accept the fact that most people ridicule network marketing because they don't understand it. The average person is intelligent enough but mentally unengaged, and to fully comprehend the magnitude of opportunity that network marketing presents you have to study it. Most people would rather go to happy hour or watch a ball game than seriously consider your company's compensation plan. This is not an insult. It's a statistical fact. If the average person really understood network marketing, chances are they would get involved. It's ingenious, and anyone who understands the principles of marketing and distribution will see that. Once your new person understands that the laughter and ridicule they experience say more about the prospect than about the profession, they have a mental foundation to work from.

Next, prepare them for the five major objections. Survey the most active distributors in your company and ask them to list the five most common objections they encounter in the field. Next, ask them to give you their best response to these objections. Once you have this information, role-play with your new people until they can recite the proper responses by heart. They aren't fully prepared until they can repeat the responses quickly and naturally. This takes time and patience, and it's a critical part of their mental training. Once they get good, get tougher in the role-play. Change the words of the objections around and try to throw them off. Then reverse roles and let them play the prospect. This gives them a chance to see their mentor in action. You had better be prepared, and you'd better be good. I can promise you that any successful trial lawyer could take the witness stand and endure the emotional assault of the best prosecutor in the world. If you're a true leader you'll be able to do the same. Put in the same practice time you're asking your new distributor to invest. If you don't, you can be sure you will get caught. Once you do, your credibility is gone.

Finally, explain the brain's primary purpose. To cap off this introductory phase of mental toughness training, explain to people how their brain works. The brain's primary purpose is to preserve and protect the mind and body. When an event occurs, the brain asks three questions: (1) What is it? (2) What does it mean? (3) What do I do?

Let's say the event is a prospect rejecting the new distributor. The average person has been conditioned to interpret rejection as a negative, and even psychologically threatening, event. As a result, they respond defensively and sometimes aggressively. The rejection itself is not the problem. The real menace is in the meaning that the distributor has assigned to it. The good news is that the meaning of an event is only a perception, and perceptions can be altered through reprogramming. The significance is that if you change what rejection means, you automatically change the response to it. Train your people to interpret every rejection as being one step closer to sponsoring the next person. Train them to understand that rejection is what accounts for the big money that is paid out to top distributors in this profession. Have you ever heard of a retail salesperson making a million dollars a year? No, because the rejection factor is low and the customer comes to them, so more people can do it successfully. It's simply not worth that much in the marketplace because so many people can do it. It's all supply and demand. Once they understand that rejection creates the barrier of entry for 99 percent of network marketers to become successful, they will get excited to know they are among the top 1 percent. Let them know they are part of an elite group of people in the profession who understand how the business really works. You will have to program them to believe this by emphasizing it over and over until they're mentally tough enough to stand on their own.

Get help with the programming process. As leader and coach to your organization, it's your responsibility to shape and mold your people into competent network marketing professionals. That being said, you can't do it all. You can get them started and encourage them along the way, but you're going to need help. Train your people to invest in books, CDs, and seminars on topics like mental toughness, motivation, and vision building—anything that keeps world-class ideas in front of them when you're not there. Remember they are surrounded, as we all are, by middle-class thinkers. Consciousness is contagious, so be sure they are exposed to the best of the best. Ninety days of this type of programming and exposure should be enough to enable them to stand on their own. If they are still dependent on you after that, move on and invest your precious time in someone else. Everyone has the ability to access their mental toughness, but many choose (consciously or unconsciously) not to tap into it. In a profession where momentum is critical to your success, you don't have time to wait for the slow movers.

Make a commitment today. Decide that you will become a mental toughness expert to ensure your success. Begin with these simple steps, and you'll be well on your way.

Steve Siebold is the author of *177 Mental Toughness Secrets of the World Class* (www.mentaltoughnesssecrets.com). As president of Gove-Siebold Group, he speaks to and trains networking professionals on how to get mentally tough. He can be reached at (561) 733-9078 or by visiting www.govesiebold.com.

CHAPTER 9

Belief: Why It's So Vital, How to Build It, Who's Responsible

Art Burleigh

Belief—with enough of it, we can achieve just about anything; without it, we're essentially paralyzed, blind, and disoriented, and any shot at success is pretty dim.

FORMING BELIEFS

This is where it all begins—for all of us.

Who talks with you the most? You do. Your own internal conversations—what you think about—are what will ultimately form who you become, what you do, and what level of success, accomplishment, and satisfaction you'll ultimately achieve.

Since you're already smart and involved enough in self-development to be reading this book, some of these ideas may seem rather obvious to you. But if we're trying to grow a better network marketing organization—one that's stronger, bigger, more self-sustaining, and one that finally creates its own momentum for continued growth and renewal—then we know that a bunch of people on our team need our training and help. This chapter provides some helpful guidelines and reminders. New distributors often need help in realizing how critical their own beliefs are to achieving success, and they need understanding in what areas to focus on for building belief along with tips on how to do that.

Let's first look at where most people are starting from. What key things affect our internal conversations, our thinking, our beliefs?

Four key elements come into play here:

1. Mental nourishment, our programming (positive or negative—usually it's a mix). This is the data sphere and emotional environment

we grew up with and which we allow ourselves to be surrounded by now.

2. Our experiences and references that form our reality—what we know to be true for us so far—the results of all our efforts to date.

3. Our current beliefs that have helped us get to where we now are and/or have held us back in areas where we can't seem to get ahead faster.

4. Our vision—what we hold to be inevitable about where we're going and what we're destined to achieve. Too often, this is a weak area that needs serious new, sustained effort so that a bigger vision will drive our self-motivation to propel us into the actions that enable us to accomplish our big dreams and goals.

The six inches between our ears—that's the real battleground for virtually all of us. That little space is the canvas where it all plays out—what's holding you back *and* what's going to propel you to the achievements that'll finally get you all the things you want.

With the right attitude, strong belief, vision, self-motivation, and doing the smart actions, this network marketing industry can provide you with a vehicle to achieve the peace of mind you so desire, the time freedom, the financial freedom, and the ability to move from money to meaning and from receiving to contribution. It can be the way to move from a posture of fear that maybe there's not enough money in the universe to enrich you, too, to a place where you operate from abundance and share success secrets that empower others so that you become attractive, credible, and influential. From that place, you can then draw those same kinds of people to you and your network—and you'll grow better in that process, get even more of what you want, and help countless others to do the same!

One big challenge is that mere desire for all that stuff isn't enough. To get to that level of success requires us to work on our belief systems and on our vision and self-motivation—and then, of course, to take all the actions that will yield results required for success.

What we believe affects everything that we do and achieve (or don't). If our beliefs are strong enough in four key areas, we'll get involved, develop the needed skills, and take the actions needed to achieve success. Many people are challenged by the fear of rejection in presenting the huge benefits of their company's products or services and business opportunity. I was at first. Because action overcomes fear, and stronger beliefs propel more action, the fastest way to conquer that natural fear of rejection is to work hard at first.

Building your belief in four key areas:

1. Belief in your company's products/services.

2. Belief in your company.

3. Belief in network marketing.
4. Belief in yourself.

If you're weak in any one of those areas, your chances for success diminish. Many are weak in the last two areas especially. If you're brand-new, you may be weak in all four.

After some personal work, once you get strong in those four key belief areas, you'll have posture—big time! And with posture, you're unstoppable because you then own what your network marketing business is all about. You own knowledge—either personal or third-party, from stories—that your company's products/services work and have big value! And your own belief that your company's strength grows as you and your team spread excitement about its many benefits to new ears and others get involved with you.

BUILDING BELIEF IN YOUR COMPANY'S PRODUCTS OR SERVICES

Use them more, and get others to use more, too. You and your family should use all of your company's products or services that you possibly can—so you're a product of the product and you're personally enjoying all the benefits possible that your products/services provide. If you don't do this, don't expect others on your team to do so.

If you're offering wellness products to the world, know that baby boomers are very willing to invest in their most valuable asset—their health! Eleven thousand boomers are turning 50 every day and they're concerned about anti-aging and longevity. As you plant more seeds by getting more and more customers using and enjoying the benefits of your products or services, more success/satisfaction stories will develop, and that's all valuable third-party validation for building stronger belief in what you offer.

When more people in your sphere of influence are using your company's products/services and being coached properly by you, more will generate some positive results. More excitement spreads from there—even if you don't personally achieve the speediest results you might have hoped for. If it's a good product/service, it'll probably produce important results for most people in time, including you. Tune in to all those success stories. That validation will build your belief in your products/services faster.

Other ways to strengthen your belief: Plug into all the tools your company offers, especially the weekly live training and business briefing calls. Listen in on your company's conference calls to hear all the new success stories and how other (new!) people appreciate and benefit from what your company offers.

Stories Build Belief

The more success stories you've heard and know, the stronger your belief systems will become. Often, one story on a conference call will have a lasting impact on you—and you're stronger after you hear that call. Your posture is different because of that increased strength.

People love to hear stories. Share the best success stories with your prospects. And tell the stories with passion (which helps to grab and keep their attention!) Remember, *you* have "the cookie" (your company's lead product/service and business opportunity!). And many prospects will want that cookie, too, if your belief in it is compelling enough to make it seem so desirable that it's irresistible.

What stories from your company inspire and drive you? And what are you doing to learn them so well that you can tell them to others? I strongly suggest you adopt a constant habit of mine: tape-record all of your company's weekly live conference calls so you can hear them again and easily share them with your family, with other key team leaders, and with prospects.

Facts tell, stories sell! People remember stories! Stories deliver emotional impact. They make your business offering seem much more real, and people love to hear them. Stories build belief. So, if your company or success line offers live conference calls, make sure you plug into them so you'll learn all the new stories from your company.

Benefits of Recording Conference and Training Calls

- Avoids family conflicts at home, lets you time-shift your listening.
- You can share the call with your spouse/partner at their convenience.
- Lets you hear more calls—so you learn more success stories.
- You can hear great calls again and again and share them with others.
- You can rewind the tape to catch something you missed.
- Lets you go to bed earlier in the more eastern time zones.
- A family member or friend can tape for you.
- You'll acquire a treasury of valuable stories!

And the best way to learn those stories, and also learn the valuable information on the many excellent business and personal development training albums that are available today, is to listen and relisten to them when you're exercising, walking, driving, and so on. You'll learn lots more by hearing stories and trainings over and over again. That process will build your belief system stronger and stronger—and that's one of the most valuable investments you can make in yourself.

BUILDING BELIEF IN THE COMPANY

People long for a greater sense of community today—especially since 9/11. Capitalize on this by encouraging your team to attend your company's events—they'll have a powerful effect. At just one location, you'll get to meet many of the key company executives and support staffers, plus you'll get to meet, talk with, and learn from the key field leaders from all over the country (or world).

Another smart move is to visit your company's main offices and manufacturing facility. Even if this requires a trip of thousands of miles, it's a key step in strengthening your belief in the company. You may be with your company for decades, so the more you know about it sooner, the better representative you'll be for all its offerings, and the more confidence and belief you'll have in the company, its products, the support it offers and the viability of your long-term relationship.

Call ahead and let the company know you're coming. They'll be happy to receive you and set up a tour. Meet the key people there that you interact with already—the customer service and shipping people, the phone receptionist, those who handle applications and order processing, and as many key executives as you can spend even a few minutes chatting with. If you show up with cookies and/or flowers, they'll appreciate that! Very few distributors actually do this, so chances are your company will warmly welcome your visit.

The most successful distributors have been to a ton of events, have visited company headquarters, and have engaged in lots of personal development to build their belief in all these areas. So it's really important to make continuing investments in yourself—to feed great inspirations to your mind from the experience of your company's events and conference calls so you develop stronger beliefs and better skills. And you'll learn from other industry leaders who've already made the mistakes you should avoid—they'll teach the necessary course corrections to get onto a success track faster.

BUILDING BELIEF IN THE INDUSTRY

Study this network marketing industry. Read the books by its major leaders. Attend the generic, industry-wide training events ("masterminds") that are put on in the United States several times a year by various successful teams of leaders and noted industry and personal development trainers. You can also subscribe to the industry support journal, *Networking Times*—just go to www.NetworkingTimes.com and check it out. Your belief in this industry will certainly grow stronger, of course, as you create more personal success with your own networking business distributorship.

BUILDING BELIEF IN YOURSELF

No investment is more important than the one you make in yourself! So make that investment by engaging in lots of personal development through the wealth of resources available today.

Mental Nourishment

Most people are challenged in this area because of the "lack programming" they've been exposed to since childhood. This is a big topic that's not discussed in much depth here, but virtually all of us need to overcome our own lack programming through constant, strategic reprogramming. This starts with being aware that the challenge is there, then being watchful and taking positive steps to burst through and beyond that strong lack programming that holds many people back in the herd.

Read from good, uplifting, empowering books recommended by leaders in our industry at least 15 minutes a day. Feed your mind with that nourishment and benefit from the experiences others have already had (and mistakes they've made). Figure out how to extrapolate their tips and lessons to what you need to do. Get inspired to take new and different actions, to build stronger beliefs, and to get better results.

Listen to tape and CD training albums by many of the people in this book and other industry leaders. Find them through Networking Times, Nightingale Conant, and other resources your upline can recommend. Most people have more "ear" time than "eye" time—they can listen to trainings while they're driving, walking, exercising, washing dishes, or doing chores. Turn your car into a college for higher learning. There's so much excellent training material available these days.

So many people need to hear from you, and get listened to by you so that rapport is created. Strong rapport opens up two-way communication, and others will listen to you differently when that happens. Your prospects might not fully understand the huge value of "the cookie" you have right away, but with repeated exposure, some of them will get it and want what you've got! Follow-up can yield huge rewards down the road.

Do all the stuff just discussed and start generating some growing checks from your network marketing business. It may take a little time, but you'll come to know that you can succeed with this industry as your belief in it grows.

WHO'S RESPONSIBLE FOR BUILDING ALL THIS BELIEF?

You are, of course. You must build it and continue to reinforce it—or else its natural fragility may drag you down, discourage you, and distract you from your path to success. If your upline leaders are smart, they'll be helping you build these beliefs, but if they don't, just realize that maybe they're not as serious about succeeding in this business as you are!

And if your company's owners and executives are really smart and experienced, they'll know that they, too, need to do all they possibly can to help you, and all your field colleagues, build these four key belief areas as well. Obviously, this means running the company really well, finding/creating, manufacturing, and quickly shipping/providing exceptional products or services that the public can develop a strong and lasting desire for.

This isn't easy. That's why the truly great companies last for many years and decades, and many others wither and disappear as they ultimately fail in key areas and disappoint themselves, their distributors, customers, and vendors. If they're a good company and they have a track record of strong performance, you're smart to give them the benefit of doubt when mistakes occur and things happen to occasionally disappoint you or your field colleagues. No company is perfect; mistakes will occur. If you courteously bring those mistakes and concerns you have to the attention of your company's customer service staff, things should get worked out. If they don't, you can seek upline help and/or help from a company manager or exec. If the company's management is smart, they'll be responsive to legitimate field concerns and get things fixed ASAP. Sometimes, you'll have to call on the strength of your own belief systems and vision to reassure those in your downline who get unnecessarily anxious about company mistakes.

If your company has a field advisory board, your colleagues there can usually help accelerate the correction of glitches that can adversely affect the field's belief in the company. Every leader on that advisory board wants the field's belief to be as strong as possible in all four key areas.

RECOGNITION PROGRAMS

A strong company's recognition program can go a long way to help distributors build stronger belief in themselves, in the company, and in the network marketing industry. If your company doesn't have a program like this, you should consider starting your own for your team and help it expand company-wide by working with other field leaders who can influence your company positively.

Most people never get recognized for much, if anything. So network marketing's ability to foster recognition of personal achievements has enormous value—it builds self-esteem, confidence, and belief in one's self. And as those wonderful benefits occur, the strengthened field makes the company even stronger.

VISION AND SELF-MOTIVATION

No discussion of belief would be complete without exploring the huge role that vision and self-motivation have in building stronger beliefs and facilitating increasing accomplishments. How do you believe in something that hasn't yet happened for you? Visualization creates that breakthrough.

YOUR ATTITUDE REALLY *DOES* DETERMINE YOUR ALTITUDE

Your attitude is composed of all these elements of belief. It becomes your outlook on things—what's possible and what still needs work. With strong belief, virtually anything is possible; certainly success in network marketing is, with enough work engaging in smart actions. Without belief, however, one's hopes for success in this business (or any endeavor) are effectively doomed. We all have a choice—to build our beliefs or not. What you truly believe is what you become. Where you believe you'll get to is the limit of how high you'll go. If you get there, and you then want more, you'll simply need to expand your vision and create new, empowering beliefs that can propel you even higher! Change your beliefs, and you'll change who you are, what level of contribution you'll make, and what level of rewards, satisfaction, and influence you'll ultimately enjoy.

Art Burleigh's background is in corporate law and marketing. He worked his way up from the mail room at Universal Studios into the law department in the 1970s while attending law school at night. Art then got involved in marketing, but he was always looking for a way to obtain some equity in what he was doing and maybe also develop residual income. Network marketing hooked him in 1988. Twelve companies later, he feels he was blessed to find the company he's now been with for more than nine years. He worked part-time for over four years before going full-time. Since late 2000, Art has been chairman of the Executive Field Advisory Council for that company. His team of more than 150,000 distributors now spans the North American continent. Together, they've moved more than $93 million in products for this company, and they've taken home over $54 million in team commissions.

Art and his wife, Marlyn, have been married for 25 years and live in the Los Angeles area. Their son, Seth is finishing up his undergrad studies at Berkeley. Because Art and Marlyn believe that travel isn't a luxury—it's homework for a meaningful life—they've benefited from the strong residual "mailbox money" their network marketing business has consistently generated by taking numerous family trips over the years *and* their commission checks always poured into their mailbox every week while they were gone.

Art and Marlyn now work their network marketing business full-time from their home, and they enjoy helping others discover a way to create an extra stream of strong, recurring income so they can enjoy more options and get where they really want to go in life—much sooner, and in style!

Art's web site at www.ArtBurleigh.com offers valuable support tools, insights, and training resources for those seeking to accelerate their quest to enhance their lifestyles through the mastery of network marketing.

CHAPTER 10

The Stages to Achieving Freedom Well Earned

Dan Conlon

Network marketing is the great equalizer. People of diverse backgrounds find new opportunity in network marketing every day. I know a woman who owned a residential cleaning business who now makes millions from her network marketing business. I know a CEO of a $300 million company who replaced his seven-figure income and found new opportunity and freedom through his networking business. I have seen people from all backgrounds—teachers, lawyers, medical doctors, realtors, hotel bellmen, blue-collar workers, and men and women from all levels of the corporate world—find freedom through network marketing. All have a personal story about their success that is both instructive and inspiring. Each of them faced unique personal challenges and obstacles while building their businesses. Overcoming these personal challenges is the price you pay for your freedom. Each of them now enjoys a great lifestyle and uncommon success, filled with personal satisfaction and freedom. Each of them earned their freedom and lifestyle through hard work, commitment, focus, and persistence.

It doesn't matter what you have or haven't accomplished in the past, how long your resume is, what education credentials you have or don't have; it is about knowledge and action. Freedom is about choice and a decision to act. Your commitment to take action and learn from your results and consistently pursue your goals will determine your level of success. I believe everyone can commit to an action plan and achieve a new level of personal success. The freedom achieved through network marketing is unparalleled.

During my 20-year experience in network marketing, I have had to do battle with my own fears and insecurities, modify my own bad habits and attitudes, and struggle with my lack of any real business training. My success has been as much about mastering myself and developing the proper discipline and attitudes as it has been about developing the fundamentals of building a network marketing business. I find that as I meet these challenges for myself, I am better equipped to help others.

Through the years I have worked with individuals with proven skills who quickly climbed to the top of our profession and made it look easy. It is always exciting to work with people like this. They paid a price for developing skills somewhere else and brought those skills to the opportunity. I have also worked with people who were new to business, marketing, and promotion and watched them struggle with their own fears and personal issues. But by making the commitment to work on the fundamentals of our business model and stay focused on their goals, many have earned a level of freedom they had only dreamed possible. Frankly, I have also seen people of capacity do it all wrong, get frustrated, start and quit all within their first month. Success is not determined by what you think you know about network marketing, but by learning simple, proven methods that work. So, if you are willing to work for a better life and more personal freedom, network marketing may be the perfect solution and business model to give all that you are looking for and more.

We often learn more from our mistakes than our triumphs. Experience usually begins with failures and disappointments, which if seen as opportunities for learning can be used to fuel new successes and develop new skills and abilities. The harder you work, the more experience you gain. The more experience you gain, the smarter you work and the more successful you'll become. My goal is to share with you a road map to develop the requisite skills and abilities needed for success, and to introduce you to the three different stages of business development.

Some people start a network marketing business to develop a part-time business to earn additional income. Others want to replace their full-time income and make a career change. Yet others will embrace the upside potential of network marketing and the power of leveraged income and build true wealth. That's your choice, and the plan of action you develop will reflect your goals. I have had the good fortune to work with a group of men and women, my upline, who have earned more than $250 million in personal income from their networking businesses. What I have learned from them has been invaluable, and what I have learned from my own experience in building a network marketing business has changed me forever. It helps to have mentors and coaches around to guide and support growth. Whether your goals are big or small, grand or humble, welcome to the adventure of a lifetime.

STAGE ONE: GETTING STARTED

Getting started is the most difficult part of any new venture. Adding something new to an already busy life and career can seem impossible at times. Stage one will demand more from you than you would give to a regular job. But it is *your* business, and the rewards are worth the effort. It's like learning to play chess. You have to learn the basics first. Each piece on the board does something completely different, and you need to learn how to deploy them effectively. Knowing how the pieces move is not enough; you also have to respond to your opponent's moves. As you progress, you begin to learn different strategies to respond to each situation. It takes time, a willingness to learn, and patience.

Success in network marketing is greatly facilitated by a well-developed training program, one that has proven effective in helping people reach their goals. Spend time with your sponsor and upline to learn the basics of their system for retailing, recruiting, and training. One of the benefits of a network marketing business is that you join a network, a group of men and women who have been in the business longer than you and have a track record of success that you can duplicate. Follow their lead and you won't have to reinvent the system. Your upline also has a financial interest in helping you reach your goals. You can look to your upline leaders to teach you the system they have developed to support your company's duplication process. They can't make you successful but should be willing to help you get started right. Your goal is to learn all you can from them while you're starting your business, and then develop your own proficiency, independence, and freedom. You are in business for yourself but not by yourself.

The business model of network marketing works. Learning how to successfully navigate the terrain of building a business may require different amounts of time, energy, and effort. Typically, people start their networking businesses part-time. In stage one you will focus on developing confidence in your company and in the industry of network marketing. Learn your product line. Develop basic marketing and promotional skills. Learn how to invite, qualify interest, set appointments, present your business, and pursue follow-through strategies, and how to most effectively enroll new members onto your team. Depending on your current skills and experience, this may be easy or may require a commitment of time and energy to develop the fundamental skills for success. Stage one is the initial building phase. You will learn, teach, master, and train others to use these basics throughout your career.

Action Plan

Developing an action plan for your business is the first step toward success. Write down all the reasons and motivations that describe why you chose to start a business. Your well-thought-through reasons will become the driving force behind your success. Define your purpose for being in business and a vision of where you're going. Set goals for immediate action. Set a specific schedule of your work hours. It is easier to get off to a fast start and build consistently than it is to start slowly with an inconsistent effort. Consistency is a behavior or a principle of success that is critical to a good start. Following

your action plan and holding yourself accountable to specific measurable results each day, week, and month will ensure that you make progress toward
your goals. In this stage clarity, commitment, consistency, and action are four
principles of success that determine how fast you reach your goals.

Prospecting

Our primary job as networkers is to help people to help themselves to a better
life. We help people build a better life through the use of our products and
services and economically through their involvement in our business model.
Your success as a team builder is secured by developing the business skills and
the personal skills required to attract, enroll, train, and develop the talents of
others. Prospecting is the art of finding others who also have the desire to
build a business of their own.

Therefore, as networkers, we must stay focused on this objective. We
can only help people reach the goals they are willing to set for themselves. We
can't make people successful. To truly help others in this business, our
prospects must want something new or be open to positive change in their
lives. Our prospects must realize that their current circumstances need to
change, and that to live the life they aspire to they need to change, develop,
and grow as individuals. And finally, they come to understand that our business model can deliver exactly what they want and more. That understanding
fuels their commitment to change and grow. Without that commitment to
change and grow, they are not prospects, just suspects. Learning this lesson
will help you to stay focused on working with the right people and to invest
your time wisely. Talk with a number of people in order to get practice. I
teach dozens of different prospecting techniques, so that anyone can find
three to five techniques that will work best for them.

Feel Like Quitting?

In stage one you will need to monitor your expectations. As you build your
business you will be in contact with many diverse people. Some will have
real interest and some will seem interested but are just being polite. You
will have expectations about their interest and potential contribution to
your business. Disappointments come when we assume others are more interested then they actually are. Qualifying real interest will help you keep
your expectations in check. As previously stated, you can only help people
to help themselves to a better life. In stage one, feeling like quitting is an
acceptable human emotion. However, actually quitting is unacceptable.
Make a commitment that is longer than the time it takes to develop proficiency—your learning curve. That way you set yourself up for real success
rather than disappointment.

Success is a mind-set, an attitude, a commitment, a burning desire, first requiring energy, excitement, and enthusiasm about the prospects for personal gain. Learning something new means you will make mistakes as you progress. Most adults dislike the feelings that come with making mistakes. Anticipate this and respond appropriately. Think it through in advance; choose how you want to respond to the challenges that will come, and prepare for them. If you expect business building to be easy, without challenges, you will be disappointed. If you take the business seriously, accept these challenges, and take responsibility for your actions, you will have a real formula for success. Responsibility means the ability to respond. When we take advantage of our freedom to choose and are accountable for the results we achieve, we become more powerful in the creation of the future we want.

STAGE TWO: A FULL-TIME BUSINESS OF YOUR OWN

In this phase of your development, you have learned the basics of a successful and profitable network marketing business. You are ready to take your businesses to the next level. Armed with your proven skills and new work schedule, you will find it easier to recruit people with greater capacity and skill. At this stage, you understand how to play the game and have mastered the basic strategies. You are beginning to see several moves ahead and are not surprised by your opponent's moves. On a good day, you play brilliantly.

The hallmark of this stage of the business is leading by example. You do as you want others to do. You recruit, train, and develop new leaders who bring new excitement and energy to your team. You now have the time required to build toward the big financial returns. You can now expand your business more strategically, moving beyond your local and regional areas to national and then international markets. When you start focusing your full-time efforts on the advancement of your business, momentum will really pick up.

I remember my own decision to quit my job as a welder and become a full-time networker. I had matched my full-time income within the first 90 days and began eliminating my debts with the extra income. Then in my ninth month, my wife called me at my welding job to tell me our check had arrived. It was now three times my income as a welder, and she was calling to tell me to quit my job and come home. I couldn't believe what she was saying. A few months earlier she was not sure that I should be starting a home-based business. Now she was asking me to leave my job of 13 years, an invitation to be free. Of course I said yes!

The Challenge of Self-Employment

When you start your networking business, you become the CEO, with the responsibilities of charting the course for the future of your business. You also become the management team responsible for the implementation of that vision. You also become the head of the human resources department responsible for recruiting and training the talent required to accomplish the objectives of the management team. You also take on the responsibilities of the head of marketing and promotion, and customer service. Juggling all these responsibilities will challenge you to step outside your comfort zone and learn new skills.

To develop a big networking business requires clear strategic thinking and a commitment to developing the right human resources to reach your goals. Stay in the building mode with a focus on recruiting stronger and more developed talent. Learn the discipline of being self-employed, and stay focused on your goals and objectives. This is an interesting challenge. You will now have much more free time to manage or mismanage. You can go golfing or stay home on a beautiful day and make the calls to new prospects. Hmm! The choice is now yours. There is no longer a boss checking up on you to see if you are getting things done. This is a new opportunity to discover your own undeveloped talents and can be one of the most rewarding and freeing personal experiences you may ever have.

Personal Development

Personal development is the process of developing more of what you have as latent potential within. Reaching your full potential as a human being consists of two different processes. One is the process of acquiring new characteristics and attributes such as patience, courage, determination, self-confidence, and trustworthiness. The second process is correcting old habits, the wearing away of the rough edges of your personality, like shyness, fearfulness, or unworthiness. This is the process where we lose or release the behaviors that no longer work for us. Stepping outside your comfort zone is an act of courage. It's also where the excitement is and where real personal growth begins.

An analogy that best illustrates this point is to look at our behavior like driving a car. We control the steering, transmission, brake, and the accelerator. The steering keeps us moving in the direction we want to go. The transmission is our human potential and current skills. The accelerator is our focus, excitement, and confidence that power us forward. The brakes are our fears that stop us or hold us back. When used appropriately, they provide for safe mobility. However, when we step outside our comfort zone, we respond to our fears and or excitement by putting our foot on the brake or on the accelerator and sometimes both. How we use these controls determines how fast we grow and reach more of our potential.

STAGE THREE: PRIVILEGED LIFESTYLE—FREEDOM

This stage is the culmination of all your plans and efforts. You have worked hard and learned much. You have well-developed skills and proven command of the business. You think and act on long-term goals and objectives. You are free! You have developed a group of strong full-time leaders. They are trained and growing without your involvement. They look to you for guidance and support on the bigger issues of planning and leadership development. You have the respect of your peers and the admiration of your corporate leaders. You are now the chess master. You see the outcome of the game before you move your first piece. You know all the gambits; you know where your opponent is going before he or she makes the next move. Each move you make flows seamlessly into the next. You are rarely surprised; you are in control of the board.

Leadership

Most of the leaders I have met in network marketing have worked hard on both themselves and their businesses. Many are articulate, have a great sense of humor, are great storytellers, have great product knowledge, have a deep understanding of the fundamentals of network marketing, and have high energy, natural excitement, and have a well-developed self-image and confidence. They inspire the best in the people around them. By working on yourself as much as on the business, you can develop your own style of leadership.

At this stage, your consistent efforts have paid off. You love this game, both for what it has given you and for what it has allowed you to give others. You have earned the right to true freedom! Your experiences have made you a better person and a better leader. You have met your own personal challenges and those victories have fueled your confidence and personal success. It is never easy, but you did it! Freedom at this level is its own reward. When others say you are lucky to have such success and freedom, you'll know with certainty that the freedom you have is a freedom well earned.

Dan Conlon is a husband, the father of two great children, a mentor, and a personal development coach. Dan is also the author of several network marketing training systems that focus on practical, easy-to-follow strategies for both the beginner and veteran networkers. Dan has been in network marketing for more than 20 years and has written several articles for *Networking Times* magazine.

He believes the mechanics of success in network marketing are simple and straightforward, that anyone can achieve a new level of personal and professional success by following simple, proven systematic methods.

Dan's mission is to help people help themselves to a better life. As a leader with NuSkin Enterprises, Dan has been instrumental in launching the company's three divisions, including NuSkin Personal Care, a premier line of anti-aging skin care; Big Planet, an Internet-based technology and e-commerce company; and most recently Pharmanex, an innovative leader in the health and wellness industry. Dan is actively building a global business, and his hands-on approach is both instructive and effective. Dan's down-to-earth style and straightforward business practices have helped thousands of individuals find their own unique path to success. Dan speaks globally to groups with an inspiring message suitable for all companies and organizations.

To reach Dan Conlon with questions and to obtain additional training resources, call (262) 375-9322 or (888) 570-1916. E-mail your questions to Dan at danconlon@bigplanet.com. Visit Dan's web site at www.danconlon.com.

CHAPTER 11

You Are Only a Couple of Sentences Away from Terrific Success in Your Network Marketing Career

Tom "Big Al" Schreiter

At my live workshops, I ask the attendees, "How many of you started your network marketing business a little bit slow?" Nearly everyone's hand goes up in the air. And then I tell them how I got started.

In 1972, I got started in network marketing. After one year and 10 months, I had no distributors and no retail customers. A leader came to me and said, "Hey, Big Al, you're doing really, really bad."

Great. I needed that encouragement.

The leader continued, "Big Al, if you want to improve your business, here are five things that you can do."

I quickly grabbed a pencil and took notes as the leader told me:

- "First, you've got to improve your attitude." (Ouch, that was getting pretty personal, but hey, maybe it could use a bit of improvement.)
- "Second, you have to build a strong belief in the business." (Well, that made sense. If I believed stronger, more people would see my conviction.)
- "Third, you need to set some goals." (I am sure you have heard this dozens of times, but for me it was a brand-new concept.)
- "Fourth, you need to get motivated, because people are attracted to motivated people." (Sounded like a great strategy to me.)
- "And fifth, be positive. Anyone can be negative, but leaders are positive." (Yes! I would strive to block out all of the negatives and be the positive leader that people wanted.)

Well, here is what happened. I improved my attitude, built a strong belief in my business, set some goals, got motivated, became more positive . . . and it didn't work!

I did all five things, and my business was still at zero. I found out that all of these things are great hobbies, but when you are face-to-face talking with prospects, they don't work.

Now I know what you are thinking. Not only are you skeptical, but you are also thinking, "Wait a minute! I read a motivational book every morning, I play CDs in my car on how to be more positive, I do running high fives with my downline, I jump off a chair every morning waving my bonus check while singing the company song . . . and you're telling me these things don't work?"

Yes. When you are face-to-face, talking with prospects, these things don't work.

Skeptical? Take this test.

1. When you first got started in network marketing, did you have a good attitude? Did you think, "Yeah, I think I can do this"?

2. When you first got started in network marketing, did you have a strong belief in your company? Did you think it was a great company?

3. When you first got started in network marketing, did you set some goals? Did you plan to get some extra paychecks, a new car, quit your job, or travel?

4. When you first got started in network marketing, were you motivated? Did you feel like saying, "Yeah! Fire the boss! This is my chance!"

5. When you first got started in network marketing, were you positive? Did you say, "Yes! Here is my money. Let me get started now."

And finally, how fast did you get started?

If you are like most people, you will admit that you had a good attitude, had a strong belief in your business, set goals, had personal motivation, and were positive . . . but you still started slow.

And now, the attendees at the workshop realize the problem. Even though they had these five great assets, they still weren't successful. And then I tell them what made the difference for me.

In my case, I was missing a little thing called skills. Skills are knowing exactly what to say, and exactly what to do when talking to a prospect. And if you don't have skills, well, it's going to be a hard, hard career.

Let me give you an example. Imagine you go to the greatest motivational workshop in the history of mankind. At the end of the workshop, you're levitating. You are floating one foot above the ground and simply glowing with enthusiasm and motivation. So you levitate out of the building, you levitate down the sidewalk, and you levitate right up to the very first prospect you see, and . . . you smile. You glow. You vibrate with enthusiasm. But you don't say a word. Do you think the prospect is going to say, "Hey, let me join your business. You look like somebody who is motivated and has set some goals." Of course not.

If you don't say something, and if you don't do something, nothing is going to happen.

It's what you say and it's what you do that counts when you are face-to-face with your prospect. And if you don't know what to say and if you don't know what to do, well, you're toast, roadkill, dead meat . . . it's ugly. You have to say something and do something in order to prospect. People won't just come running across the street asking you to join just because you have a goal chart at home.

So the real key is, "Can I learn exactly what to say and exactly what to do to attract prospects to my business?" Because your prospects don't see the home office, they don't see the mission statement of the company founders, they don't see the big computer. All your prospects see is you! So your prospects have to make up their mind based on what you say and what you do.

And you can learn those skills. And the great news is that you don't have to be a superstar, possess an outgoing personality, be a pushy salesperson or a professional hugger, or have great courage. All you have to do is to learn exactly what to say and exactly what to do—and you can build a big business.

Want more great news?

Most people are only a few sentences away from success in their network marketing business. By learning a few key icebreakers and a few key prospecting questions, they can get all of the presentations they need. And that's all we ask the prospects to do in our network marketing career. Simply look at our presentation and then make a decision that is best for them. That's it.

So are you still skeptical that skills make a difference? Let's look at learning how to fly an airplane. Now, as a pilot, I am going to teach you how to fly an airplane. Excited? I take you down to the airport and we find a small single-engine airplane. I strap you in, close the door, wave good-bye . . . and just before you take off down the runway, I throw in a CD on goal setting.

What's going to happen at the end of the runway?

Crash and burn.

So I run down to the end of the runway, pull you out of the wreckage and say, "Winners never quit, and quitters never win."

I drag you to the front of the runway, find another plane (this time we rent it), and strap you in the pilot's seat. I close the door, wave good-bye, and just as you are rolling down the runway, I yell out, "Get motivated!"

What's going to happen at the end of the runway?

Crash and burn.

Again I run down to the end of the runway, pick you up from the wreckage, brush off the little singed bits, and I say, "You need to focus. You need persistence."

Then I drag you back to the front of the runway, put you into another airplane, strap you into the pilot's seat, close the door, wave good-bye, and just as you are rolling down the runway, I yell out, "Get a better attitude!"

What's going to happen at the end of the runway?

Crash and burn.

At this point you say to yourself, "I see a trend. And the only way for me to stop the pain is to quit!" And you quit.

It didn't matter how positive you were, or how much you believed in flying. If you don't have the skills, you will crash and burn. And this happens to new distributors in network marketing all the time. When they first get started, they have a great attitude, a strong belief in their business, goals, and motivation, and they are extremely positive, but they don't have any skills. So what happens?

They talk to a few friends who tell them that they are crazy. When they talk to relatives, it gets uglier. And when they talk to strangers, well, because they didn't know exactly what to say and exactly what to do, they get rejected and humiliated, and your new distributors think that the only way to stop the pain is to quit!

Sound familiar?

Need another example of how skills make the difference?

Imagine that I am a new distributor and you are my sponsor. My job is to make some chocolate chip cookies. So you send me into the kitchen. I look around and say, "Gee, nothing looks familiar here. I think that thing over there is a spoon." What are the chances that I am going to be able to make chocolate chip cookies?

Zero.

You open the door to the kitchen a bit, look inside, and see that I haven't made any chocolate chip cookies yet. You feel sorry for me and want to help me. So, you toss into the kitchen a CD on goal setting!

When you come back a few days later, what do you see inside of the kitchen? Do you see chocolate chip cookies?

No. You see charts on goal setting on the walls. Pictures of what chocolate chip cookies should look like. And I have a goal-setting group together and we are discussing what it would be like to be able to make chocolate chip cookies.

Well, you want to be helpful, so you yell, "Get more positive!" And then you leave for a few days.

When you come back and look inside the kitchen, here is what you see. I have written hundreds of affirmations and I am chanting, "I am a chocolate chip cookie." But still no cookies.

You try to help me by yelling, "Get more motivated!"

I immediately write a cheery song about chocolate chip cookies, dance the chocolate chip cookie dance, and cheer with enthusiasm . . . but still no chocolate chip cookies.

The only way that I can make chocolate chip cookies is if you give me a cookbook that tells me exactly what to do. No amount of positive thinking or motivation will do the trick. I have to have some skills. I have to know about ingredients and what to do with the ingredients. Now granted, I may not make the best chocolate chip cookies in the world the first time I try, but I will be able to make chocolate chip cookies. Skills make a difference. And insufficient skills are what hold back new distributors from contacting people and exposing their business.

Most new distributors talk to a few people who tell them, "I am too busy. You are crazy. I don't do those sort of things. I am not a salesman. It's a pyramid. I can't see myself doing that business."

And what happens?

The new distributor quits because he hates getting the constant rejection.

Instead of getting the new distributor motivated to go out and get constant rejection, why don't we do this? Why don't we teach the new distributor the skills necessary to get the prospects to say, "Yes, tell me more"?

Let's teach our distributors exactly what to say and exactly what to do to get prospects to lean forward and ask us for a presentation.

Tom "Big Al" Schreiter writes the "Fortune Now Newsletter for Leaders" and is the author of six books on network marketing. With more than 30 years of network marketing experience, Tom gives live workshops throughout the world. You can reach him by e-mailing bigalnews@fortunenow.com.

You can read some of his books and newsletters free at www.fortune now.com and at www.sponsoringtips.com.

CHAPTER
12

A Sense of Urgency

Charles E. "Tremendous" Jones

f you could add one personality trait to improve yourself as an effective, successful network marketer, what would you choose? Courage? Wisdom? Enthusiasm? Confidence? We could go on and on and still probably miss the one you might choose. I heard a speaker say it was important to be inspired but still more important to have the desire, the will to want to. I most heartily agree with him. I also like Dr. Norman Vincent Peale's six-point success formula: (1) work, (2) work, (3) work, (4) forget self, (5) set goals, and (6) get along with others. We've all heard many formulas, and they all will work if we will.

Most are ready to accept these success formulas but for some reason never get them into high gear. You've noticed many in the field of network marketing who have great potential and every reason to be tremendously successful, but nothing seems to happen in their organizations. What is it that chains so many of us to the pit of mediocrity? What is it that dampens the fires of greatness that are lit so many times in our hearts?

Perhaps my findings are not the only solution, but with all my heart I believe the fires of greatness in our hearts can be kept aglow only after we develop a sense of urgency and importance of what we are doing that goes beyond just enrolling others to make us money. I mean a sense of urgency to the extent that we feel it is a matter of life and death; and for many trapped in jobs they hate and lives of quiet resignation, it *is* a matter of life and death. For in growing, we are alive, and in quitting on our dreams, we are dying in a sense. If you don't believe this, talk to anyone who has lost the sense of urgency of getting things done and has been drifting in complacency, mediocrity, and/or failure. If you are without a sense of urgency in the building of your network marketing business, you know what I mean.

A sense of urgency is that feeling that lets you know yesterday is gone forever and tomorrow never comes. *Today* is in your hands. It lets you know that shirking today's task of speaking with a new prospect will add to wasted yesterdays marked by procrastination. Postponing today's work will add to tomorrow's burden. The sense of urgency causes you to accomplish what to-day sets before you. The sense of urgency can change a dull, shabby effort in building your business into a sparkling career filled with positive expectation and accomplishment. While this may not be the complete solution, I think we can all agree this will be a tremendous step in the right direction, moving your business forward. Right now, decide to take on a sense of urgency in your work. Believe that you can, and then act accordingly.

To help our sense of urgency help us, let's look at seven "tremendous" laws of leadership that will support your networking accomplishments and follow that up with an examination of two important qualities essential to any endeavor—discipline and loyalty.

SEVEN "TREMENDOUS" LAWS OF LEADERSHIP

1. *Learning to put excitement in your work.* Why is it that some people work and work at their network marketing business, and never have anything to show for it? And others spend fewer actual hours work-ing their business and accomplish more? The secret is learning to put excitement in your work.

    If I'm not learning to get excited about the tasks involved in business building that I don't like, I'll never get to be very excited about the aspects that I do like. Everybody in network marketing looks for the right opportunity to change their lives. Sometimes you'll hear, "I'm looking for the perfect company that fits me." I say, "I hope you get something better than that." We need to learn that no company or income opportunity can make you successful on its own, but anyone who can put excitement into their daily efforts can make their opportunity successful and touch the lives of many others in the process.

2. *Use or lose.* There's a law that says we all have certain attributes, characteristics, and talents. If you use what you have as you go about building your business, you'll develop more skills and attract more help; but if you don't use it, you'll lose it. One night, as I was coming out of a seminar, a person asked, "Do you think it's possi-ble for someone to be excited about their business, be thrilled about its potential and successful in attracting others to it, and then, three years later, be sick of the whole thing and sorry they ever heard of the whole business?" Here's a perfect example of one who doesn't know the law of use or lose. Once he was in his glory, using all the talents he had, and as a result was successful. But one

morning, because he wasn't using what he had, he began losing it. People stopped showing up to expand and duplicate success. And one morning he woke up and asked, "What went wrong? Who let me down?"

The answer is that nobody let him down. Nothing went wrong. Because he wasn't using what he had, he was losing it. And the people who lose it always blame somebody else. Remember nobody is ever a failure until they blame someone else. Responsibility always means looking in the mirror, rather than placing blame elsewhere.

3. *Give to get.* In network marketing and in life in general, leadership is about learning to give whether or not you get anything in return. If you ever give to get something, you're not giving; you're trading. And there's a big difference between giving and trading.

If a person gives whether or not they expect to get anything in return, then they are learning to give. If you give whether or not you get anything, you get a greater capacity to give more, whether or not you get anything in return. And out of this begins to develop a reservoir of reserve and readiness that becomes a tremendous asset. You can lose your reputation, you can lose your home, you can even lose your family, but you can't lose your capacity to give once you've begun to live this law.

4. *Production to perfection.* Someone going about their business-building efforts will say, "I'm a perfectionist. I believe in doing everything perfectly, including prospecting, following up, enrolling, and training. And if I can't do all aspects of my business perfectly, I won't do any." That's the person who never does anything. As a result, he gets to be right about keeping his perfect record in place. But what is he sacrificing in the process?

There's a law that says if you're not learning to make something happen today, you'll never know more than your own whimsical, shallow dreams. Production will teach you a little about perfection, but perfection will never be more than your own fantasy. Give up your need to be perfect and build your business with a commitment to being excellent, instead.

5. *Exposure to experience.* In the beginning of life, suppose everybody receives an imaginary key ring. Every time a person is exposed to another situation they get another key of experience for their key ring. Soon, the key ring begins to fill with thousands and millions of keys of experience.

As a person gets exposure and experience, they get to use the same keys over and over again. The law of exposure to experience gets better with the years. Finally, a person gets to know which keys unlock which doors, while the inexperienced don't know if they have a key. All they can do is fumble around and hope to add another key of experience to their key ring.

Network marketing offers each of us the opportunity to expand and grow daily. It gives us the chance to meet new people, learn new lessons, and develop new experiences to become the person we choose to be. If we have the courage to experience new challenges and learn from each, our business expands and we get to grow as individuals. If we opt to play small, not speak with prospects who may reject us, and avoid situations where we may fail, our business suffers and we wonder why we are not having the success for which we once hoped.

6. *Flexible planning.* This is the age of the planner. Everybody's planning, planning, planning. In network marketing, don't ever tell anyone that planning alone will do it. I believe you have to have a plan to move your business forward deliberately, but the real law is not planning; it's flexible planning. Flexible planning says, "Plan on it going wrong." If we expect to experience challenges, we'll be able to creatively overcome them and be back on the track to success.

You say, "What if it goes right?" We will just have to work it in. Growing is learning that nothing ever goes wrong except to make you more right. Learn to embrace problems. Welcome them. Know that in every problem is the seed of a way to overcome them and achieve greater success in your business. Give up your right to invalidate yourself when things do not go as you had hoped. Ask yourself, "What might be missing for me to address to bring about the results I'm looking to accomplish?"

7. *Motivated to motivating.* Which would you rather be: a miserable motivator or a happy motivated flop? I would rather be a happy, motivated flop, because if I can be motivated long enough, I'll get to be motivating, and if I can be motivated long enough, I'll eventually become a motivator. And I'll get to enjoy what I get. That's not the case with the person who has learned to motivate everybody but themselves. Our problem isn't motivating them, but keeping them from demotivating me. The motivation will flow when you are totally committed and involved.

Motivation is a natural result of a positive expectation of your ultimate success in this business. If you believe you will be successful in building your business, you'll be motivated to do those things that will result in accomplishment. To the contrary, if you expect to fail, why bother staying in action? You expect it will do little good to speak with people about your opportunity. They'll probably not be interested anyway, so why go through the trouble? We get what we expect, so check your belief level first if your motivation is lacking.

DISCIPLINE AND LOYALTY

We live in a world where these two great words—discipline and loyalty—are becoming meaningless. Does this mean that they are worthless? On the contrary, they are becoming priceless qualities because they are so hard to develop in the first place. And should you be one of the fortunate few who have caught the vision of how network marketing can contribute to your life and to the lives of others you introduce it to, your battle has just begun. This is because the greatest battle is to keep what you've learned through these two priceless qualities.

Discipline is that great quality that few people use that enables them to be constructively busy all the time in the pursuit of their goals. Even in discouragement, rejection, and defeat, discipline will rescue you and usher you to a new place to keep constructively busy while you forget about doubt, worry, and self-pity. Oh that more men and women in this day would realize the absolute necessity of discipline and the degree of growth and happiness to be attained from it. In network marketing, maintaining the discipline to prospect and follow up those prospects every day will surely go far in ensuring your ultimate success. Discipline is essential to produce a result in any action plan, but it is even more critical when things are not going well. It's too easy to return to what is convenient rather than maintain the discipline to stay in action despite the challenges and disappointments.

Most people think that loyalty is to a thing or to a person when actually it is to one's own self. Some think that it is to a goal or an objective, but again it is to one's own convictions. If loyalty has to be earned, then it is deserved and is hardly more than devoted emotion based on a temporary feeling. No, loyalty is the character of a person who has given oneself to a task, and this person will always realize that out of a loyal heart will spring all the other virtues that make life one of depth and growth.

Be loyal to yourself and go about your daily efforts with a disciplined sense of urgency, expecting that you will touch countless lives with your products and income opportunity. When you spend your days introducing others to your business with a passion that speaks your enthusiasm for what this awesome opportunity can do for others (and for you as a result of you contributing to them), you will give forth an energy that attracts others to you. They will see and feel your commitment to share the gift that network marketing can be and will want to partner with you, inspired by your belief and positive expectation.

Charles E. "Tremendous" Jones, CPAE (Council of Peers Award for Excellence), was born in Alabama and grew up in Pennsylvania. He now resides in Mechanicsburg, Pennsylvania, with his wife, Gloria. They have six children, seven grandchildren, and two great-grandsons. He received a Doctor of Humane Letters from the Central Pennsylvania College and Doctor of Christian Education from Canyonville Christian Academy. Jones entered the insurance business at age 22 with MONY Life Insurance Company. At age 23, he was awarded his agency's Most Valuable Associate Award. Ten years later, he received his company's highest management award for recruiting, manpower and development, and business management. At age 37, his organization exceeded $100 million in force, at which time he founded Life Management Services, to share his experience through seminars and consulting services.

For more than a quarter of a century, thousands of audiences in the United States, Canada, Mexico, Australia, New Zealand, Europe, and Asia have experienced nonstop laughter as Mr. Jones shares his ideas about life's most challenging situations in business and at home. He is the author of *Life Is Tremendous*, with more than 2,000,000 copies in print in 12 languages. Two of his speeches, "The Price of Leadership" and "Where Does Leadership Begin?," have been enjoyed by millions on video, on cassette, and at conventions. He is featured in the *Leadership by the Book* television series with Ken Blanchard, *Dynamic Achievers World Network* television series, the Automotive Sales Training Network satellite training service, "Insights into Excellence" video training series, Nightingale's "Executive Treasury of Humor" cassette series, and two 30-minute color films by Sales Masters, *The Leading Edge* and *Learning—A Tremendous Experience*. More than 1,000 companies throughout the world have used the films.

Mr. Jones is the president of Life Management Services, Inc.; CEO of Executive Books; member of the advisory board of Investment Timing Service; chairman, Pneumedic Corporation; member of the National Speakers Association Hall of Fame; and member of the Speakers Roundtable. In 2001 he was recognized by the National Speakers Association as one the top 20 speakers of the twentieth century. E-mail him at Tremendous@ExecutiveBooks.com and visit his web site at www.ExecutiveBooks.com.

CHAPTER 13

The Art of Persuasion

Nido Qubein

Do you want to boost your selling power and effectiveness in network marketing? Then add power to your persuasion. But how can you add power to your persuasion? How can you become more effective at persuading your customers to buy and become more effective at persuading your prospects to join your team?

Let's look at the way skilled professionals put power into their ability to persuade. Let me share with you 10 secrets I've learned from some of the most persuasive people in America—10 ways to add power to your persuasion. I call them the 10 Ps of persuasion.

1. BE POSITIVE

One of the most successful insurance salesmen in America is a country fellow from south Georgia, who says, "You can no more sell something you don't believe in than you can come back from some place you ain't been." Successful salespeople are positive people. Successful network marketers are, too. They have positive mental attitudes about themselves, the companies they represent, the products or services they're selling, the prospects they're attempting to persuade, the country they live in. They're positive about everything. Enthusiasm is contagious. When you're excited about life and the work you're doing, you can persuade with power, because you can get other people excited.

2. PROSPECT

Successful networkers have learned to direct their persuasive power toward people who have the mental and physical resources necessary to achieve success in this business. In addition to offering their opportunity to everyone without prejudging their suitability, successful networkers also pinpoint those prospects who are likely to possess the qualities necessary to ensure long-term success and therefore profitability. They look for people who are coachable and for those who have shown a propensity for doing those things that have resulted in accomplishment in other areas of life and business.

In short, the powerful persuader prospects deliberately, targeting purposeful efforts at people who have the desire, resources, motivation, and willingness to make sound decisions to move their businesses forward, and the potential for attracting other successful people.

3. PREPARE

Red Motley, who started *Parade* magazine, said that the average person will work like crazy to get a sales appointment or an opportunity to make a business presentation, then blow the opportunity with a poor presentation after the prospect has agreed to the interview.

You don't persuade busy people by rambling on for 40 minutes about features and benefits of your products or company. Usually, after such disjointed presentations, neither the networker nor the prospect can summarize what's just been said. Professional networkers always do their homework. They know that the better they're prepared, the more persuasive they'll be when they walk in to make a presentation. They research to find out everything they need to know about the prospect. They plan what they will show and what they will say, and they practice, practice, practice.

4. PERFORM

Amateur networkers are easily let down when their prospect turns out to not be interested in their income opportunity or their potential customer refuses to make a purchase. How could that customer not want these great products? How could that prospect not see the value in this marvelous opportunity? They must be idiots!

The customer and prospect were not idiots. Either the novice networker simply did not create sufficient value to persuade the customer to buy or the prospect to join or, perhaps, the products or opportunity were simply not a fit.

Remember: People don't typically know the benefits of using your wonderful products or joining your extraordinary company. Communicating this extreme value is *your* responsibility. If you don't make a strong presentation, you can't persuade your prospect to buy or join.

Powerful persuaders are like stage actors playing to a full house. They are artists at making their presentations. They're entertaining and informative to watch and hear. At the same time, they are authentic and persuasive in communicating value. To achieve top levels of success in your network marketing business, you have to make your presentations count by communicating rich possibilities for your prospects to step into while creating true value for your products or services.

5. BE PERCEPTIVE

Powerful persuaders are alert to everything that happens during a prospect's interview. They are not preoccupied with personal problems, with airline schedules, or even with the next call they are going to make. They know that building their network marketing organization always begins with focusing on the presentation at hand. Powerful persuaders tune in to their prospects and look for the motivating forces in the life of each. Once they discover that motivating force, they play to the motivation. To add power to your persuasion, learn to read your prospects and to discover the motivations they have to want to join you in partnership to build a residual network marketing income.

6. PROBE

Novice networkers often do a lot of talking, in the belief that dumping lots of information on their prospect or customer is surely the way to get them to see value in their company, products, and opportunity. They ramble on, clueless about what may be important to the prospect or how their company's offerings might contribute to their lives.

That's why silence is so threatening to most novice networkers. The instant a prospect pauses to take a breath, the amateur will jump in with a sales spiel or some additional information, just to break the silence.

But powerful persuaders use questions to diagnose the needs and concerns of a prospect much as a skilled physician uses them to diagnose the problems of a patient. They become masters at asking penetrating questions, and they use those questions to draw prospects into the selling or enrollment process.

7. PERSONALIZE

The most powerful word in selling and prospecting is "you." The emphasis on "you" marks the difference between manipulative and nonmanipulative presentations. Manipulative prospecting is self-centered. It focuses on what the networker wants and needs. Nonmanipulative prospecting is client-centered. It focuses on the needs and desires of the prospect.

A person who is looking at the business proposition you are offering wants to know just one thing: What's in it for me? If you want to add power to your persuasion, personalize every part of your presentation to meet your prospect's own personal needs and wants.

8. PLEASE

Powerful persuaders seek to close sales or enroll new distributors by pleasing their prospects. When prospects become excited about the idea of owning what you're selling, they become customers. When they become excited about realizing how your income opportunity can have an impact on their lives, they become associates and partners in your business.

Professional salespeople know that they can't force their prospects to buy. Their challenge is to make them *want* to buy. So they seek to please them in so many ways that they create the desire to buy. Successful networkers know that they can't make their prospects build a networking business. Sure, they might talk the prospect into enrolling and maybe even buying some products, but if the prospect is ever to build a significant networking business, the prospect must eventually become self-motivated and take the consistent and persistent actions required to achieve significant levels of success.

9. PROVE

Savvy networkers don't make statements they can't back up with facts and stories to demonstrate their points. And they don't expect their prospects to accept at face value everything they say. They are always prepared to prove every claim they make—to back up those claims with hard data, with test results, and with testimonials from satisfied customers and successful business builders. One of the best ways to persuade by proving is to give proof statements from people who are happy with your products or services. Third-party endorsements go a long way in building credibility for your claims and for your products.

Facts combined with testimonials are very persuasive. Learn to use them, and become a powerful persuader. An old cliché says, "Facts tell and stories sell." The masterful networker uses facts to appeal to the logical, left-brained aspects of the prospect's personality while adding stories to entertain and enroll their emotional side.

10. PERSIST

Call on good prospects as many times as it takes to persuade them. About 80 percent of sales are made on the fifth call or later. It takes at least three follow-up contacts to enroll most successful network marketers. Yet studies have shown that:

- Fully 50 percent of network marketers call on a prospect one time and quit.
- About 18 percent call on a prospect twice and give up.
- Some 7 percent call three times and call it quits.
- About 5 percent call on a prospect four times before quitting.
- Only 20 percent call on a prospect five or more times before they quit.

It's that 20 percent who enroll the majority of future associates and generate 80 percent of the sales through their persistent efforts. You don't have to become a dynamic personality to consistently sell or enroll. You don't have to put pressure on people or outtalk people to accomplish your objectives. In fact, putting pressure on your prospects is ineffective in producing a result or in developing long-term leaders. It also leaves so many prospects who do not choose to become involved with a very bad taste about those obnoxious, pushy network marketers!

The most effective thing you can do is to apply your own intuitive skills and savvy to these 10 ways to add strength to your persuasion. To master the art of persuasion—as well as selling and enrollment—you must also learn to recognize and work with different personality types.

There are eight different types of personalities:

1. *The balkers.* These people are indecisive. They can't make up their minds. It takes a lot of patience to deal with them. Sooner or later, you have to support them in moving the action in a forward direction by asking, "What would keep you from making a decision to join us today?"

2. *The talkers.* You can control the talkers by asking questions to keep pulling them back on track. Use simple questions they can answer "yes" or "no" interspersed with questions that allow you to develop rapport, identify what's important to them or missing from their lives, and support them in seeing how your offerings can contribute to their lives.

3. *The clams.* Keep drawing them into the conversation with questions to make them talk. Ask for advice or for their opinions.

4. *The skeptics.* With the cynics, use a lot of raw data. Pour on the proof statements and documentation. Keep getting agreements as you go along. Never argue or make these skeptics wrong. Instead, listen to their concerns and assist them to see the value you are presenting.

5. *The sarcastic souls.* Sometimes they're hard to take, but keep your cool. Find out what's behind their sarcastic remarks. Laugh at their sarcasm. Listen to the concerns that underlie their words. Support them to see the value.

6. *The egotists.* Resist the temptation to tell them off. Feed their egos by asking their opinions and giving them compliments. Win them over by giving in on all minor issues. Empower them to choose your company and join your team.

7. *The bullies.* They get their way by acting tough. Be nice, but stand your ground. Don't run, don't fight—just stand. In the end, this is a business in which we get to choose who our business partners will be. Perhaps you might decide not to invite some people with poor attitudes to join you.

8. *The timid ones.* Take it nice and slow; don't rush them. Concentrate on building their confidence. Network marketing is a business where anyone willing to work on themselves along with their business can be successful.

You have to deal with different types of people in selling your products and services and in interviewing for potential business partners. The better you become at discovering and dealing with each of the different personality types, the more successful you can be.

Remember, prospects always do things for their own reasons—not for yours or mine. You're thinking: "I wish this prospect would go ahead and make a decision. . . . I need this enrollment. . . . Besides, I've got another appointment!"

But the prospect keeps thinking: "Why should I spend this much money? Is this the best opportunity I can find right now? Can I really become successful in this company? What's the big rush?"

If you want to move an evasive prospect to action, you have to give that prospect a strong benefit for acting promptly. And here's where you can usually separate the novices from the real pros. The novices start to become desperate. They forget about maintaining their all-important posture and instead become needy. This energy may further turn off their prospect. After all, who wants to partner with a desperate person?

That's not a visionary prospecting strategy, not the high-level posture that works effectively with people who are supposed to be attracted by your professional skills. In fact, it often creates precisely the opposite effect from what you want. The prospect starts thinking: "Maybe this person is not such an expert, after all! He or she must not have much business! Maybe I'd better take a closer look at this whole thing!"

Real professionals take the opposite approach. They develop rapport and determine what is important to or missing in the prospect's world. They create true value, showing prospects how they can impact their lives for the better with the products and/or income opportunity. They focus on the prospects' key benefits for becoming involved in the business immediately. Their energy says, "I'd love to work with you in partnership to create a life-changing income for you and your family—but I am certainly *not* attached to you having to do anything!

It's called "hot button" selling and enrolling, and it works like this. You find the prospect's primary motivation for buying products or joining your business and zero in on that motivation. You keep asking questions until you find the prospect's strongest reason for acting promptly, then you reinforce the client's own reason.

One of the simplest and most powerful formulas for success I've ever discovered came from Frank Bettger, a man Dale Carnegie called the best salesman he ever met. Frank Bettger said, "Show people what they want most, and they will move heaven and earth to get it."

So I always figure that if people are not willing to do whatever it takes to get moving, I have not yet discovered and shown them what they want most. When you have done that, you don't have to worry about pinning down evasive prospects. They'll pin themselves down.

Learn how to persuade more effectively, and you will boost your selling and enrolling power.

Nido Qubein is an international speaker and consultant. Visit his web site at www.nidoqubein.com, write to Creative Services, Inc., P.O. Box 6008, High Point, NC 27262, or call (800) 989-3010.

CHAPTER
14

Why Won't They Listen to Me?

Kim Klaver

When you talk to someone about your business or product, have you ever wondered why it's so hard to get them to listen? You use the scripts and blurbs the company or your upline has provided—showing the solid technical or scientific track records. But still, getting someone good to listen seems to be almost impossible these days.

You may be happy to know you are not alone. In describing the death of the once hugely successful TV ad engine (for cereals, personal care and cleaning products, for example), marketing guru Seth Godin writes that unlike 25 years ago, "you could never afford to introduce Cap'n Crunch today, regardless of who made your commercial. Kids won't listen. Neither will adults." His conclusion about the challenge of marketing today: "Consumers are hard to reach because they ignore you."[1]

Over the past few years, my students have told me the same thing. When they start to talk about their business or the product, the other person's attention somehow wanders off, and they mutter, "Oh, that's nice. Say, what's for lunch?" If the old TV audience isn't listening anymore to the usual commercials and the standard pitches, neither is the audience that is being presented with network marketing products and opportunities. This may be in part because over the past decade in our industry, there have been massive changes and often failures that have affected us all. It has become a familiar story: promises made and not kept, hype and allure that turned out to be false once someone got into the business.

I believe the direct sales/network marketing business model is one of the most sophisticated business models available. We have plenty of evidence that it *does* work, in spite of the many network marketing companies that are no longer in business, and in spite of the many who have attempted to build a successful business but were unable to make it work. I am person-

---

[1]Seth Godin, *Purple Cow* (New York: Portfolio Books, 2003), 12, 15.

ally so certain of it that I recently started my own direct sales and networking company.

So let's get back to the first question: Why won't people listen to you anymore?

I believe there are two reasons people ignore us. Both have to do with the actual words and phrases people use when making their presentations, long or short, formally in a meeting or informally in the elevator.

1. *For presenting the business.* The use of certain words meant to impress the listener, but which turn off the good ones and attract the weak ones.
2. *For the product.* The use of words meant to impress the listener, but which in fact result in the familiar eyes-glazing-over scene, and you know the rest.

Let's take them in turn.

PRESENTING THE BUSINESS

There are five things people throughout network marketing land say in their meetings that tend to shut down all good people—because those people *know* better. Here they are.

1. It's easy. Anyone can do it.
2. You can make big money almost immediately in this business.
3. Everyone will want this product/service. It sells itself.
4. Ours is the best deal/company/pay plan/management in the history of the world/out there.
5. All you have to do is talk to people you know.

These five statements are intended to impress someone with the ease with which one can become successful. And perhaps they're meant to give the listener some encouragement and a can-do attitude so they'll say yes. However, each one is either false or ignorant, and anyone who has had any business experience, including anyone who has spent a day doing network marketing, knows it.

Ask yourself these very five questions, as you remember your own past one to nine years in the business.

Has it really been easy? Is it easy today? Have you found that "anyone" can do it?

Did you make big money immediately?

Did the products/services really sell themselves?

Is it really the best company for everyone? Or maybe just for someone with your values? (Compare those who prefer the adventure of a start-up to someone who prefers a more conservative, established company.)

And last, have you found any truth to the fifth statement—that all you have to do to become a success is talk to people you know?

Many people have told me that going to people they know has been the very worst thing they ever did—for their network marketing career and their personal relationships. (No place to go for Christmas dinner.) Bottom line, I think we all know none of these promises are true. But my students, who agreed, they told me they said those things because they didn't know what else to say—and that anyway, that's what their upline said and told them to say.

That is a big problem, because here's who these five promises *do* attract: the desperados—those who are hoping for a quick financial or personal fix. Since there is no business without obstacles, they drop out at the first sign of trouble, adding to the dropout statistics that make us look so bad to some people.

Now ask yourself this question: Whose fault was it that they dropped out, as so many seem to do? Shall we blame the recruit who's "just lazy" and not committed or can't see the big picture? Or might it be the pitch itself that draws in precisely the kinds of people who can be goaded into thinking it will be a piece of cake to succeed? Could that be the reason that the dropout rate is so high? That we're unwittingly asking for entirely the wrong ones with the "five worst things" programming?

I, for one, vote to stamp out the constant and pathetic repeating of the "Five Worst Things to Say to a Good Prospect" from all company literature and trainings, in meeting rooms, and on leader-led telephone conference calls around the country. Read: Let's stop attracting the wrong people to our profession. It is *not* easy, and not everyone can do it. Do you think that's how Google and Apple and Microsoft attract their people? By advertising that their job opportunities are easy and for anyone? No wonder the dropout rates are so unbelievably high in our field. We're attracting mostly wrong ones with our recruiting verbiage.

Why not start asking for the best ones, and have fewer of them? In this case, less may indeed be more. Wouldn't fewer people drop out if they were more qualified in the first place, because we start *asking* for people who know it is *not* easy to succeed in a business of one's own? People who stop asking "How fast can I make money?" and instead ask: "What does it take to become successful in this business?"

PRESENTING THE PRODUCT

Do you represent a product line that you love madly? And you can't figure out why, when you present or describe your products, the other person's eyes glaze over, or they suddenly have to go now? I cataloged hundreds of scripts and phrases that people told me they were using to describe their products—nutritionals, personal care, and home cleaning products, Internet and telecom services, skin care lines, candles—you name it, I got samples. After thousands of hours of discussion and review of these, I noticed that there were certain characteristics of the language they used that caused listeners everywhere to turn off—including the very people who used them, when someone presented the same words to them.

There's something about the way a seller talks, and everyone reacts pretty much the same way. I noticed three characteristics of what I now call "seller talk." It's immediately recognizable to anyone who hears it. When I ask my students, "Can you tell when a seller starts talking?" they all say "Yes!" And when I ask if they tend to go toward that person or away from them, they all cry out, "Away!" But what if you didn't know you were sounding like a seller?

Here are the three dead giveaways that tip off the listener that the speaker is a seller. Most of them represent language that is again meant to impress the listener. Only it has the opposite effect, as my students have learned over many years of getting all those glazed eyes and "What's for lunch?" comments.

1. *Generalities.* General, vague nondescript words that speak to no one in particular. If you use words that speak to no one in particular, who will respond? For example, in response to the question that so many people in our profession dread, "What do you do?," we hear responses like:

   I'm in the wellness business.

   I help people get financial independence.

   I do telecommunications.

   Ask yourself, if you heard any of those, would your ears perk up or not? Would you lean in closer wondering what they did?

2. *Technobabble.* Jargon, technical terms, scientific names, names of the products, the name of the company, names of diseases, and so on. Technobabble is any words a 13-year-old would not understand. For example, say someone asks you the question, "What do you do?" Say this response out loud. It's one of many I got in my script

classes. "Oh, I'm a wellness consultant. I market unique, patented nutraceuticals."

Or, "I have my own home-based business, and I educate people on how they can protect and build their immune systems with glyconutritionals. These are the same nutrients as in mothers' breast milk, but we don't get them so now we have autoimmune diseases on the rise and . . ."

Or, "I do ABC Company, the greatest company in the history of the world."

What normal consumer would have the vaguest idea of what these three people are talking about? And why would they care? Their words are total jargon and technobabble—to the listener. Remember, you're talking to a normal consumer person—someone who has not learned any of the jargon you had to learn when you signed up. Were you saying any words like those above before you got trained by your company? Would you respond to someone who spoke to you this way if you asked them what they did? Would you really want to find out more?

3. *Hype.* There are three kinds: promises, chest-beating, and screaming.

> *Promises.* Those are the usual promises about something good about to happen to the prospect in the future. For example, you will lose weight with this product. You'll get rid of X with this product. This will save you money . . .
>
> Question 1: Can you really predict the future for someone else?
>
> Question 2: Who else makes these promises about *their* products? Hmm. So, how will you distinguish yourself if you sound just like everyone else they hear?
>
> *Chest-beating.* "This is the most wonderful, the greatest, the most fine and fabulous product out there." These comments, when made by a seller, are suspect, are they not? Do *you* believe everything advertisers tell you on TV, radio, Internet, or newspapers? Claims made by people who sell stuff are suspect, aren't they? It's not about truth, but perception. If the seller is saying it, can it really all be believed? Respect your audience. They're just as smart as you. Why expect to influence someone else with words that you wouldn't believe yourself, if you heard them from another seller?
>
> *Screaming.* Overstating and exaggerations. For example, "Earn $3,000 to $5,000 per month!! Easy!! We do the selling for you!!" This is the BEST BAR NONE weight loss product ever

invented!!!!!" On web sites, screaming appears as TOO MANY WORDS IN CAPITAL LETTERS, red type, and lots of fonts and exclamation points.

According to Strunk and White, the bible of writing style: "When you overstate, readers will be instantly on guard, and everything that has preceded your overstatement as well as everything that follows it will be suspect in their minds because they have lost confidence in your judgment or your poise."[2]

So now what? If you take out all the words in your product presentation that are any kind of seller talk, what's left? What could you say instead?

Well, how about telling a story? A real one? Like your own? Instead of trying to impress someone by repeating the clichés or technobabble you've heard, what if you tell your personal, authentic product story? The assumption behind this strategy is this: There are others out there who will want the product for the same reasons you did. After all, aren't there people who might want a product that could maybe do for them what it has for you? Someone who feels the same way you do about wanting to, say, lose weight without surgery? Or who wants to get rid of those irksome little aches and pains—but without drugs? What about reaching out to them? You know, like-minded people?

Telling your product (or service) story can be accomplished here with a simplified two-step process. The formula is laid out in detail in my new book *If My Product's So Great, How Come I Can't Sell It?*[3]

First, go to the remembering room of your mind. (*not* the impressing room—the remembering room.) Complete this sentence: Before I started using this product, I was someone who . . .

Put a couple of *very* specific "befores," such as: "Before I started using this product, I was someone who had achy knees when I went up and down stairs. Eight months ago I fell down the steps and hurt my knee. And ever since I had to have therapy because it hurt so bad. My doctor gave me some drugs, which helped, but they gave me stomach problems and I was worried about other side effects."

Then the formula adds a phrase like this: "Then I tried this [other] product, and after [time period—not to exaggerate] I noticed that . . ."

So for example, here's how this student's remembering room script ended up: "Before I started using this product, I was someone who had achy knees when I went up and down stairs. Eight months ago I fell down the steps

[2]William Strunk Jr. and E. B. White, *The Elements of Style*, 4th edition (Boston: Allyn & Bacon, 2000), 73.
[3]Kim Klaver's new book is available at http://whowho911.com or (800) 595-1956.

and hurt my knee. And ever since I had to have therapy because it hurt so bad. My doctor gave me some drugs, which helped, but they gave me stomach problems and I was worried about other side effects.

"Then I tried this new cream and rubbed it on my knee. And almost right away, I noticed the pain in my knee was almost gone. I immediately stopped the drugs and one week later I stopped the therapy. It's been five months now and my knee feels fine. And I can exercise again like I did before I got hurt."

That is her personal story about this particular product (her company has others) and she chose it because the change she got with it meant the most to her. This is right from her remembering room. She was not trying to impress or attract anyone else. This was all about her story.

So now, you try it. First, pick the fix or change you got that meant the most to you. Start either with the problem you had, or the fix you got—the before and after you care about. You must do that by going to your own remembering room. Stay in there. Do not go to the impressing room. That's very easy to do and you'll know it happened when seller talk starts coming out of your mouth.

The remembering room experience is about one thing—describing you and your before and after. You go there to remember and describe your before and after—not to impress, play to, or "get" anyone else. This will be about finding people like you, remember? So we start by describing you.

Next we'll put your story into what I call a "first date script" format. This particular script is designed to answer the question: What do you do? (The *If My Product's So Great . . .* book shows many other uses of the script.) Let's try it. Someone asks you, "So what do you do?"

First you'll see a 37-second first date script, then the seven-second version. You can choose when to use either. Read this out loud so your ears can hear.

> *You:* I market a product for people who have achy knees when they go up and down stairs, like I used to. Eight months ago I fell down the steps and hurt my knee. And ever since I had to have therapy because it hurt so bad. My doctor gave me some drugs, which helped, but they gave me stomach problems and I was worried about other side effects.
>
> So I tried this new cream and rubbed it on my knee. And almost right away, I noticed the pain in my knee was almost gone. I immediately stopped the drugs and one week later I stopped the therapy. It's been five months now and my knee feels fine. And I can exercise again like I did before I got hurt.
>
> Do you know anyone who might like to know about a product like that?

Here is the seven-second version response to "What do you do?"

You: I market a product for people who have achy knees when they go up and down stairs, like I used to. Do you know anyone who might like to know about a product like that?

Go ahead and read these out loud, and see what your reaction might be if you met someone who said each one in response to your asking them "What do you do?"

The results thousands of my students have obtained with this kind of response have surprised nearly all of them. Maybe because it's such a friendly, non-seller-talk kind of authentic response. They've gotten referrals from people they never dreamed would give them any. And they've made sales that will warm any heart.

I believe that the greatest obstacle to getting good people to listen to someone's business or product presentation has been the urge to try to impress the other person. For the business presentations, the "Five Worst Things to Say," while intended to impress, are perhaps the greatest turnoff to a good person, because they know better. Instead they seem to attract those who are weak and vulnerable. This, of course, adds to the drop out rate, since they're not the right ones for our business. At least, not now.

For the product presentation, the urge to impress has led to massive use of seller talk, which everyone says they'd move away from if someone did it to them.

So there you have it. Be authentic. Respect your audience—your listener. Tell your story—your mini-movie. That's what will connect and endear you to them.

So now you tell me: What do you do?

I'm listening. . . .

Kim Klaver, aka Ms Stud, has been selling things she loves since she was eight. The little Dutch girl with broken English sold more Christmas cards door-to-door in her neighborhood in Grand Rapids, Michigan, than all her friends.

In her debut as a professional direct seller, Kim retailed more water filters than anyone in the company's history—nearly $60,000 worth in her first month. Five years later with another product she loved, Kim achieved the highest position in the shortest time in the National Speakers Association's history. For the next eight years, she shared her secrets with the entire network marketing industry through her books, audios, and classes. Her web site http://whowho911.com, with 5 million hits a month, has become the biggest in the industry.

Kim's study of language began at MIT in 1970 where she nearly failed the introductory linguistics class. So, she wrote *From Deep to Surface Structure*, published by Harper & Row in 1971. It became the basic textbook for the introductory linguistics course at MIT and other U.S. universities. At Harvard in 1972, she earned a master's degree in teaching and wrote language tests for children. Harcourt, Brace published the *Bilingual Syntax Measure* in 1972 and 1973.

Today she's CEO of her own direct sales and networking company, Uptown Av, Inc. (http://uptownav.com). The company markets whole food nutritional supplements for people who want a dose of good nutrition in a capsule—people who know they don't eat right, or health nuts who want high-octane supplements.

You can reach Kim Klaver by e-mail Kim@uptownav.com or (800) 595-1956.

CHAPTER 15

Finding Passion in Your Business

Kathy Coover

Do you know the most vital step to take before beginning your new network marketing business venture? It's a step that's often overlooked or even viewed as not being important, but I promise you, it's one of the most important things you can do. Before you get started, you need to do some soul-searching to reflect on your vision and purpose in life. My personal vision is to impact people's health and help others become successful. Your vision may be entirely different, and that's absolutely fine.

BUILD YOUR BELIEF SYSTEM

Each of us has an intrinsic purpose—some special reason why we are here, living now, in this world. It is our basis for being, the passion that generates our master plan. Discovering or defining your passion is one of the most helpful things you can do for yourself. You must build a belief system so strong that nothing can shatter your goals. The moment you carry the conviction of belief—fueled with absolute passion—is that moment your dream will become reality.

Passion for the Industry

Build your belief in the industry of network marketing. Some naysayers will try to take your dreams away and discourage you from joining the industry. Read some of the outstanding books on network marketing to get the facts and the figures on the industry.

Passion for the Products

Build your belief in your company's products. Educate yourself on the products and speak with passion about them. You must develop a powerful story to share with others—why you love the company and why you are sharing their products. It is the music you sing to others. Your enthusiasm is infectious. It radiates in your face and in your voice, and others will instinctively want to join you.

Passion for the Compensation Plan

Build your belief in your company's compensation plan and share this with conviction as well. Let others know what sets your plan apart from others. Speak to why it is so powerful in supporting distributors to create residual income. Borrow success stories from other people in your company if you are just getting started. Stories are what get people excited about the business.

Passion in Your Abilities

The very most important element to success is to believe in yourself. You can do this, and you can do it with intensity and with passion. Believe you can. The only thing that stands between you and what you want from life is the question of whether you have the will to try it and the faith to believe that it's possible.

PUT A PLAN TO YOUR PASSION

Once you have your belief structure and passion in place, establish your goals and your business plan for building your organization. Make a commitment to work your business consistently and persistently and stay laser-focused on your goals and dreams.

If you wish to go to the top, you will need to stretch yourself and build your team through many modalities. Start with your warm market first. If you don't approach your warm market, someone else will. Learn to acquire referrals from your warm market. You will never run out of people to talk to if you ask for referrals. For example, you can say, "I just started my own business and I am looking for some entrepreneurial people who want to generate a secondary income. Do you know anyone?" Develop some approaches that are powerful and will create curiosity. Then use the tools available to you from your company's web site, CDs, DVDs, brochures, catalogs, and the like. The key to building a massive organization and income is to create duplication within your group. People are not duplicable, but systems and tools are. Develop a system for recruiting for your organization.

By using the company's tools, people whom you are approaching will think to themselves, "I can do this! I can hand out and refer people to the company tools." Then ask your people who have reviewed the tools this simple question: "Have I given you enough information to make a decision to-day?" When they say yes to your business, it is imperative to get them into action as soon as possible. Set a time to interview your new distributors. Find out what their goals are and why they are pursuing the business. Once you establish their needs, help them achieve their goals.

Every successful business begins with a plan. The following interview will help you develop your plan and should be conducted with every associate you enroll. (Take notes to keep on file, and record name and date of interview.)

1. What is it about the company that attracts you?
2. What is it about the network marketing industry that attracts you?
3. What could possibly hold you back from taking full advantage of this opportunity? What obstacles do you foresee (spouse, time, money, confidence, etc.)?
4. How much money would you need to add to your income this month to be happier or more comfortable? How much money would you need to add to your income in the next six months to feel good about your business?
5. When your business is successful, what do you see being different in your life in one year? in three to five years?
6. Are you willing to learn and follow a proven system? Are you willing to refer people to a web site and give CDs and DVDs to interested people?
7. Write down the days and times you will reserve for your business. How many hours per day? When will you do this? What time will you use to follow up with contacts?
8. How much time are you willing to invest initially per week?
9. How much money can you invest on a monthly basis to get your business going?
10. Do you like to work on the phone? Do you like to work on the Internet?
11. Do you have a large circle of influence?
12. Do you enjoy working with people and making personal contacts? Where do you come into contact with people in your daily activities (shopping, PTA, gym, organizations, etc.)?
13. What resources do you have available (computer, fax, membership in organizations or clubs)?
14. What is your commitment level to be successful?

There are many ways to build your business. Develop your plan and help your new associates develop theirs.

- Warm market/referrals (best way for most).
- Three-foot rule (talk to everyone around you).
- Direct mail/postcards.
- Advertising.
- Sampling the products.
- Internet.

By using this interview, you will be able to determine if this new distributor is an A player, B player, or C player. An A player is someone who will do whatever it takes to be successful. A B player is someone who will pursue the business part-time and will put in moderate effort. A C player is a customer and will use the products only.

By making this distinction, you will be focused on the people who want this as a business. People need your financial product! Work with the people who have the same goals as you do. Don't try to drag people into the business or across the finish line. The key is to find the A players and help them become successful. Help the B players achieve their goals, and the C players can be loyal customers. Build a strong, nurturing relationship with them and work as a team. This is a fun business!

One technique I have used over and over is the "10 Name Quick Start." The key is to create urgency with your new distributors. Tell them, "I have a system that will rapidly explode your business. I need the names of your top 10 people today. Think of all the people you know who have a burning desire to change their financial status. Think of all the entrepreneurial people you know who are already successful and have a positive attitude, people who have a desire to make a difference in the world. Write their names down, phone numbers, addresses, and e-mail addresses, and get them to me by tomorrow. I will personally call all of these people with you and we will jumpstart your business into the profit mode."

I always make an offer like this: "If you get those names to me tomorrow and someone becomes interested, I will send them out one of our company CDs." I then start calling their people with them, and if I run into an energetic person who seems to be excited about the program, I make them the same offer: "Make your list of 10 people and I will call all of them with you." By doing this, I am working deep into my team and creating depth that will drive the checks. Do this; it works. Keep on going and work even deeper. You will never run out of names this way and will have an unlimited source of referrals.

My personal experience with building three successful network marketing businesses is you have to sponsor a lot of people to find the ones with desire and motivation. Once you find these people, help them become leaders. Work with them by doing three-way calls, home presentations, and meetings. Develop self-sustaining leaders who can stand on their own. Have fun with your team. Build that loyalty and relationship that are unstoppable. Creating that team concept can be your way to building the long-term relationships that are crucial to your success.

One exercise I do every morning before getting up is that I ask myself this magic question: What do I have to be grateful for? After reflecting on these positive things in my life, I start my day with zest and passion for the world. I also have written down all these things that I am grateful for and keep them by my desk so I can reflect on them throughout the day. This keeps me laser-focused on my goals and keeps my heart passionate about what I am doing.

Discovering, defining, and acting in accord with your purpose naturally leads to passion. Many of us try to get passionate about our goals. That doesn't always work because passion comes from being who we are, not doing what we can. Our vision generates passion—the driving force, the desire and zest for life that are unstoppable! Lead your business with enthusiasm and joy, and you can achieve your objectives. Network marketing is free enterprise at its best. Develop a passion and love for it, and it can be the vehicle to realizing all your dreams.

For 18 years, Kathy Coover was a practicing dental hygienist. Although she loved her profession, she was looking for something new to do with her life that had the potential to profoundly impact others. In 1990, Kathy became involved in network marketing. That's when all the excitement began.

Kathy escalated to the top of three separate companies and has generated millions in income. With the first company, she built an organization of 40,000 people and had 10 separate million-dollar earner legs. She eventually sold that business and then duplicated her previous success record in the next company. Kathy was the fastest person in the company's history to achieve Diamond status, and she was also the first female to accomplish this amazing level of success. Kathy continued to work hard and became a Double Diamond, producing nine Diamond organizations. Through her success, she has helped several people become six- and even seven-figure earners.

As a nationally recognized and respected field leader and trainer in the direct sales industry, Kathy has developed training and support systems that have helped tens of thousands of entrepreneurs achieve new levels of success.

Today, as co-founder and senior vice president of Isagenix International (www.isagenix.com), Kathy continues on the path to phenomenal achievement as Isagenix International enjoys record-breaking success. Kathy's involvement in a company that helps people gain better health and build real wealth has made her passion for this industry even stronger. As a firsthand witness to Isagenix's ability to improve people's lives, Kathy is proud to offer people a true opportunity to build a business they can count on for the rest of their lives. She can be reached at kgcoover@aol.com.

CHAPTER 16

Finding Your North Star

Shannon Anima

I went back to the grocery store last week and asked for a refund for some cheese I bought and later couldn't find in my grocery bags. The store cheerfully refunded my money and apologized for their error. As you can probably guess, I found the cheese this week moldering beneath some leafy greens in the bottom of my refrigerator. This is not a big moral dilemma, just a small one: Shall I bother to own up and return the $6 to the grocery store?

Not a big thing, but life tends to be made up of the small choices that accumulate and create a clear path of action (or nonaction) when the bigger decisions come up. I'm talking to a potential customer for my networking enterprise and she is ready to purchase some products; do I point out that the package plan is a better bargain for her, if it doesn't benefit my business as much?

In some circles, network marketing has a bad name, and sometimes there are individuals and companies that deserve that reputation when their core values are lost to greed. Ironically, it is often the snake oil salesman advocating virtue and good deeds who has a rationalizing explanation for dishonest maneuvers in business. In business, as in the rest of life, the guilty seldom own their selfish choices and are adept at shifting away from responsibility.

If my name and my integrity are associated with the network marketing industry, I want it to reflect honorable ideals. I am constantly in a state of inquiry about my own motives and intentions in my business. It can be an awkward balance at times to avoid being immobilized by indecision while questioning motivation. It's a follow-the-heart kind of intuition that will help to hold you to your right path, while refusing to inculcate the rhetoric of every presenter and company official.

At 3 A.M. in a hotel room after a sumptuous celebration buffet, my husband and I were offered a very lucrative opportunity to work closely with a top earner in our company. Although we were very flattered as neophyte

119

networkers, something in my internal radar felt off course with the offer. We declined. Only a few months later, this individual left our company under a cloud of innuendo and accusations. I don't know the whole story, but I'm glad I listened to those angels whispering in my ear. Your conscience or moral intuition is an acute detection device for scams and scammers. Sometimes this detection device is too sensitive and it prevents us from seeing possibilities or even listening to ideas. And occasionally the scam artists do slide through undetected, though likely your hindsight will say "I told you so" and list the hints that were dropped.

When I was first presented with my current opportunity, my internal detector said an automatic "no." In fact, I said no for five years before I would listen to the information and dare to challenge my own biases. This is often where our new prospects begin, with their thumbs on the reject button before we have even pressed play.

When you approach a new person with your network marketing message, their resistance to your approach is often about a perceived values conflict. When they hear "network marketing," their internal radar dials negative. Their internal fears may be beeping warnings like these:

- *Greed and injustice.* This is a pyramid where those at the top make money, and everyone else doesn't.
- *Deception.* Sales are made by giving false information.
- *Shame.* This is a shameful way to make money, and others will look down on you.
- *Unlawfulness.* These companies work illegally and break laws. You would have to feign an interest in others to find business partners and clients. Dishonesty lies ahead.
- *Purposelessness.* You would be wasting your time and energy selling items of little value to gain profit.

When you get underneath the surface of the often unspoken concerns our potential partners may have, it is apparent that they are having a values crisis. How could they hear any information about the benefits of binary plans, the power of residual income, or the potential of our products, when they fear their own values are being put at risk?

Balderdash! Let's have a look at how these fears are based on False Evidence Appearing Real (FEAR), and how we can address these concerns up front with integrity and transparency. Maybe you have experienced some of these fears yourself, and possibly you still retain some of these concerns. This is important internal work to embark on to align ourselves fully with values in our business. Otherwise, both peace and success will always elude us, as we project our fear and sense of unworthiness at our prospects.

As an industry and as individuals, we have to begin by addressing the values issues. The kind of people who will contribute to our industry, our businesses, and our planet are the kind of people who need to know how network marketing stands as an ethical and contributing sector of the world business community. As ethical, discerning kinds of people, we need to examine ourselves, our motives, our industry, and our businesses.

In my training programs with both new and longtime distributors, we go back to the basics. The basics, the foundation for our business and our lives, are our own values. By taking some time to be thoughtful about our own values, we are able to shape our lives and businesses with purpose and integrity. (See Figure 16.1.)

Values are our principles, our standards of conduct, our personal evaluation of what is important in life. Values give our lives meaning; living a life in accord with our values is living a life of integrity, in alignment with what we perceive to be important. When we have an awareness of what is of most importance to us and we live it, we achieve true success in our own eyes and hearts.

After a rapid rise through the ranks in my company, I was rear-ended in a car accident and injured my neck and shoulder. As I convalesced with gratitude for the residual income arriving weekly with my postwoman, I hit a doldrums in my attitude toward my business. I had difficulty motivating myself to make calls and approaches. I resisted my own advice about reading and rereading my goals, and began to question whether I wanted to achieve them at all.

After a few months of treading water and feeling uncommitted, I went back to the basics with a values assessment. I had to reassess my goals for achievement in light of my personal values. In the process, I realized that I hadn't been paying enough time and attention to my spiritual practices and my health regime while I was on my rapid business ascent. My reluctance to go full throttle in my business was a warning from my values thermometer that I had let things become unbalanced. I had to reframe my goals for achievement in accordance with my needs for self-care, contemplation, and creative expression. When I affirmed my values, reframed my goals, and made space in my schedule to prioritize my values, I felt renewed enthusiasm for my business and experienced a phenomenal growth phase. Now I was attracting individuals with the maturity and integrity to live their lives with the drive, vision, and balance to achieve their values-based goals.

Networking is a highly ethical way to create wealth and growth in our lives and share that wealth and growth with others if we approach it with clarity about our values. Take some time to do your own values assessment. You might want to approach it as a full day retreat and include some time before and after the writing exercises for walking, meditation, and prayer. You

Love: Approach everyone with love in your heart—your friends, family, and downline. Smile, and feel the love in your heart before you make your next phone call.

Respect: I need to convey respect not only to my customers but also to myself. I can convey respect when I am a good listener, when I am open to the outcome, when I can allow no to mean no until it means yes. I respect myself when I believe in what I am doing, no matter what anyone else may say or believe.

Service: Read *How Can I Help?* by Ram Dass as your next network marketing manual. I love the synchronicity of networking. When I call I know it has a purpose, that I have a service to offer; I won't know until we have our conversation whether that is a listening ear, a little encouragement, a warm voice, or an amazing opportunity.

Joy: Joy is connecting with people heart to heart. Joy is hearing that someone is feeling better than they have in years because of your products. Joy is contributing abundantly to your favourite charity with the abundance you receive.   What is joy for you? How can you bring some joy into your business and your life every day? Be positive!

Trustworthiness: Calling back when I say. Being on time for meetings. Appearing businesslike. My business has taught me and is teaching me to be a more trustworthy person.

Persistence: Do it every day whether you want to or not, whether you feel like it or not. You may have downline who depend on you. You may have your own family who depends on you. Or you may depend on you. Just do it.

Purpose: Be clear about your purpose. Purpose is one of our royal values; it guides our lives like a North Star. Network marketing may be your purpose in life, or you may have another purpose that the income and influence you gain through your business will help you to achieve.

Figure 16.1   Connecting with Values in Your Business

could share this project with a friend, a business partner, or with a team on a training day. Or you can take just 15 minutes every day for a week to reassess and reset your life's purpose with meaning and integrity.

Values Assessment

A. Write out the 10 most important things in your life:

1. _____

2. _____

3. _____

4. _____

5. _____

6. _____

7. _____

8. _____

9. _____

10. _____

B. Remember a time when you were a kid that you experienced as joyous. Describe it fully.

C. What do you want to accomplish and enjoy in the rest of your life? Write for five minutes without interruption. If you run out of ideas just write "I'm out of ideas" until a new idea comes along.

D. What would you want to do, who would you be with, and where would you be if you had just six months to live? Imagine that you would be healthy but know your life will end in six months. Write for five minutes without stopping.

E. Put these 12 values in order from first to last according to their importance to you:

- Creativity
- Freedom
- Achievement
- Trustworthiness
- Excellence
- Commitment

- Service
- Integrity
- Respect
- Joy
- Persistence
- Love

F. What other values would be on your Very Important Values list?

G. Now make it a Foundation Five Values list.

1. _____

2. _____

3. _____

4. _____

5. _____

H. Reread all you have written about your values, about what is of deepest importance to you, about what brings you joy, and about what fulfills you. How do you want to express your values in your life beginning today? Write for five minutes without stopping.

Unless we have truly taken the time to answer these questions for ourselves, we will not be able to convey to others at the conscious and subconscious levels the clear message that we are working with absolute integrity in an industry of real contribution.

When approaching new prospects, take the time to inquire about their lives, their interests, and their goals. Reflect back not only the story you've heard but also some of the values you've perceived within the story. "Dennis, I can tell that contribution and service are really important in your life." "Alice, I can hear that you really value health, and that excellence is a value you live in your business and your life. Is that true for you?" When we reflect back the values that we perceive, we tell our prospects that they are being listened to at a deeply meaningful level. We convey that we care. When we share some of our own goals and values in our lives and our business, we indicate that we are trustworthy and principled. Begin with values.

Help your downline members to be clear about their goals, as well as about the values that are foundation to the goals. Values connect not just to the head and the emotions, but to the soul and spirit level with our friends and business partners. By examining values, we develop depth in our partnerships and personal growth that is fundamental to business growth.

My top five values today are: contribution, compassion, creativity, love, and gratitude. These are posted in capital letters in the front of my daily planner. As I plan my week and set goals for the months ahead, I want to know that I am living a life that fulfills my foundation values. I want the hours of my day to reflect contribution and love, my evenings to include rituals of gratitude, and my life to have ample downtime for spontaneous creativity. As I reflect on the past week and my accomplishments and mishaps, I evaluate with compassion and refocus with love.

This week, in my business, I am running a raffle for the Children's Hunger Fund during a public education event on Saturday. What a great opportunity for contribution. I have sent gratitude cards to two new friends who gave me opportunities to speak about my business. This afternoon I have carved time from busyness to finish writing this article that combines creativity with contribution. Every Sunday, I free the day to love my family: watching soccer games, helping with homework and chores, making soup for the week. This Sunday is all about my daughter's 12-year-old birthday bash and spa facials with some of our new products! I have love and gratitude for this network marketing business that allows me multiple opportunities every day to live my life by my own values and to share that opportunity and intention with many others whose hearts yearn to live authentically on their own terms.

Shannon Anima stumbled into network marketing after resisting it vociferously as her best friend tried every company and plan that came her way. Like so many others, she accidentally became a network marketer after struggling for a long time with the symptoms of the "woman who does too much" disorder. She was exhausted and ill, and while visiting a friend, tried her latest products to combat a lingering case of the flu. Within that first month, symptoms she had had for many years seemed to fall away and she had more energy than she had felt in a very long time.

You know the rest of the story: those weekly checks, and the joy of helping others to regain their health and to establish financial security. At the time she began her network marketing career, she had a very strong reason for joining: She needed the products and needed groceries. Shannon was living in a run-down trailer, and was a single mom to two terrific daughters.

She believes that with determination, honesty, and a dream, any of us can shift our life direction through the gift of network marketing. These days, Shannon has a snug writing room in her home by the ocean. She offers life coaching and training in self-development through values and vision for business and balanced life. Watch for her new book *Parenting with Purpose*. Together with her husband, Dr. John Snively, a biological dentist, Shannon assists others to find health and freedom. To reach her for business or health consultations or to reach John for biological dental consultations you can write to synergy.group@shaw.ca or view her story on their web site, http://synergygroup.usana.com.

CHAPTER 17

Values-Based Selling

Linda Avery

There is plenty of conversation these days about values: family values, core values, Wal-Mart values, you name it. Yet a true understanding of values has become muddied over the past few years. "Values" has become one of those words that sounds like it may have moral substance and great significance . . . but often people are not sure why or how. What I can tell you, though, is that values in your business can make all the difference in your success. And the more attention you pay to values, the more lives you can change for the better.

Let's talk about what values are *not*, and then see if there is a definition that will serve you well in your business. Remember the stereotypical used-car salesman (poor guy!), who has been much maligned for being a glad-hander and, well, not a very good listener (that's putting it mildly!). These salespeople are still around, but they're not getting quite as much business as they once did. Something about their approach turned people off.

If you've encountered this kind of sales approach, did you believe that the salesperson cared about you? Did he or she understand what was important to you? Did she listen to you, or did she tell you what to think? Did you get a word in edgewise? Did you buy the car and then spend the next four years kicking yourself because you did? Did you get red in the face and threaten to knock his block off? Was it a pleasant experience that felt like a win-win? Did you go back, eager to do business with him?

Let's examine the dynamics of that old selling ploy where the seller tells you what you want. Let's discover what *not* to do in selling. Remember, in network marketing, when you are recruiting and sponsoring, you are literally selling your business opportunity and yourself to others.

First of all, the ineffective seller (that's you) talks too much. A rule of thumb in selling is, "Let the buyer talk. You listen." Why, you might ask, shouldn't I tell the buyer all about the great advantages of my business? I'm the one who knows everything, after all." *Au contraire.* You know very little about the buyer, your prospect. So listen instead. Listen to what's important to other people.

When you listen, this is what you'll hear. We call it listening for values. Your prospect comes to you with problems that your business opportunity may be able to fix. The problems could be money troubles, time constraints, poor working relationships, a boring lifestyle, a hectic existence, or an unfulfilling life in general. There are many, many others. Get the picture? You are listening to discover two things:

1. What the buyer needs.
2. What the buyer values.

When you hear the answers to those two questions by actively listening to your potential recruit, you can match the buyer's needs to your business program. Nearly every network marketing opportunity has plenty to offer a wide variety of people. *Variety* is the key word. You can match your program to the person you are talking to, one way or the other. But remember, that doesn't mean every prospect will sign up with you. So what? Move on. The goal is win-win, and you can do it. You accomplish this by listening for values.

Let's look at a typical network marketing scenario where Maggie wants Earl and Shelly to join her network marketing business. Maggie is a true believer in her company and the opportunities she sees and that she's beginning to experience. She's gung ho, bright-eyed and bushy-tailed, enthused, and she desperately wants her favorite young couple to come into business with her. Now, is she likely to listen to Earl and Shelly, or is she more likely to launch into her sales pitch and stop only when the clock strikes twelve?

You guessed it. If Maggie tells them everything she thinks they want to know, she will miss the opportunity to discover what they think they need to know. Suppose Maggie tells Earl and Shelly how much fun the business is, and how many places they could all travel together. Suppose she is really sold on the Saturday night ballroom presentation at her national convention where everyone dresses up and wears their best jewelry. Suppose Maggie tells them how much fun it is to sit down with people and present sponsoring interviews.

Now, just suppose Earl and Shelly are nearly insolvent, fear public speaking, hate to travel, do not have evening wear, and have no jewelry. How likely are they to relish joining Maggie's business? Not at all likely. Maggie may be baffled, but the young couple is not. They see that the business Maggie is offering won't solve any of their problems. You see, one of Maggie's top values in life is having fun. For Earl and Shelly, having fun is on the back burner. What they value is financial security. Like two ships passing in the night, the couple and Maggie make no connection.

You can solve Maggie's kind of problem. It may have happened to you when the person you thought would be "so perfect" for the business turns away and says it's not for him, or not for her. You scratch your head and ask, "What's wrong with these people? Can't they see the opportunity here?"

The answer is no, they cannot. They cannot see it because the business that was presented had nothing to do with them. "So how can I make it important to them?" you may ask.

Values are the keys to knowing who people are and what matters to them. Values function like a code of ethics by which people live. The expression "That's what makes them tick" holds the key here. Your values are what make you tick. Those same values may not apply to the people you prospect. Values get you up in the morning, take you through the day, and go to sleep with you at night.

Let's take a look at some of the more common values people live by. Here is a partial list:

Acceptance	Joy
Adventure	Order
Appreciation	Participation
Belonging	Peace
Comfort	Perfection
Communication	Pleasure
Contribution	Power
Creativity	Recognition
Family	Relationship
Freedom	Respect
Harmony	Safety
Honesty	Security
Humor	Spirituality/God
Independence	Trust
Integrity	Work

You may see some words that feel very important on that list, and others that are not as essential to your daily life. Yet, whether or not we can identify these for ourselves, the values we hold dear are part or our operating systems as human beings.

Have you known parents who are very neat and orderly who cannot get over how their teenage children keep their rooms messy and in disorder? There is conflict there that sometimes breaches the bond between parents and child. Yes, let's accept that a teen may simply be acting out against her parents. Yet, something fundamentally different may be going on. Perhaps the teen values creativity, joy, respect, and peace more than she values neatness and order. Is it possible that people could actually come from very different places on the values continuum? Sure it is.

Back to your business. Everyone you have on your prospects list—that is, everyone you think you should present your business opportunity to—is *very* different from you in some ways. Let's look at Ben and Mary's prospecting skills. The Monsons are a couple that Ben and Mary think would be absolutely fabulous in their Food4Vitality network marketing opportunity. Ben likes the business because he is a health nut and Mary likes it because she loves meeting people. They both love the people they get to work with, and they can see themselves earning five-figure monthly commission checks by the end of the year. Ben is especially happy about the money he plans to earn, because he is saving to buy a Humvee. He has darned good reasons for loving his business. Ben and Mary are very excited and cannot wait to tell Judy and Ray Monson from the country club all about it. (Did you notice the word *tell*?)

Ben and Mary launch right into all the things they like about their business as soon as they sit down with their friends at the restaurant where they met. After a while, Ben notices that Ray frequently looks toward the exit and then back at his watch, and Mary watches Judy fishing around in her purse and no longer paying attention. Neither of them is focused on the presentation.

By now, you know what is wrong with this picture. The Monsons have no interest in why their friends are so excited about their business opportunity because it has no connection to them. They have plenty of money, and they think Humvees are an unnecessary extravagance; Ray loves his job, and Judy is suffering from empty-nest syndrome. What none of these four people realize is that there are some very good reasons why Ray and Judy could find satisfaction in the business opportunity. The only problem is that the Monsons haven't had a chance to talk about what's important to them. Because, you see, what they want and what their friends want are very dissimilar, yet the business opportunity could fit them very nicely. Let's find out how.

Before we move on to a solution to this problem, however, let's look at what is missing in the scenario. Ben and Mary haven't yet learned that the Monsons don't care very much how they feel; the Monsons have their own concerns and are listening for something that fits them, not what fits their friends. Sound about right? We all want to know what's good for us. Just don't make the mistake of thinking that what is good for you is necessarily what's good for your friends.

How could Ben and Mary approach their friends in a way that would bring them into the conversation about the business instead of driving them away from it? They could listen. Now, you may be asking yourself, "Yes, but what are they supposed to listen to? The Monsons aren't speaking."

Let's listen to a conversation the Monsons recently had with each other in the privacy of their home. If Ben and Mary had known this, they might have proceeded differently.

"You know, Ray, since the boys have gone off to college, I just don't have the same energy I used to have. I used to love seeing them off to school, helping them with homework, taking care of their clothes, cooking for them. They were my life."

"It sure does feel different around the house with the twins gone. Home seems pretty empty. I didn't think about how their absence affected you."

"Well, it's not that I'm just twiddling my thumbs, but here we are with everything we need, yet life doesn't seem to hold the same interest for me. Maybe I'm just bored."

"Why don't you get involved in more country club activities? You know, cards, lawn bowling, golf, things like that."

"Really, Ray, I would think you know me better than that. I want to be helping people, not whiling my time away on myself. I want to make a difference in people's lives."

"Funny thing—today Ben asked to sit down with us and share something he and Mary recently became involved with. He seems pretty happy about it. Want to meet with them and see if it interests you?"

"Absolutely. I'm open to anything."

Would Ben and Mary have given the same presentation of the business if they had been privy to the Monsons' conversation? Let's hope not. They would have heard that Judy does not value money, fun, cars, or hanging around with fun people. She values accomplishment and helping and making a difference in the lives of others. Ray seems supportive of his wife and an all-around nice guy, so Ben and Mary should see a golden opportunity here.

Ben and Mary live in a world where do-overs are commonplace. They get to do their presentation over again. But because they still don't know about the Monsons' conversation, what can they do to find out what you just found out? They will need to listen this time.

When Ben and Mary greet their friends, Ben motions them to a table at the restaurant and asks them about their twin boys. How are they? Where are they going to school? What's it like at home with the boys out on their own? What changes have come about in Ray's and Judy's lives?

Ben's questions are open-ended. He waits for whatever responses his friends have. Ben and Mary are genuinely interested in this change in the Monsons' lives. They both engage in active listening. As Mary listens between the words, she hears wistfulness in Judy's voice and hears her desire to be doing something important for people, something helpful.

The more she listens, the more excited she gets because she sees how their Food4Vitality business would be a great way for Judy (especially) and Ray to work with people who don't always have the time and money they need to make their lives work optimally. Judy has all the time and money she needs, so she may find it very satisfying to help other people achieve the same things she has, namely to get more time and have more money.

It doesn't stop here, though, because Ben and Mary must continue to listen for any other values they hear. The more Judy talks, the more they realize that she values helping others find fulfillment in their lives, and she values family. Notice how none of these values are the same as the ones Ben and Mary revealed in the prior conversation?

Notice how listening reveals more than telling? Make no judgments about what your prospects say, but ask clarifying questions to get more information. For example, Judy may say, "I don't just want to spend my time doing things for me. That isn't what gets me out of bed in the morning."

"You must have loved having the boys around when you could see that they got off to a good start every day."

"I did. So many young people leave a dark house in the morning, trudge out to the school bus, and never have any warm, family time before they leave for school. Lots of children don't even get breakfast at home in the mornings."

"Family is really important to you, isn't it, Judy?"

"It is. And you know what, if I could do something to help other children experience what mine did, now that's something that I could get excited about."

Bells and whistles are now going off in Ben's and Mary's heads (and maybe yours, too). This is an open invitation to support Judy's vision of helping families. Mary then adds, "I work with so many single moms and couples now in my new business. It's so satisfying to see them get their lives back on track."

She could stop there, but adds an anecdote to make her point. "One of my distributors, a single mom of two high-school-aged girls, had to work two shifts at her job to make ends meet. She was gone when the girls left for school and often asleep when they came home. After six months of following our business plan, she was able to quit working at the plant, and found a single-shift job at a nursery. She now spends time at home building her business and being with her girls. She's added $1,500 a month to her income without having to work that extra shift. And the girls love having their mom around."

What do you think Judy is thinking after she hears this? She doesn't care about earning $1,500 for herself, but she sees the chance to help other mothers and young people change their lives. She wants to help other women get what they want.

Mary and Ben struck gold because they listened for it. Judy's values, and all prospects' values, are golden. They are what will motivate and sustain yours and Ben's and Mary's and Judy's businesses.

A wise friend once told me an observation attributed to Abraham H. Maslow, "When all you have is a hammer, every problem looks like a nail." In network marketing, you will have to determine what hammer you have been using. Your hammer consists of your values, and especially your most important values. If your hammer is fun, or money, or travel, or hard work, then you might be inclined to approach all your prospects as if you can fix their problems with your hammer.

Think about it. Network marketing businesses offer many, many opportunities for people. Not everyone wants money, even if you do. Not everyone wants to have fun, even if you do. Not everybody wants order in their lives, even if you do. Therefore, treat each prospect with respect and with anticipation about discovering their values. You will get to hear what is important to them. Their problem is often something missing in their lives: time, money, lifestyle, recognition, respect, relationships, freedom. You can show anyone how your business opportunity would be the perfect fit.

Mary's closing question to Judy (knowing that Ray will support her) is, "Judy, if I could show you how to work with women who need more time with their kids and better opportunities to make money without working themselves into the ground, would you be interested in hearing about it?"

Now, do you think Judy is going to refuse? I don't.

What Ben and Mary learned to do and what everyone in network marketing will benefit from is looking at your business opportunity from many different angles. Make a list of some of the values your business honors. My business offers these opportunities/values (add whatever you think is appropriate):

Lifestyle change	More time
Freedom	Adventure
Recognition	Prosperity
Relationships	Contribution
Security	Joy
Power	Communication

This is the short list!

Try it again and come up with 10 values that can be found in your business.

Hold your business in one hand and your prospect in the other. Then listen for what your prospect values, and listen for what is missing from his or her life. Begin to tailor your presentation to match your prospect and ask your closing question, "If I could show you . . . would you . . . ?" and your business will take off.

Now, lest you think all of this is a trick to get your prospects hooked into the business without them knowing about it, think about this. Would you deny someone the opportunity to have a satisfying and fulfilling life? Would you begrudge people's lifestyles that make them happy? Would you take away someone's joy at accomplishment? Of course not. Few people know how to get beyond the survival level of work, paying bills, and planning retirement. Yet, most people, if they had the time and money, would like to make much greater contributions to the human experience than they are making now. Judy wants to help women make their lives work. Tammara would like to support hundreds of poor children in third-world countries through a monthly donation program. Jack wants to hone his leadership skills so he can be a model for young, fatherless boys in his community. Jeanne wants to help her niece through college. And Randy wants to be a professional speaker in order to affect thousands of people's lives. Yet none of these individuals currently has the time or money to live their dreams. Can you show them how with your business opportunity?

Withholding your business opportunity from your prospects is wrong. Why? Because if you listen carefully enough, you will find that very few people are truly satisfied with their lives. Loneliness, poverty, unemployment, lack of respect, boredom, and disempowerment are just a few of the things that people contend with every day. Physicians are forced to quit medicine because malpractice insurance premiums are too high. Teachers are forced to quit because the pay is too low. Travel agents' jobs are being taken over on the Internet.

You have something to share with all these people!

Most people might not be able to list their values unless they have been to a workshop where values were identified and clarified. Yet everyone knows what they like, and everyone knows what it feels like to be blindsided, irritated, worried, harried, angry, disorganized, or confused, don't they? All these emotions and states of being are a direct result of values being either ignored or violated.

People get worried when they feel they cannot control events in their lives. They feel disempowered to do the things that must be done in order for them to stop worrying. People are confused when they have no clear direction.

If you value clarity and you don't find it, you may become angry, confused, or irritated. Take your pick. On a very small scale, if you value order and your office is a mess, you may find it difficult to work well. The mess distracts you and makes you feel irritated. This is how it works. Values are essential to honor people's definitions of themselves.

Businesses have values, too. What values in your business will fit the needs of each of your prospects? You won't know unless you listen for their values. Listen, not speak.

When you have found a perfect match for your business and your prospect, then you have added one more brick in the strong foundation of a business that will grow big enough to poke a hole in the sky.

It's really that simple.

Linda Avery, M.A., has 16 years of experience in network marketing. She built an international organization in one of America's top network marketing companies. She is a professional business coach, freelance writer, and writing instructor. She and her business partner in South Carolina, Constance Dugan, co-own The Heart of Business, offering business executive coaching, public speaking coaching, business editing, and women's business and personal workshops. Contact Linda at (253) 627-1441 or by e-mail at linda avery@earthlink.net.

CHAPTER 18

Recognition: The Driving Force

Brad Hager

"They come for the money, but they stay for the big neon sign that says love and recognition."

It was years ago when I first heard a mentor make that statement. I instantly reached for a pen, for I knew it was one of those rare pearls of wisdom occasionally given out by those who have gone before us. However, it would be years before I would come to realize how vital these words are to building a large, successful organization with true staying power.

According to the Direct Selling Association, the number one reason people get into network marketing is for financial gain. The second factor is to obtain time freedom and more control over their own lives (which incidentally is very rarely obtained without first getting more of number one). These being the facts, we can clearly see what approach we should take with prospects when attempting to enroll them into our business. By focusing on their hot buttons, anyone can go out and build a large, successful organization, get rich, and live happily ever after, right?

Wrong.

While sharing your opportunity with new prospects, the preceding motivators should definitely be revealed. But, contrary to what some people teach, there is more. To build it big, it goes beyond getting involved and sponsoring a few people.

I'll never forget my first few years in this business when I would ask the larger money earners what I needed to do to get my business going and to start making those big checks. I received the same two answers that many of you have gotten in the past. The first was simply "sponsor more people"; the second answer was "do more of what you're already doing." Duh!!! I immediately thought to myself, "What I'm doing is *not* working, so why would I want to do more of it? So that I could fail faster, I guess."

I think you'd agree it doesn't do a lot of good to continue putting people into your business if the old ones are quitting faster than you can sponsor new ones. I'm reminded of a lady who approached me not long ago to inform me she had sponsored 42 distributors who had all quit. Needless to say, she looked at me funny when I told her to please stop sponsoring people. I then went on to explain to her that something was obviously not working. "Don't you think you should figure out how you messed up the last 42 before you sponsor any more?"

I learned a long time ago if you're going to make residual income in this industry, especially large amounts of it, the name of the game is get them in, keep them in, and move them along. The sad thing is that many people work very hard learning how to put them in but very few figure out how to keep them in and move them along. Therefore, after a few hard months of sponsoring, many get discouraged and quit or move on to another company, thus creating the revolving door effect so many organizations are plagued with today. These people falling by the wayside give our industry a bad name. They're like that TV show called *Where Are They Now?* You know—the one where they do a segment on a movie star or singer who had the one big hit and fell off the face of the earth. The same thing happens here. Some people sponsor a lot of others and get a few big checks the first few months, but they never figure out how to keep them in and move them along. When the checks go away, so do they.

Recently, a gentleman approached me and proceeded to ask how he could have prevented his last 10 personally sponsored distributors from quitting. What could he do differently to keep them in? My answer was simple: "Get them a check." The money is the number one reason people get involved, so help them get what they came for. People who are making money are less likely to quit than those who are not. A philosophy that has served me well is "what gets rewarded gets repeated." It is also true that rewards and recognition should be swift and abundant. A check is a reward. Help your people get that reward as soon as possible. In today's fast-paced environment, people are not into delayed gratification. If they go too long without getting rewards (i.e., checks) they either quit or move on. It has been said, "Volume never goes down in network marketing. It just moves to another company." Too many people join our industry and go into a recruiting or retailing frenzy, creating a check for themselves. What they fail to do is slow down long enough to help their people earn a check. The irony is they then wonder why their people quit. What they fail to realize is getting them in is not the same as keeping them in. Remember, they come for the money. Getting them a check is the first step in keeping them in.

It would serve all of us well to understand that people are recognition driven. If you doubt me on this, go down to your local bar on karaoke night. While some are very talented, just watch and listen (if you can bear the pain) to those who can not carry a tune. They step up to the microphone and embarrass themselves for three or four minutes, all so they can be recognized by the crowd's applause. Heaven forbid if someone tells them they were good . . . they go back for round two! This leads to more applause and more recognition. You and I get more misery. Remember, what gets rewarded gets repeated.

Still not convinced people are recognition driven? Perhaps you should view one of the many reality shows so abundant on television today. You'll see people eat bugs, swim in shark-infested waters, and do a host of other grotesque and hazardous acts. Many get disqualified or beaten out by their opponents and get nothing. Do you think they do these humiliating acts for the money? No. For most, their job pays more than they will earn from winning. Most are merely seeking recognition, the opportunity to be seen, to be appreciated. When it comes to recognition, the old adage is that "men die for it and babies cry for it." If you've ever been in the military or had children, you know both are true. I personally know this all too well. My two-year-old wants nothing more than mommy and daddy's approval and attention, and he'll cry as long as it takes to get it.

Those same desires for attention and recognition have followed us into our adult lives. Just as children want their parents to acknowledge them when they learn and accomplish new things, our downlines want their accomplishments recognized as well. This is why most companies have pins and awards to signify different levels of achievement. While some will never realize the significance of recognition and the pin system, if they stick around they eventually will. I'll never forget the guy who told me he wasn't into this "recognition thing." "Just send me my checks and I'll be happy," he said. The first time he got a $30,000 bonus check and no one recognized him for it, he wrote the company a letter and complained about it.

In the largest study ever conducted on job satisfaction, money and benefits were not even ranked in the top 10 items that make the most profitable and productive work environments. You must realize even though it is the number one reason people join your business, it's not the money that drives them away. History has proven that people will work for less money as long as they feel appreciated. The same is true with your downline. If you don't respect them, they will leave you. I can personally attest to this. I once walked away from a company where I had a large check and more than 65,000 people in my downline because of lack of respect. If you don't acknowledge them, you are, by default, disrespecting them. One of the worst things you can do is ignore your downline.

In the corporate world, companies that do recognition have a less than 4 percent turnover rate. Wouldn't you like to have a retention rate like that in your downline? It has been said that the greatest motivational force in the world is when someone else believes in you. You would have to search long and hard to find a more effective motivational tool than recognition. The good news is that most network marketing companies have recognition programs, and the majority do an adequate job at it. The challenge is that very few do a *great* job at it. The reason is that most employees and owners alike don't understand the value of recognition and how to do it effectively. It makes matters worse that very few distributors understand it well, either. Most believe recognition is the company's responsibility. I learned a long time ago not to rely on the company to motivate my organization. I take recognition into my own hands, and I suggest you do the same. Understand that performing recognition effectively does not come naturally to most people, even the top income earners. But the great news is it can be learned. I encourage you to learn the incredible art of motivation through recognition.

My best advice for people in this business is to develop a "catch them doing something right" mentality with regard to their downline. Better put, praise them to profit. The best leaders learn to celebrate virtually everything, from advancing through the various compensation plan levels to achieving record-breaking months, from adding new enrollees to making new retail sales. They also use many forms of recognition, from a congratulatory voice mail or e-mail to a steak dinner, from a bottle of champagne to a trip to Paris. I believe that we should recognize our people with plaques as big as doors, and trophies as big as the people who earn them.

The bigger the accomplishment, the bigger the reward should be. For example, one of our personally sponsored distributorships recently achieved a top pin. My wife and I surprised them by picking them up in a limo and taking them to a private jetport where a leased private Learjet awaited our arrival. Once airborne, we enjoyed the finest of champagne during our short flight to Martha's Vineyard, where we had lunch at the top restaurant on the island. After a little shopping, we hopped back on the Lear to return to Manhattan. The limo took us to the Plaza Hotel to relax and picked us up again in time for dinner at the number one restaurant in New York City. The distributorship achieved something big so we made them feel appreciated, respected, and valued by giving them an experience they will remember for the rest of their lives.

We do recognition right in our organization. We've taken our leaders everywhere from a dream week in Cabo San Lucas to first-class weekends in Beverly Hills and Las Vegas, from New York to Paris to French Polynesia. We recognize the big accomplishments and we recognize the small stepping-stones. We look for any reason to call someone's name, to stand and be applauded. Our people understand recognition so well, the other day the sound guy walked onstage to check the microphone and the crowd gave him a standing ovation! We've designed a championship ring for our leaders who achieve top pin levels. Now, I'm not talking small potatoes. Our championship ring makes a World Series ring look insignificant. Anyone would be more than proud to wear this on their finger. The ring and its diamonds are massive, and deservingly so. I believe if we can stand and cheer the sports figures and the rock stars who color their hair purple and tattoo their bodies and we hold these people up to our children as role models, then we should also give championship rings to the real heroes of this world. People like you who are reading this book, people who are teaching entrepreneurship, people who are helping parents put kids through college and showing how to bring spouses home from work so they can be with their children are the real heroes. You deserve the recognition. This business is about the stuff of which dreams are made, so I encourage you to become a dream maker.

If you're missing a great recognition program, then I suggest you start one. Here are a few recommendations on how to get going. First, start a recognition journal. Make a list of different contests and promotions you can run to increase sales, recruiting, new pin levels, and so on. What is worthy of recognition? What is it you want to focus on—a retail contest, a recruitment contest? My philosophy is: If it can move, measure it, promote it, and reward it. Simply put, if you measure it and reward it, people will do it. Select a promotion that is easy for the participants to understand. It should be something they can measure with ease. If you make it too complicated, people won't perform.

Second, determine when you will start the promotion, how long will it run, and how often you will recognize accomplishments. Starting dates are important to maximize your objectives. Consider what else is going on at this time in the company. Are there any promotions that would conflict with this one? Is this a good time of year, or are there holidays that would detract from (or add to) the promotion? Many companies go through slumps during June, July, August, and December, yet these are always some of our biggest volume and recruitment months because we line up specific promotions with fun rewards during these times. I suggest keeping promotions under 90 days while having weekly recognition benchmarks. The more often you recognize, the better the performance you'll receive. Long promotions lead to greater chances of burnout.

Next, determine what awards will be given for the promotion. I suggest you set up a promotion budget in proportion to your income. Doing this will ensure you have allotted a certain percentage of your check every month to grow your business. As your income grows, so does your promotion budget, which in turn causes your check to grow even more. Awards should be of value and motivate your team. Make sure the awards will give you a return on your investment. In other words, the promotion should pay for itself. If not, either choose another award or reconsider the promotion. Cash is not recommended as an award. Studies show that people who receive other types of awards outperform those receiving cash by 50 percent. People will spend the cash to pay bills and never have a memory or reminder of what their achievement or award was. People collect mementos, not cash. Memories of a great trip will last forever. Awards with your company's logo or symbol are great for keeping the accomplishment and vision alive.

The next step is to create awareness and excitement about the promotion. It is suggested to get as many of your leaders and team members as possible on board with you prior to launching the promotion. The more people who buy into the promotion before it starts, the better chance for success. You will also want to spend time training your leaders on how to present the promotion the right way. There are numerous ways to get the word out and the excitement up. A great promoter will use as many methods as possible to ensure success. Use everything from e-mail and voice mail blasts to hanging posters at every meeting to putting flyers and brochures on every chair. Special conference calls are great to announce and explain the promotion and awards. To be successful, a promotion must be at the forefront of everyone's mind. Most promotions fail because they are announced once or twice and then forgotten. To be successful, remember to keep it simple, say it often, make it burn. The promotion should be simple enough for a child to understand. Talk it up daily, several times a day. Make it a promotion that everyone wants to win.

Now it's time for the grand finale, time to reward the winner(s). This should be a big deal and always in front of as many people as possible. Make the fanfare as big as possible in proportion to the size of the promotion. Take pictures and put them on your web site. Videotape the award being presented and send it to all of the winners' relatives. To be most effective, present the award within a few days of the conclusion of the promotion. Remember, recognition should be swift and abundant. Make it a big deal and do it with class. If you go over and above in any part of your business, recognition is important. Done right, the returns are enormous.

When we believe in people, we motivate them to reach their highest potential. It's been written, "Look at a man as he is and he becomes worse, but look at him as he should be and he'll become what he could be." People always grow toward a leader's expectation, not toward criticism and examinations. Expectations promote progress. Promotions and recognition programs create expectations. Commit to becoming a master of recognition and you'll master many of the challenges you'll face in this journey we call network marketing.

Brad Hager has over 13 years of experience in the networking industry. He has worked both corporately and in the field. As national development director for a company in the mid 1990s, he developed a company-wide recruiting and training system that duplicated like wildfire and led that company to over $100 million in sales. As a distributor, he and his team went on to build an organization and set a company record of enrolling more than 65,000 people in three years. Brad has sat on company advisory boards and been featured in numerous magazines and industry journals as well as top-selling books. Brad is recognized as one of the leading motivational speakers in the industry. Many consider him to be the number one nuts-and-bolts trainer in the business.

Brad has trained thousands of people in effective life-skills seminars that are powerful in building not only a financial success but also a balanced personal relationship environment with family and friends. Brad believes that to grow and maintain a large income requires strong leadership skills and a willingness to change. In his trainings, he shows people how to change in the area of personal growth. Over the years, Brad's training system has provided the vehicle for exuberant people to enjoy exceptional incomes and ideal lifestyles. The training system is a gold mine that has produced many fortunes for those who follow his coaching. Brad's best-selling tape and training program entitled *Success Leaves Clues* has helped many people hit millionaire status.

Brad and his wife Marcia live in Las Vegas where they raise their son, Devin. With a seven-figure income, they are the top earners in CyberWize with over 80,000 people in their organization. To contact Brad or to get information about his system and training materials go to www.bhager.com.

CHAPTER
19

The Magic of Network Marketing: Building Real Residual Income

Barry Friedman

There is something very special about most legitimate network marketing opportunities. It is not always obvious and not always fully appreciated for what it is and what it can mean to most families. Behind all of the excitement and expectations of newfound financial freedom is the real essence of what financial security is all about. Clearly, it is very important for the new prospect or seasoned networker to look beyond the promise of huge up-front money—the $10,000 per month in 90 days to $1 million or more per month as you build your business. While this possibility can be real in many cases, it is more elusive for most.

When all of the dust has settled and the initial excitement has faded, what really matters in terms of wealth generation is how much money you are receiving each month—today—for the work that you did yesterday. That is residual income. I believe that most of us would easily opt for $10,000 per month for the rest of our lives (and our survivors') rather than $50,000 per month for a few months. When we combine the concept of residual income with that of leverage, we are indeed on our way to permanent financial security. I invite you to read this chapter not only from the perspective of how residual income can impact your life but how you can use the value of residual income to attract your prospects to your networking business.

Let's take a step back to look at the very special financial perspective of network marketing. First, allow me to provide a little background. I have been a financial planner since 1968 and a Certified Financial Planner (CFP) since 1978. During this time, I have spent endless hours with clients trying to help structure retirement plans and to help establish financial security. It has seemed that no matter how hard most people try, they have either too little time or too little money. There are, after all, not many ways to accumulate significant wealth. You need to have either sufficient funds to make the most of your limited time to accumulate or a lot of time during which to build your available capital. Sad to say, neither of these strategies works for most people. The young, who have the time in which to accumulate, rarely have the discipline to do it. The older folks, who have the burning need and some limited resources, just do not usually have the time left to reach their goal.

It has become clearer every day that just working at a job is not the answer. The old idea of working 40 years on the job and retiring with a gold watch just does not work today. We are living longer, working harder, and making less, and have even less to show for our efforts. Nine out of 10 families now need two working members just to make ends meet. Surveys also indicate that 85 percent of all Americans would like to own their own business. With that in mind, let's look at how many people are effectively addressing the problem.

In the United States, someone starts a new home-based business every 10 seconds. More than 25 percent of all Americans are involved in some sort of home business, and the numbers are even more dramatic in other parts of the world. The average successful home-based business generates more than $50,000 yearly in income, while the average working wage is only $22,000 in North America. The reason for the great disparity, to a great extent, is due to the concepts of residual income and leverage. We will touch briefly on leverage here and get into a more detailed discussion of residual income shortly.

The concept of leverage was most clearly stated by J. Paul Getty, the oil industry billionaire, who said, "I'd rather have 1 percent of 100 people's efforts than 100 percent of my own." It would be hard to state this principle any more clearly or have it make any more sense. Since network marketing is all about word-of-mouth communications with others, it epitomizes the principle of leverage. You tell someone something that you feel strongly and passionately about, and they tell someone, who tells someone, who tells someone . . . and so it goes. Before you know it, you have an organization building your business while they are building their own. Remember, most people are involved in network marketing now; they just aren't getting paid for it. Isn't that what happens when one recommends a restaurant, movie, or product? How much would you have made if you got a check every time you made a recommendation? Well, you can . . . with network marketing.

I became deeply involved with network marketing about 25 years ago when I was doing some research for a financial planning client. He was about 60 years old and was about to leave a job that he had been at for more than 30 years. His company retirement plan was to give him an income for life of about 50 percent of the salary that he barely survived on while working—not a very promising prospect. At his request, I looked into several network marketing opportunities and discovered something incredible from a financial planning perspective. That was, it seemed reasonable to assume that within two to four years in network marketing, my client could build a residual income that could equal or exceed his retirement income, and this income could continue to grow and pay not only him, but his heirs upon his death. What a financial planning tool!

Let's put a pen to this and utilize some financial planning concepts to put the picture into its proper perspective. Let's look at the concept of asset equivalency. What would be the equivalent cash asset needed to replace a reliable, continuing cash flow generated as a result of residual income from a network marketing enterprise? First of all, we must accept the premise that this type of residual income can be stated as if it were the return on a cash asset. For our illustration, we are going to assume a very safe investment equivalent: a bank certificate of deposit or (CD), in this case, one that yields a better than average return of 3 percent. Treat the following illustration in this manner: A benefactor has given you a lump sum of money and has required that it be placed in a CD. This enables you to receive the income for life and your heirs will continue to do so thereafter, provided you do not touch the principal.

Let's assume you have joined a network marketing company that offers a true residual income opportunity. You have studied well and worked hard. It is now one year into the effort and you have built a $2,500 per month residual income. From a planning view, you have created a personal asset possessing a net worth of $1 million. Assuming a 3 percent yield on your money, 3 percent of $1 million equals $30,000 per year, or $2,500 per month. Yes, you are now a millionaire!

But you are not ready to quit yet. Let's see what can happen with a bit more effort if you continue to do exactly what you were doing that got you to where you are. You are working and getting others to work in a compensation plan that has rewarded you with this income. Over the next 12 months, you do not work any harder and you do not work any smarter, but at the end of this time your monthly residual income is now $5,000 per month. That's right, you now have the equivalent of $2 million in the bank, and are earning as if your $2 million was generating 3 percent.

I think that you have the picture. Without working harder or smarter, each year your net worth increases by $1 million and your income by $30,000. You may decide to work harder or smarter, but it is also acceptable to go and spend your remaining days on the beach, as long as you have developed leaders who will continue to support their organizations. Your income should continue to grow, as will your net worth. One of the beautiful aspects of this scenario is the benefit that your heirs will receive upon your death. The income should continue and pass on to your heirs without serious erosion from the effects of estate or inheritance taxes.

There are a number of important factors to put into place to make sure that the income you have built is residual. Most network marketing businesses have the element of helping and caring for others. It is critical that you become a product of your products, that you truly care about what you are doing, that you support your customers ethically, and that you empower your distributors who themselves become leaders. Your rock-solid belief and the enthusiasm with which you present yourself and your opportunity will be the key to your success.

Let's step back a minute and examine where you are. You have now found the right company with the right business plan. You have examined the compensation plan and it works for you. Your family is supportive and you have a fire in your belly. It is now time to learn the business as well as you can and put what you learn to work. Plan your work and work your plan. Don't get discouraged because at some point along the way to success you will likely hit the wall. Keep on plugging, inspired by the reasons that had you join your company in the first place, and it will be well worth it in the long run. If you work your business with all of the energy that you can muster, you will achieve success and, as a result, life will never be the same.

Network marketing companies possess several key components that will ensure that the residual income created will last long into the future. Every element does not have to be present to the same degree in every program, but there is a relationship between the reliability of the income and the presence of the following elements:

- High demand.
- Great value.
- Limited competition.
- Affordable pricing.
- Continuous need.
- Ready availability.
- Geographic availability.
- Products or services backed by a guarantee or warranty.

It is critical that once a customer or distributor has made the initial commitment to the product or service, the revenue is repeatable without effort. What makes it work is that the benefits outweigh the costs, yielding the ability to keep on adding new customers and distributors without losing old ones.

Network marketing has traditionally been an eyeball-to-eyeball, belly-to-belly business. That method has worked for decades and will for decades to come, but in today's world of the Internet and electronic marketing, more and more people are finding success without stepping away from their telephone and computer. The best way is the way that works best for you. In a large organization, success will typically result from a combination of techniques, but never forgetting the basics of people-to-people, relationship marketing.

As a network marketing millionaire, or budding millionaire, there are now other things for you to consider:

- What am I going to do with my money?
- How long and hard do I want to work?
- What is my definition of financial freedom?
- Who do I want to bring along with me?

These are not easy questions, but ones that you surely can answer. You will also have the opportunity to do some necessary financial planning and tax planning. As an independent business owner, you are entitled to hundreds of tax benefits that can amount to many thousands of dollars each and every year. The combination of residual income and self-employment tax benefits represents some of the most powerful financial tools anyone can access. You will soon understand why the rich and famous can stay rich and famous—or at least rich.

Here is your final challenge. Given the experience of working with hundreds and maybe thousands of network marketing millionaires, the ultimate challenge may not be how to become a millionaire, but what to do when you become a millionaire. Residual income millionaires may be faced with choices that they have never dealt with before in their lives—choices like:

- What time do I want to get up today?
- Do I want to work today?
- Where do I want to be today?
- What do I want to do today?
- How do I want to spend the rest of my life?

Network marketing can be a vehicle for doing as much good as possible for as many people as possible, and getting paid for doing it! There are people who have some very definite personal goals that can be attainable with the level of financial security made possible by a million-dollar residual income. These might include:

- Gaining a long overdue education.
- Sending someone to college.
- Doing mission work or contributing to charity.
- Creating a new home for oneself or one's family.
- Having the means to afford all the material things that make life fun and exciting.

There is no right or wrong when it comes to making these choices since they are so personal. Financial freedom can certainly be a worthy goal for which to strive. How you obtain it and what you do with it are up to you. Network marketing can give you the best shot at joining the top 2 percent of earners in America. It is up to you to make it happen.

Barry Friedman, CFP, began his business career in 1959 after graduating from Lafayette College with a degree in business administration and a major in marketing. His early career was spent as a sales promotion and marketing consultant, specializing in the financial services and direct sales industries. In 1968, he became a financial planner and has held workshops and seminars for tens of thousands of people around the country.

After many years of being on the road 200 to 250 days a year, he chose to settle down and become associated with one of the nation's fastest-growing network marketing companies. With his financial and marketing background, he soon became fascinated by the prospect of the perfect residual income opportunity and the impact that it could have on the lives of so many people.

He is senior vice president, sales and marketing, at AmeriPlan Corporation in Plano, Texas, and can be reached at (469) 229-4003 or barryf@ameriplanusa.com.

CHAPTER
20

Creating a Steady Stream of Prospects

Randy Gage

director on my frontline called to ask if I would accompany him on a one-on-one presentation. This was kind of surprising, because he had a nice size group, and hadn't needed help with a presentation for months. I asked why.

It turned out the guy he was prospecting was the CEO of a multibillion-dollar public company, a guy who was in the business pages and financial publications every week. As CEO, he made several million dollars a year in salary and had stock options that were worth millions more. He attended the same church as my guy, and my guy had prospected him the previous Sunday. How could I resist?

We went to the appointment, which was in his office. (Now that's a mistake, but I went along with it because that's how it was set up.) His office was bigger than the home I lived in. Really. He had a conference table there that must have cost at least 50 grand.

I was a little on edge, but we sat at the end of that table and I did my presentation. He sat through it very attentively. When I was finished, he admitted that it was quite fascinating, but explained that he couldn't get involved. It turns out that his contract with his employer actually prohibited him from doing any other business ventures, as his company thought that would be a conflict of interest. He did go on to say that he was delighted my guy had found the opportunity, and even recommended some people he thought would be good for the business.

So I learned a couple of very important lessons from that encounter.

First was the realization that even some of the highest-paid people in the world are still slaves to their jobs, and don't own their own lives. Very interesting. The second thing I learned from this gentleman and many subsequent experiences is this: The easiest people to get presentations with are busy, successful people while the hardest people to set appointments with are the broke people who need the opportunity the most! Why? Because that's why they need it the most. They might be lazy, closed-minded, or just so busy meeting with their parole officer and watching the Jerry Springer show they don't have time to meet.

I quickly learned that if I wanted my new distributors' organizations to grow rapidly, we needed to compile their lists and then go after the most ambitious, successful, and busiest people on the lists first. Show me a person who works two jobs and also has a booth selling at the flea market on Sundays—and I'll show you a person who will find time to see your presentation.

The reason many new distributors don't employ this approach is just mistaken belief. They are afraid to approach the best prospects on their list, because they don't feel qualified to approach people who have more education, make more money, or have a more important-sounding title than they do. This is a big mistake! These people are actually the best prospects. I've found professionals like doctors, lawyers, and accountants are great prospects. They have learned fairly rapidly that even after all of their schooling, training, and prestige, they are still victims of the trading-hours-for-money trap. As a result, they are usually quite open to finding out how they can harness the power of leverage for financial security.

If you will adjust your sponsoring strategy to reflect this reality, you'll see a lot more growth. Here's a technique to make it easier. The best way to go after the most ambitious, busy, successful people on your list first is using the credibility of your sponsor. Using your sponsor negates the "hometown prospect" syndrome. You put your prospects in front of your sponsor. Depending on what system you use, this could be a three-way call, a full-scale conference call, or meeting them for a two-on-one presentation.

There are some real and very positive benefits from this.

First, it negates the fear many people face. They can be in the background of the initial presentation, deferring to their sponsor so they are less nervous about contacting these high-powered people. They get started in the business a lot faster.

Second, they are learning a very important skill: the first step of the sponsoring presentation. And they are learning it by actually watching their sponsor model the behavior, instead of some role-play or other imaginary situation.

The next benefit is an apparent one: New distributors grow their organization much faster. A fast start invariably leads to faster growth, which carries all through the organization as this replicates level by level.

But the most important benefit concerns the confidence it develops. Instead of being fearful and procrastinating or analyzing everything, new distributors are immediately immersed in doing the business and being productive. Because they have approached their best prospects already—and have some of them in the group—they are much more self-assured about approaching the rest of their list. It creates an ongoing cycle of confidence and competence, which filters down the fast-growing organization.

Let's talk a bit now about meeting people. There is more to the business than just approaching the best prospects on your name list. The other important component is meeting people. Yet, most people in the business will never reach even the beginning stages of the leadership ranks for one simple reason: They don't know how to expand their prospect universe and meet new people. What a waste that is since the real culprit here is ignorance because the ability to find and attract prospects is a fairly simple skill to learn. It can be done fairly readily within your warm market. The key factor is the type of approach you use initially.

There are actually two different types of approaches to use with prospects: the direct approach and the indirect or mystery approach. Most distributors in network marketing know only one—the indirect or mystery approach. Here are some examples of this approach:

"Chuck, you seem like a sharp guy. I'm wondering if you ever explore opportunities to make a second income. I'm expanding my business, and I'm looking for a couple of key people. I'd love to sit down and discuss it with you."

"Chuck, I've got a high-volume marketing business [or, I'm working with some people who have a high- volume marketing business], and we're expanding in this area. We're looking for a couple of key people, and I thought you might be interested in taking a look."

"Chuck, have you ever thought about being your own boss? I help people open their own home-based businesses, and I've got something I want you to check out."

The indirect approach works very well with the casual acquaintances you will meet as you go about your life. However, it's not very effective with your family and close friends. They respond much better to the direct approach.

A direct invite looks like this:

"Hey, Chuck. It's Randy. Got a minute?"
"Sure."
"I've got a quick question for you. What do you know about network marketing?"

This approach can also be done by substituting the name of your actual company in place of network marketing (e.g.,: "What do you know about Shaklee?").

I've found the direct approach was a breakthrough for my business, and so has everyone I've taught it to. That may surprise you if you have the belief that people are skeptical about the industry and you think you need to keep things a secret until late in the process. I used to think that. But experience has given me a different belief. Now I believe that most people are fascinated with network marketing!

Here's where I get this belief. For about three years, I did my own little unscientific experiment. Every time I was on an airplane (which is often) and people asked me what I did, I replied, "I'm in network marketing."

Frankly, I was just curious about the possible reaction. Would people give up their seat and go back to the economy section? Would any try to jump off without a parachute? Would anybody attack me? A fascinating thing happened: Nothing. In more than three years, I never had one negative response. Probably about 20 percent of the time, they may ask if it is something to do with computers. If so, I ask them if they have ever heard of companies like Amway, Herbalife, or Mary Kay. Naturally they have, and then I explain that those companies are involved in network marketing. That usually leads to a comment I often hear from the other 80 percent, something like one of the following examples:

> *"Well, you know, I tried that once. I was in Herbalife a couple of years ago, but it never really worked out for me. But I know a lot of people who do real well with that."*

> *"I was in Amway back in the 1980s. I never made any money with it, but we had just had a baby, and I didn't put a lot of time into it. But my old sponsor is still in it and he makes a lot of money in the business."*

> *"I tried Shaklee back in 1999 and it didn't really work out for me but I have some friends who joined a few years before me and they just built a 20,000-square-foot house and they have two Mercedeses and a Ferrari! They must be making a fortune."*

These responses demonstrate how much fascination there is with the industry. This is a subject people want to know more about. They're either in network marketing or they know someone successful in network marketing or they want to be in network marketing or they used to be in network marketing, and they're thinking about getting back in. The amazing success stories they've heard have them very curious what all the fuss is about.

If you're still suffering from the belief that people think it is a pyramid or it's a chain letter, or fear that most of them will respond negatively, think again. My experience with the direct approach has shown me nothing but positive reactions, and, in many cases, very well qualified leads.

What makes the direct approach so effective is the fact that in reality, almost everybody you know already knows that you're in network marketing. How? Because your friends all talk about you when you're not around! So, when you call up with the indirect approach, they wonder why you are being sneaky and mysterious, and they respond with skepticism. It insults their intelligence. When you approach them with respect, they respect you and the opportunity a lot more.

That doesn't mean you will never get a negative response. Once in a great while, you may. They might tell you that they had tried that five years ago and spent a lot of money on water filters that took them several years to sell at the flea market. Believe it or not, that's not necessarily a bad response. It's good to find out up front if there is any negativity. Then you can come back with something like:

> *"Well, you know, the industry has changed a lot over the last couple of years, and I've got an opportunity that I'm very excited about. Since you have experience in the business, I'd really love to sit down with you, have a cup of coffee, and have you evaluate it for me. Would you be willing to take 30 minutes and take a look at this with me?"*

Even a skeptic can't resist an opportunity like that! They'll agree to meet you, thinking they are going to save you from yourself. Once they see an actual presentation, they'll probably discover that the problems network marketing experienced during its developmental years (front-end loading, hype-driven compensation plans, etc.) have since been corrected. And it's highly likely that they will end up joining.

Remember, there was a reason that they joined in the first place. They had that dream to be their own boss, get rich, or experience the network marketing lifestyle. Chances are it isn't dead—just in hibernation. Your presentation could be the impetus that revives it!

In reality, most people don't know the real scope of network marketing. If they did, they'd be in it, and already be millionaires. What they have is a superficial, distorted view, based on their two- or three-week experience from five or 10 years ago. Perhaps they were front-end loaded in some shady company or got duped by a pyramid scheme posing as a legitimate company. But that tells you they did have a desire to build a residual side income business at some point. When they really sit down and take an objective look at it, most people will see the soundness of the business today.

The direct approach absolutely gets right to the point, and it's very effective. It lets you know exactly what your prospect's perception of the business is, so you can respond appropriately. In actuality, though, the people who still hold a negative view of the business today make up a small minority. Network marketing companies are trading on the stock exchange and have been featured positively in publications like *Inc.* magazine, the *Wall Street Journal*, and *Success* magazine. If you are open and professional in the manner in which you bring it up, most people are willing to spend 30 minutes with you to take a look at what it's about. The direct invite really has the potential to transform your business.

So how do you know when to use either approach? The secret is knowing which person to use which approach with. For casual acquaintances or people who respond to marketing campaigns you run, I still favor the indirect approach. This works very well with them, because casual acquaintances will take you at your word.

If it's somebody you met at the mall that you had a 15-minute conversation with, and you call them up later and let them know that you have a marketing business that's expanding in the area and you're looking for a couple of key people, they'll simply accept that, whereas your brother or neighbor may be much more likely to challenge you. So with friends, neighbors, and relatives, I definitely like the direct approach.

Prospecting and presenting make up the engine that drives fast growth in this business. The savvy network marketers are the ones who know how to create a steady stream of new prospects to look at their business. This gives you the opportunity to work with only the best and brightest people. You control your growth, and you build a business with the people you enjoy.

Of course, the best part of all this is the magic of duplication. Whatever you do at the top of the organization duplicates down through the whole group. So what you do expands exponentially. And that makes for some pretty astounding growth!

Randy Gage has been called "the Millionaire Messiah" because he believes that you are meant to be rich, and it is a sin to be poor! Through his books, audio programs, and workshops, he travels the world, teaching that health, happiness, and wealth are possible for all who desire it. Randy reveals how to harness the power of thought and intention to manifest success in all areas of your life.

Randy is a tireless champion of the network marketing industry as a vehicle for people to create prosperity. His prospecting audio *Escape the Rat Race* is the top prospecting tool in the industry. Through his Internet-based coaching program, "Breakthrough U," Randy works directly with success seekers in more than 40 different countries.

He is the author of six books: *How to Build a Multi-Level Money Machine*, *Prosperity Mind*, *The 7 Spiritual Laws of Prosperity*, *101 Keys to Your Prosperity*, *Accept Your Abundance*, and *37 Secrets about Prosperity*. Randy is also the author of more than four dozen other audio and video learning resources, such as "Duplication Nation," "The Midas Mentality," and "Prosperity." His works have sold over five million copies, and been translated into more than a dozen languages. To find more about Randy, go to www.RandyGage.com.

CHAPTER 21

Creating a Simple Yet Effective Method of Operation

Art Jonak

"An excited distributor going down the
wrong road will get to the wrong place faster."

—Anonymous

Here's a typical growth cycle for many network marketing organizations. They grow to 30 distributors, and then shrink to 10 or 5. Then they grow again to 30 and shrink again. Grow again to 40 and shrink. Then the organization fizzles and finally disappears. It rarely gets to 300, 500, or 1,000 distributors.

A healthy organization should grow one, two, three, or more levels deep down each organizational leg every month.

If you sponsor someone who has owned a successful business, she might sign up 30 distributors on her credibility alone, and then have very little, if any, new growth after the initial surge.

You hear the same story all the time. You go to a local meeting and see the chamber of commerce guy on stage and learn how he signed up a ton of new people in his first month. And then, the next month, he's nowhere to be found.

This is what I call the "Superman Syndrome."

You want an organization that grows without you, that doesn't even need you, one that doesn't even know who you are! Wouldn't that be great! Ultimately you want to work your way out of a job. I once asked Tom "Big Al" Schreiter what success in network marketing looked like. He answered:

"It's when you're collecting a great weekly bonus check from
your program and 95 percent of your team doesn't even know
your name."

156

So, how can you make that happen? I'll share my experience regarding what has worked for me. It's not gospel and you can disagree with any part of it. My suggestion, however, is to try it on like a jacket. If it fits, use it. If it doesn't, stop using it.

STANDARDIZING THE OPPORTUNITY AND PRODUCT

Every network marketing organization should have a standard method of operation by which they sponsor, train, and duplicate. Network marketing programs have three common elements: the opportunity, the product, and the distributor. The product is the same for everyone in your company. No one in your company has a different product line than you do. Regarding the opportunity, does your company offer a different compensation plan for people with a college education than for those with no education? Does the compensation plan pay some occupations more than others? Is there a glass ceiling for women, like there is in corporate America? Does your plan discriminate against distributors over the age of 65 or under the age of 25?

Of course not! The opportunity and the product are the same for everyone.

That leaves the distributor. Success is a function of the skills the distributor learns. It involves the techniques he teaches and the viewpoints he takes about his business. These make the biggest difference in the size of his weekly bonus check.

As your sponsor, if you go out there and become a huge success, it will not be because of me. It will be because of you. And on the flip side, if you go out there and fail, it will not be because of me. It will be because of you.

As your sponsor, I'm not here to work for you. Instead, I'm here to work *with* you, to teach you the skills necessary to build a large, successful network marketing organization.

This is where a simple method of operation for your team can help. You want to create a pattern that is the same every single time, a pattern your team can develop that's easy enough to encourage the learning of new skills. Create a solid method of operation for your team, and the chances your group will be able to consistently share the message of your opportunity and product will increase exponentially.

You want to create one method of operation and stick with it for a long period of time. If you don't stick to one simple method of operation, here's what could and probably will happen. Imagine you're going through your mail and between all the bills, offers, and advertising, you find a letter from your networking company. You rip it open and pull out a bonus check!

"Well," you think, "I might as well cash it and go shopping!" On your way to the bank you notice about 50 cars, bumper to bumper, in a parade procession. Suddenly the lead car accelerates to over 100 miles per hour. Your sense of adventure kicks in and you decide to follow the procession leader setting the pace. You rush past 15 other cars just to keep up with the speeding car, which then makes a U-turn, followed by a right turn and then a sharp left turn. Luckily you happen to be Mario Andretti's second cousin, so you're able to stay on the leader's tail. However, 20 of the other cars can't keep up and drop out. The lead car speeds up for a mile, zips down an alley, runs a traffic light, and disappears into heavy traffic. Even you can't keep up. So, you decide to quit trying.

How many of the 50 cars do you think are still following the lead vehicle?

Probably none. That's why a successful procession leader follows a set path, at a steady pace. This way everyone following the procession can reach the ultimate destination together.

As a leader, you are like a procession leader for your team. The question is, "Are you following a proven path or are you zigzagging around, hoping everyone will keep up with you?"

If you don't have single and simple method of operation, here's what might be happening on your team. Your sponsor shares her method of building the business. You agree to use it and share it with your new distributors. Three weeks later, you attend a regional rally and the guest speaker shares a different way of building the business. You and some of your distributors decide to try his way while other distributors decide not to. A few weeks later, you read an article on the Internet about another great way of building your business. You decide to give it a shot. You forward the article to your leaders. Some of them decide to try this new way. Others on your team won't. Six months later, you're wondering why your group grows only a few levels deep and then fizzles out. And why many of your leaders are inactive and why your bonus check is getting smaller.

Here's the bottom line. It's hard to build momentum on your team if you change systems every few weeks, or even every few months. Pick one way and stick with it. Looking for that one secret magical way to build your business every couple of months could end up costing your team a great deal of time and money. A fragmented organization cannot compete with one that has a set path, a set method of operation.

A method of operation can be as simple as:

1. Getting a handful of customers.
2. Getting a handful of customer getters.
3. Repeating the process.

Find a method of operation that your entire team can learn and get re-sults from, especially the brand-new distributors. Teach it over and over and over again. Teach it on your conference calls, after your meetings, and through your actions. Have everyone experience it. Don't teach anything else until they get the basic method of operation down. If someone's check is flat it tells me that he has made his business too personality driven and not driven by a simple and effective method of operation.

THE METHOD OF OPERATION LITMUS TEST

As you build your business, ask yourself whether what you're doing and ask-ing your team to do is something that can be done:

- In depth, 10 or 15 levels below you.
- By somebody you don't even know, because the vast majority of peo-ple on your team you won't even know.
- Working thousands of miles away from you, because eventually the majority of your organization will not be in your backyard.
- By a brand-new distributor, somebody who has never really been successful, and who is getting ready to approach someone with a lot of success. Remember, that's really big!

Begin with the end in mind by putting the focus on what you are per-sonally doing. If what you are doing on your first level is not something that can be done in each scenario just listed, then the odds are you'll never create any depth on your team. What you'll constantly get is you and your 10 team members, then 20, then back to 10, bouncing back and forth. But you'll never develop any significant depth.

We want a presentation format that is so simple and duplicable that when somebody hears it, they will always say:

- "I can do what you're doing."
- "I won't have a problem doing what you're doing with the people I know."
- "I have the time to do what you're doing."

The problem I see with most approaches used by distributors to get a person started is the person ends up thinking: "Yes, you've got a great com-pany. Yes, I agree with everything you're doing. Yes, it's all great, really great. But you know what?

"I can't do what you just did.

"Nor do I want to do to my friends or associates what you just did.

"And I don't have the time to do what you just did."

In essence, you won the battle but you lost the war and immediately the duplication has stopped.

Successful network marketing leaders know there is an opportunity when someone says no to what they are offering. If someone tells you that your opportunity or product is not for them right now, you want two things from them:

1. "Yes, you can continue to keep me updated."

2. "Yes, I can give you referrals."

Again, if your approach is complicated, cumbersome, and very aggressive, most people will say:

1. "No, I really don't want you to do this to me again."

2. "No, I would not expose you to my associates."

A REVEALING CASE STUDY

My friends John and Brian joined our network marketing company during the same week. Both were in their late twenties, and had similar backgrounds, similar centers of influence, and similar lifestyles. After six months, Brian's group was about the same size as John's. After 12 months, Brian's group was 10 times bigger than John's. After 24 months, John had about 100 distributors in his group and was making about $1,000 in residual income each month from his business. Creating $1,000 a month in passive, ongoing income after only twenty-four months of part-time work is pretty darn good. Outside of network marketing, it would be pretty hard for the average person to do. However, Brian's group was 50 times larger and so was his bonus check. Yes, Brian's check was $50,000 per month and growing!

I'm sure you'll agree those are H-U-G-E numbers, especially after working the business for only 24 months! Same backgrounds, same company, same compensation plan, different results. Why? Probably a number of reasons. However, the fact that Brian had a simple, effective, and focused method of operation was without a doubt the single biggest reason.

KEEPING THE MAIN THING THE MAIN THING

Successful businessman Frank Aucoin coined the phrase "Keep the main thing the main thing." And what is the main thing? Simply this: How many times today was the story of the opportunity and product told on your behalf by you, by your team, or by an event?

At first, the number of times the story is told will be based 100 percent on your own efforts. If you share the story twice that day, the number is two. Once you sponsor someone who agrees to share the story twice a day, then the story is being told four times a day on your behalf: twice by you and twice by your new distributor. As your organization grows, the story can be told hundreds, thousands, even tens of thousands of times per day. However, the odds of this happening are greatly increased if you have a simple and effective method of operation.

THE BIG QUESTION

How can the story be told perfectly every time, 10 or 15 levels in depth, by brand-new distributors we don't even know who live thousands of miles away from us? How can it be told by a dud, somebody who's never really been successful, who is getting ready to approach someone with a lot of success?

Learning a 30-minute presentation is daunting. Not only will it take weeks and even months to learn, it's an unreasonable request of your distributors. Think about the last time the average person had to give a presentation. It was probably in high school and they dreaded every second of it!

THE SOLUTION

Let's go back to Brian. Brian's method of operation was simply based on the effective use of a third-party tool to tell the story. The definition of a third-party tool is basically anything you're not. A third-party tool can be a tape, CD, video, DVD, conference call, meeting, three-way call, web site, and the like. You are using third-party tools when you're not personally verbally sharing the facts on the company and product. A third-party tool will tell the story perfectly every single time. Distributors simply need to learn to point prospects to third-party tools. It's much easier to teach a distributor to point to third-party tools than it is to have them memorize a full presentation. If you use a third-party tool to tell the story, you'll end up talking less so you can talk to *more* people.

Brian knew that in order for his distributors to be successful, they had to always *be the messenger and not the message!*

Most people get involved and think it's their job to personally tell the world about this business. It's not. The people who make the most money are the ones who use third-party tools to share the story.

If you are taking an hour to do the explanation, you might do great and sign up your prospect—but they'll say, "I can't do what you did!"

Instead, Brian stuck to a simple enrollment process:

1. Pique the prospect's interest.
2. Get them the information.
3. Sign them up.
4. Repeat the process.

So let's go through the process and the skills a distributor would have to learn to be successful.

First Skill: Where to Find Prospects

Learning to create prospects is something every organization should be able to help you with and too broad a subject for this article.

Second Skill: Piquing a Prospect's Interest

You can pique interest with an opening sentence like: "Are you the kind of person who keeps an open mind to a business opportunity?" Or "Would you be open to learning how to make an extra weekly paycheck?" If the prospect says yes, the tendency is to tell the prospect about your opportunity. Stop! Just pique interest and hand the presentation over to the third-party tools. Don't spill the beans. Talking will kill your business. Only lead them to the tools, and let technology do the presentation for you.

Third Skill: Creating Interest in the Third-Party Tool

Use an audio, a video, a web site presentation, a recorded message, a faxable slide presentation, a three-way call with your sponsor, a conference call, or a CD presentation. You could say something like: "Take a look at this. It'll knock your socks off. It may or may not be for you but it'll take only 14 minutes of your time." Or "What's on this video is making many people a fortune. It may or may not be for you but it'll take only 14 minutes of your time." Or "I think you'll really like the part near the end about how most people do our business every day, but they just aren't getting paid for it!" Or

"Be sure to listen for the part about the two-year story. It's really funny! I laughed out loud when I first heard that story." Or "I'm going to loan this CD to you. But I'll need it back in three days because I have others waiting to listen to it."

You get the idea.

Once you've directed them to the third-party tool, here's what you'll say:

Absolutely nothing!

If they ask questions, simply tell them the CD does a much better job of answering their questions than you can.

During the time it would normally take you to give a 30-minute presentation to one prospect, you could've handed out 10 CDs. Same amount of time, but in one case, the story is told one time; in the other case, it's being told 10 times.

Fourth Skill: Effective Follow-Up

Handing out 10 CDs is effective only if the prospects actually listen to what's on the CD.

Here's an example of effective follow-up. Call the prospect and ask:

You: "Did you have a chance to listen to the CD yet?"
Prospect: "No."
You: "How long does it take you to drive to work?"
Prospect: "About 20 minutes."
You: "Perfect. That's how long it takes to listen to the CD. Could you do me a favor and listen to the CD on your way to work tomorrow?"

Call them the next day and ask: "Did you have a chance to listen to the CD yet?" Continue to create interest in the third-party tool until they listen to it. Your job is to have them hear the story in its entirety. After all, they have a need for what's on the CD; otherwise they wouldn't have agreed to listen to it. Once they hear the story and decide the opportunity or product is not for them, fine. But don't let them decide until they've heard all the facts. The information could end up changing their lives for the better, forever.

Once the prospect has listened to the CD, all you need to ask is this: "What did you like best about what you heard?"

If they say nothing, thank them for their time and ask them for referrals. "Do you know anyone who would be interested in earning an extra weekly paycheck working from home?"

If they say they like the product, sell them the product. If they say the like the money part, ask them if they are ready to get started. If they are, sponsor them.

If they have a few questions, get them to a meeting or on a three-way call with your sponsor.

Fifth Skill: Three-Way Calling

A three-way call is when you, your prospect, and a third person get on one phone call together. Here's an example of the three-way call.

> *You:* "Mr. Sponsor, this is Bob. Bob, this is Mr. Sponsor, my partner I told you about."
>
> *Sponsor:* "Julie tells me you are interested in an income opportunity and have a few questions. The money part of our business is very exciting, but before I tell you my story and answer your questions, let me ask you this: What has Julie done with you so far?"

And here's the magic—the moment of truth and why this works so well.

> *Prospect:* "Well, Julie asked me if I'd be interested in making an extra paycheck from home. I said yes. She then asked me to listen to a CD. After a few days, I did. She then asked me what I like best. I told her the money and that I had a few questions. She then put me on the phone with you."
>
> *Sponsor:* "Excellent. Let me ask you this: Is there anything that Julie did with you that you can't see yourself doing with someone else?"

Bingo. Suddenly prospect Bob realizes he will not have to become an expert on this business or on the product to effectively build an extra weekly paycheck with your company. The rest is easy. The sponsor shares his or her story, answers any questions, and ends the call with:

> *Sponsor:* "Is there anything else you need to know before you get started?"

If Bob says yes, the sponsor answers the questions and then again asks: "Is there anything else you need to know before you get started?"

Once Bob says all his questions have been answered and he is ready to get started, the sponsor turns the call over to Julie and lets her help Bob get started in the business.

And it gets better! During the process you are also training your distributor, Julie. She is learning the answers to the most frequently asked questions so that after 10 or 15 three-way calls she'll be able to do three-way calls with her new distributors.

THE MAGIC OF THIRD-PARTY TOOLS

During the sponsoring process, all prospects wonder: "Can I do what you did?"

If you follow this simple method of operation, they realize that you said absolutely nothing about the company or product. So the resounding answer is, "Yes! I can do this business!"

Resist the tendency to become an expert. If you do, you may actually end up losing credibility. Stay humble. Let the experts be a third-party tool and your sponsor. It's the most efficient and effective way to get the story told in its entirety, perfectly every single time—and have it told hundreds, even thousands of times per day on your team.

Using third-party tools allows average people to make above-average incomes and allows above-average people to make extraordinary incomes. It allows your team to grow one, two, three, or more levels deep down each organizational leg every month, thus breaking the typical growth cycle that many network marketing organizations experience.

As one of the new breed of rising network marketing stars, Art Jonak has one of the feel-good stories that keep the dream alive for many. Twelve years ago he had to count on food stamps to buy milk for his newborn daughter. In his quest to get out of debt, he worked two jobs and delivered pizzas at night. His relationships were horrible. Every aspect of his life was spiraling downward—fast. So he joined network marketing. And like a lot of people, he struggled mightily for the first few years of his network marketing career. But he never gave up.

Art became an avid student of the industry. He read network marketing books, listened to audio programs, and attended every event he could. He began a program of regular self-development. In other words, he did all of the things your sponsorship line has been telling you to do.

Today he's blessed with a fast-growing network marketing organization, a prospering bank account, and a wonderful lifestyle. He and his wife just celebrated their first wedding anniversary in Italy and Dubai.

Art has built organizations with distributors numbering in the thousands, and helped dozens of individuals reach significant leadership positions and income levels in the business. He specializes on the marketing side of network marketing, teaching others the skills to create prospects, develop recruiting systems, and produce duplication through the organization. Art is the author of the "One-Minute Sponsoring Tips for Network Marketers" newsletter.

The success and duplication that Art is developing led to him being featured in the best-selling books *Wave 4* and *"The Wave 4 Way to Building Your Downline*. He also wrote the monthly technology column for *Upline* magazine, and is a frequent contributor to the "Fortune Now" newsletter. He is one of only 600 individuals certified by the University of Illinois as a network marketing professional.

Art was one of the early pioneers of online network marketing. He developed an Internet-based viral prospect-creating system for his company, which is one of the most automated recruiting systems in network marketing. His MLMPlayers.com site is one of the highest-ranked MLM training web sites in the world. But he doesn't just build his team on the Internet. He has created a worldwide methodology for growth including global conference calls, opportunity meetings, and live trainings. Most importantly, he's done it in a way that provides replication.

Want to get a glimpse of what type of lifestyle a network marketing business can allow you to live? Browse through Art's lifestyle photo gallery online at www.MLMPlayers.com/gallery. Art offers everyone his "One-Minute Sponsoring Tips for Network Marketers" newsletter free by simply visiting www.MLMPlayers.com. Art can also be reached directly at art@artjonak.com or by calling (281) 271-1105.

Sponsoring a "No"

Beatty Carmichael

Have you ever presented your business to a prospect and gotten to the end of the presentation only to have the prospect tell you, "No, I don't think this is for me"? I've had this happen lots of times.

When this happens, you have two options: You can say, "Okay, I guess it's not for you," and leave, or you can say, "That's okay, we can handle that. We'll just get you started anyway"—and you enroll him and build a big business.

How do you do this? It's a simple technique called "testing the waters." Here's how it works.

Let's walk through the "testing the waters" concept through the eyes of a distributor at the end of a presentation. In this example, I have just helped a new person, Joe, get started. Joe has followed a few prospecting methods I taught him to get started, and one of the prospects he found was Harry.

When we meet with Harry, we do our best to recruit him. We try to build a relationship, find his hot button, and come up with the reason why he will get involved in our business. He's sitting back and is just a little gun-shy. He's seen "these types of things" before and he isn't very excited. He gives me some sort of excuse: "I just don't think I have the money. I don't have the time. Let me think about it. Please call me back next month." All these things are wrapped up in one, and Joe's over there wondering what's going to happen with Harry. I'm going to ask Harry, "Well, let me ask you, Harry, hypothetically, and this will never happen . . ." and I'm going to put Harry at ease. As an aside, why do you think Harry is telling me these things? It's a lack of belief. In almost every case, it's a lack of belief and that's why these prospects give you an excuse.

How many times has someone asked you to do something and you told them you could not because of something? You realized in your heart that that really wasn't the honest answer; it was an answer and it had some honesty to it, but it really wasn't the real reason. You were just uncomfortable; you didn't know why you were saying no. Does that make sense? Harry is the same way. Harry has a need, but he's telling me no and I know that he's not lying to me on purpose. That's the key—on purpose. Always remember, an excuse is a bag of reasons stuffed with lies. It looks good on the outside, but inside there's just nothing to it. And if Harry tells me he doesn't have the money and I find a way to handle his money objection, in most cases I'm barking up the wrong tree and I'm still not going to sponsor Harry. I've got to find out what's really holding Harry back, and more importantly I've got to help Harry understand what's holding him back, too. Does it makes sense that until I help Harry understand why he's hesitating, I can't get Harry moving?

So, to sponsor somebody you've got to get him or her moving. You can take a ship anchored in port and try all you can to steer it but it's not going to steer anywhere because it's not moving. Once you get that ship to pull anchor and start moving, even if it's moving in the wrong direction, you can steer it and make it go in the right direction. That's what I want to do with Harry. I want to get Harry moving. Once I get him moving, I can sponsor him. I may ask a very nonthreatening, noncommittal question: "Hypothetically, and this will never happen, but I'm just curious . . . if the president of our company gave you a promissory note that if you worked this business four hours a week for the next four weeks only, and that's all you had to do, he would guarantee you a commission check of $4,000— then would you get in and work it four hours a week for the next four weeks if it's guaranteed?"

What is Harry going to tell me? "Yeah, I'd do that." Then I'll say, "Okay, great. What I think I hear you saying is . . ." and now you repeat their answer in your words. "Let me repeat what I think I hear you saying. What you're really telling me, Harry, is if it was guaranteed to make you $4,000 this month for 16 hours' work, then you could find the time and the money to do this business? But because it's not guaranteed, there are enough other things holding you back that you're not sure about this and therefore money is an issue and time is an issue because we've got too many variables left unknown? Is that what you are really telling me?"

What answer can Harry give me at that point? Is there anything besides "yes" that he can say? You see, it's not that I put Harry in a corner. It's that I now got Harry to confess to the honest truth. "Yes, if it's guaranteed, I'd do it. But it's not guaranteed; therefore I'm hesitating." Now we're on the same page. Only once we are on the same page can I answer his real objection.

The next step is to get Harry to start moving a little bit, and I need to inch him along. Now, this isn't a prefect world, so this doesn't always happen this way. But if you are sponsoring 2 out of 10 people, this little technique will probably get your response rate from 2 out of 10 to probably 5 or 6 out of 10.

What I'm going to do is start with a real broad funnel with no commitment, and by the time I get through with Harry this evening, I'm going to get a pretty strong commitment out of him. I'm going to say, "Well, Harry, let me ask you something. Have you ever seen one of these little yellow cards before?" (In this scenario, we found Harry by using a prospecting method named SizzleCards. You can see more about that at GrowthPro.com. The SizzleCard is a prospecting card that may have been left on a newspaper machine, Harry picked it up, then called a prospecting message and asked us to call him back.) So, if he responded to a SizzleCard, what's he going to say? He'll say, "Yeah, I picked one of those things up off the newspaper stand."

"That's right, that's how we got here tonight, isn't it? That's how we met you. Well, Harry, let me ask you: Next time you go get a newspaper do you think you could leave a couple of these on a newspaper machine?"

"Well, yeah, I could do that."

"Harry, next time you go to the gas station and pump your gas, do you think you could stick a couple of these on the gas pump?"

"I could do that."

"Well, Harry, next time you go to Wendy's, do you think you could leave a couple of these on the table when you leave?"

"Yeah, I could do that."

"Well, gee, Harry, if you can do that you can probably make some pretty good money with this business, because that's all it takes to make it work."

Harry's eyes are starting to open up. He's starting to sit on the edge of his seat. He's starting to say to himself, "Hey, maybe there is something to this."

Now I want to go through a simple example of how to use this prospecting technique. Before I get into that, I'll ask Harry one more leading question. "Let me ask you a question: If I could show you a way to protect your family's livelihood in the event you get downsized" (Harry had previously told me this was his hot button and his biggest concern to solve) "is that important enough to you to be willing to test the waters and see if this might work? I'm not talking about making any commitment or spending any money in this business to test the waters. But if I could show you conclusively with two hours a week for two weeks only whether or not you can make $2,000 or $3,000 or $4,000 a month, is it important enough to you to be willing to do a little test? You'll never have to talk to a single person, and I'll never ask you for the name or telephone number of anyone you know or have ever known in your life. Would you do that test?"

If I phrase my question right and know his real hot button, he's probably going to say, "What do you have in mind?" That's when I'm going to ask, "Have you ever seen one of these cards? Can you leave it on the newspaper stand, can you leave it on the gas pump, can you leave it at Wendy's? Gee, if you can do that, you can make money with this business. Let me show you how easy it is." And I share how easy it is to find prospects with our methods. It's not so critical that your prospecting method involves SizzleCards, but it *is* critical that you have an *easy* prospecting method that your prospect can believe he can do . . . and succeed.

As I go through my example and he begins to say, "I could do *that*!" I'm moving him off his "no" to a "maybe." It's not significant movement, but just like a ship in port, it's a gradual movement. I'm getting him thinking, "Hey, maybe I *can* do this." Now I'm going to say to him, "Let me ask you, Harry, in the next two weeks, by not really going out and not making a commitment to do this thing a whole lot, but just getting out SizzleCards by leaving them wherever you go, how many do you think you can get out in the next two weeks?" He's going to say, "I probably can get out maybe 200 or 300."

"Great, I'll leave you 500 just so we'll be sure you don't run out. By the way, Harry, your code number is going to be code number 38. That way, we're going to be able to track your prospects separately from mine and other people's. The code number lets me know who did the work to generate a particular prospect, so I can credit the prospect to the right distributor."

Next, I'll say, "Harry, one of the things that we need to determine is whether or not you can actually do this business. One of the steps outside of just giving out SizzleCards is making some phone calls back. Now, in the early stages, you'll never have to make a phone call if you don't want to. I'm going to help you and I'm going to teach you along the way, but eventually if you're going to make some big money with this, you may have to make a few phone calls, okay? As we start testing the waters and seeing if this is something that you can do, would it make sense to see how we make phone calls to see if it's something that you can do also?"

Harry says, "That makes sense."

"Great, let me ask you: Do you have anything scheduled Tuesday night?"

"No."

"Good. Why don't we meet about eight o'clock Tuesday night? Here's a copy of the script that I'm going to use. I want you to just listen to me as I make some phone calls so you can see how easy it is to call these people back. Again, you're not going to say anything—I just want you to listen." What I've just done is set a follow-up appointment, moving Harry another step forward.

Next, I'll continue and say, "Oh, by the way, you know since we're going to be making some phone calls together in just a few days, it would be really great if you can make a real strong effort to get out a lot of these cards. If you could get out 300 or 400 of these in the next couple of days, maybe leave 10 minutes early for work and stop by a gas station or two and some newspaper machines. When you go to lunch, instead of taking an hour, take half an hour and in the other 30 minutes stick some more SizzleCards in places and then when you come home, instead of coming straight home, take another 10 minutes and hand out some more. Is there any way possible you can try to get out between 300 and 400 cards so we could have a lot of prospects generated to call back, so we can see if this thing is going to work for you?" He's probably going to say, "Sure, I'll try."

So, I'm going to get him trying harder than he would have because we have a follow-up appointment already set.

Once we leave there, Joe looks at me and says, "Harry told you no. Then you got him to get out cards and set an appointment to call prospects back with you! That's great!"

I say, "That's right, who cares if he says no? He's only saying no until it works and then he's going to say yes. All I have to do is show him that it works."

Here's what happens next.

Harry starts getting out SizzleCards and finding prospects. The prospects leave the code number on my voice mailbox as part of the message they leave me. So, as I'm checking my voice mail, I find all the code number 38 prospects. I then meet Harry on Tuesday and we start making some phone calls. Maybe we talk to 15 people and five of them are his prospects. Every time I ask the prospect, "Do you remember what code number was on that card?" and they mention code number 38, I say, "Oh, I know who that is." Harry thinks, "Whoa, there's one of mine," and something clicks in his belief level. Then we talk to another code 38 prospect and he says to himself, "Wow, there's another one of mine." Click! And maybe out of five people, we set two appointments.

At the end, Harry is going to say something like, "Gee, Beatty, you just read that script word for word."

I say, "That's right, Harry, that's pretty simple, isn't it?"

"Yeah."

"Do you think that you could read that script word for word?"

"Well, yeah, I could read that."

You see, I've taken all the mystery out of building this business by having Harry listen to me make phone calls. As long as it's a mystery, the prospect doesn't know if he or she can do it, but once I expose them to what we really do, then it's simple and believable. After Harry replies that he could read that, I say, "Harry, if you can do that, you can make money with this! You've shown you can get out SizzleCards. That was pretty easy, wasn't it?"

"Yeah."

"And you see how simple it is making the phone calls, and you see how easy it is setting those appointments, right?"

"Yeah, that's pretty easy."

"Well, Harry, you know, there's one more step, and I don't know if you can do this or not. I don't know if you can show this business to somebody where they would want to get involved. Wouldn't you agree that securing your family's financial security in case you are downsized is important enough to check out the last step to see if this is something that you can do?" I'm always bringing him back to the reality that this business means he can accomplish his dream. So I say, "Is there any way possible that you can go with me on these two appointments we just set with your prospects so you can see how I show this business to them to see if it's something you can do?" So I get him to go. Now what am I really doing? I'm getting my prospect to tell me that he'll see this business presented two more times!

While we are in the car driving to the appointment, guess what we're talking about? We're talking about the business and how much fun it is and how easy and how much money one can make with it. Then we get to the prospect's home and begin presenting the business . . . and Harry is sitting there watching!

And that's how you sponsor someone when they say no.

Let's summarize briefly.

When someone tells you no, they are really saying, "I don't believe this will work for me. If it did work for me, I would get involved."

You can't answer the objection they give you because it's typically not completely true. Understand what they are really saying (i.e., lack of belief), and answer that objection.

Get the potential recruit moving forward by suggesting testing the waters.

Show the recruit how to find prospects without talking to a single person, without getting rejection, and before spending any money.

Schedule a follow-up appointment to make phone calls.

Encourage your potential recruit to give a stronger commitment so your follow-up appointment will go well.

Call the prospects back with your new person listening on the phone. Make sure he has a copy of your script so he can see there is nothing special that you are doing.

As you talk to prospects, make sure Harry knows they are his prospects. That increases his belief. When you set appointments, try to get Harry to go on the appointments with you. This gives you more time with Harry and gets him in front of seeing the presentation a second or third time. And the best part is that when new people see the business again, it's with prospects of their own!

By the time you present the business to one of Harry's prospects, even if the prospect doesn't get in, Harry typically does. Why? Because he has already experienced what it's like to build the business and realizes it's not that difficult. The mystery is gone and Harry believes he can do it!

Beatty Carmichael is president of GrowthPro, a leader in recruiting systems for network marketers. Mr. Carmichael first started in network marketing in 1984 in college. As his business and career grew, he changed companies in 1995 to a company with one million distributors. He and his business partner reached the highest promotional level in that company in 12 months and were among its highest income earners. In 1997, he formed GrowthPro to provide cutting-edge recruiting tools and training to the industry.

Today, Mr. Carmichael and his company are known for their off-line and online recruiting systems, their Sizzle Line prospecting voice mail, and their straightforward approach to training networkers how to truly build their businesses. Their approach in teaching others has been so successful that Growth-Pro is the only company that guarantees a minimum seven new recruits in 90 days or you can get a full refund of your money.

For more information about GrowthPro's recruiting systems and how to private label them for your team, or for free training and audios to help grow your business, visit GrowthPro's web site at www.GrowthPro.com or call (205) 871-2998.

Chapter
23

Leadership in an All-Volunteer Army

Greg Arnold

Leadership is truly the most marvelous mystery in existence today. Volumes have been written about it, yet no one has completely captured its essence in a manner that allows everyone to taste from its cup. Leaders come in all shapes and sizes, colors and backgrounds, religions and beliefs. Leadership doesn't discriminate in any way, shape, or form when choosing who possesses it. Leadership positions are available to anyone willing to assume its mantle and responsibilities.

Let me clear up a few common misconceptions about leaders before I tell you what I think they all possess. Not all leaders are noble, nor do they all fight for noble causes. Not all leaders are honest, nor do they all possess flawless character. Not all leaders have a burning desire to lead others; in fact, most don't. Not all leaders are courageous and bold. I doubt most leaders are thrifty, brave, or reverent, either. They aren't even necessarily Boy Scouts. The point is, most leaders simply don't look or act much like Superman or Wonder Woman. Most of the time leaders are like everyone else.

NETWORK MARKETING
ROCK STARS

Even though all leaders are pretty much the same as everyone else, in the network marketing industry they are treated like rock stars. Mere network marketing mortals elevate and deify them. They are cheered on stages around the world and quoted daily. Everyone is his or her friend. Their incomes are magnified many times over, only limited by the enthusiasm of the person telling the story. Network marketing leaders truly become legends in their own time. Network marketing leaders are rock stars indeed.

SOUNDS PRETTY GOOD,
WHERE DO I SIGN UP?

So you want to be a rock star. Conventional wisdom would tell you to work on yourself, become perfect in every facet of your life, and good things will come. Or, fake it until you make it! Go out and buy fancy watches, nice cloths, and expensive cars. Be sure you travel to each and every public network marketing event and company training party, because being seen is as important as being good.

I'll admit, I may sound a little cynical here. That may be because I am. Network marketing leadership isn't about what people think you are; it's about you being committed to and following your path. Rock stars don't play for the fans or even the money. They play because they can't live without the music. They passionately pursue their perfect song.

I see so many networkers chasing a higher status. I see them buying books and CDs, going to seminars, and trying all manner of motivational processes. They hope to find that one gem that will make them break the bonds of their cocoon of mediocrity and sprout their wings of financial freedom. The challenge is that until you accept yourself for who you are, and then forgive yourself for being a mere mortal, you aren't going anywhere. If you want to be a network marketing rock star, you have to find your passion and pursue it passionately. That is the truth that will set you free.

When you are ready, the live training and books and CDs will be very valuable to you. I hope the preceding paragraph was your epiphany that leads you to do great things. Because quite frankly, until you get it, you aren't going to get it. Until you get who you are and find a way to be happy living with that person every day, and also find out what drives that person, you aren't going anywhere.

CHANTING ON MOUNTAIN TOPS

Before you book your flight to Tibet for a little 15,000-foot soul-searching session, consider this: I have a friend whose answer to the question "Who am I?" was simply, "I'm just a guy who wants the best he can give for his family." Once he found out his passion was his family, he began to put all the pieces together. Providing the best he could for his family drove him. "The best" may be somewhat subjective, but every time he defined it as contributing to his wife's security and happiness or being for his kids' education or what kind of neighborhood they would grow up in, his passion drove him more and more. Yes, he also became a network marketing rock star, and yes, the books and CDs and seminars became very helpful to him once he found his direction and once he committed to his path.

LET YOUR PASSION
BECOME YOUR CHAUFFEUR

What drives you is more important than what you want. Way more. In fact, what you want out of life has very little to do with what you get out of life. Wishes come and go like the seasons of the year. What you want now blooms in the spring and falls off the trees in the fall. In contrast, your passions drive your expectations and your expectations drive your life. So what if you want to become a network marketing rock star. Who doesn't? If that was all there was to it, all networkers would be rock stars.

We become slaves to our expectations. When we expect something to happen, our entire physical being changes to brace for the jolt. We simply begin to act and perform differently when we expect something good or bad to happen. Your expectations are your windows into your future. When you expect something bad to happen, you prepare for it by feeling bad, shutting down physically, and boarding up the windows to your soul. Then, like you expected, it happens and it's bad. When you expect something great to happen, you get excited, you perform at the top of your game, and you open up to the possibilities. Then, like you expected, it happens and it's great!

How do you control whether your expectations are good or bad? Easy—follow your passions. Your passions drive your expectations. I'm letting you in on this little-known and seldom-practiced secret so you don't have to spend all that time and money on your trip to Tibet.

If you're passionate about helping humanity and you can do it through your network marketing opportunity, fantastic. If you're passionate about helping others succeed beyond their wildest dreams and you can do it through your networking opportunity, let that drive you. It doesn't matter what your passions are, pursue them passionately and you will become a slave to your expectations. You simply won't lose.

EXPECTATIONS DON'T LIKE TO
DRIVE BEAT-UP 1984 FORD ESCORTS

In 1993, I had been involved in network marketing for almost 20 years. I was earning about $1,500 per month between my two occupations—one as a full-time network marketer and the other working part-time in a factory to supplement my network marketing career and pay the bills. Somehow I never really chose the right network marketing opportunities. As I left each one of them I said the same thing: "I didn't really think that one would work anyway." That alone probably tells you where my expectations were and what my outcome would be each time.

One day I was reading an article in *Success* magazine that was written by Mark Yarnell. I don't remember much about the article but it mentioned that Mark lived in Reno, Nevada, which was also where I lived at the time. I began to think that if I gave Mark a call I could probably convince him to mentor me. So a few days later I acted on my newfound expectation. I looked him up in the phone book and I called him—and he answered his own phone! I asked him if I could buy him lunch and pick his brain a little. Another surprise: He not only answers his own phone, he eats, too!

I drove up the mountainside to his hilltop castle, one of two landmarks you can see from anywhere in Reno. He greeted me in person at the door and asked me in. Wow, do they really make houses like this for mortals? We chatted for a few minutes and then went outside to drive down the hill for lunch. Mark stopped dead in his tracks when he saw my beat-up old Ford with the paint peeling off and the dent in the driver's side door, which made me leave the window down so I could open it with the inside handle. He smiled and said, "Let's take my car." Obviously his expectations about what kinds of cars he would ride in were higher than mine at the time.

EXPECT SOMETHING GREAT!

I was ready to change my life that day. I expected to win. I expected that whatever Mark told me would work. I became passionate about my new path. I can tell you right now that for the most part Mark told me what I already knew. Somehow it had new meaning, though. Coming from him, I expected it to work. My expectations started to drive my life. Like Mark, I also learned that my expectations didn't like to drive beat-up old Fords, either. They liked to drive fast! They expected to drive 500-horsepower sports cars that corner like they're on rails. Expectations want to get you there fast so they can move on to the next adventure. A year later I had built an organization of more than 11,000 simply by acting on my expectations.

THE HIGHER YOU CLIMB,
THE MORE YOUR REAR STICKS OUT

Because network marketing mortals see you as a network marketing god, they expect you to be one. That means they expect you to have none of the human frailties that they or any other human being possesses. You must look just right, act just right, and have a just right family life. No smoking, drinking, swearing, or overeating. Even your teeth must be very straight and movie-star white. We hold our network marketing leaders to a much higher standard.

Leadership is tough in an all-volunteer network marketing army. When things go wrong for the troops, and they will, it's always your fault when you're the leader:

> *Rule 1:* Network marketing mortals are not accountable for any of their own actions or outcomes. If they were accountable they wouldn't quit and they wouldn't blame you. It's easier to rationalize away the responsibility for your own failures when you can blame it on your leaders. I didn't say leadership was easy, did I?

> *Rule 2:* If anything ever goes wrong for a member of your team, refer to rule 1.

The closer you get to becoming a leader or network marketing rock star, the bigger target you become for the average networker when they discover your flaws. To go along with the fame and fortune, you must develop a thick skin.

THE FORMULA FOR LEADERSHIP SUCCESS

No one can manage a team of 5,000 or even 500 dependent distributors. So you must define to them your job as team leader. Let everyone know that you are available to help him or her build his or her business. Let them know that no matter how deep they fall within your team, you will do two-on-ones with them if they are local to you and that you will do three-way calls at two in the morning if need be. Make sure everyone understands that if they want to build their business, you are there for them. In other words, you'll match their effort.

If you have a team member who gives a 3 percent effort, match it. If you have a team member giving all that he has, match that, too, when you're helping him to succeed. Let your team members know that all personal training time is spent in the field helping them to build their business and that you are available for this training anytime they wish. When you build your business this way, only your leaders will call you. That means that almost all of your time will be spent building your business.

Once someone has proven to be a leader through their actions, not words, jump all over them. Become their new best friend. Get to know them and their family. Don't worry about how deep they fall within your organization. Your relationship with your leaders is the most important part of your business. Pay attention to this. This is called overlapping leadership; practice it.

YOU SIMPLY CANNOT MANAGE YOUR WAY TO THE TOP

Over 90 percent of your team members will be good product consumers at best. Always help them to feel good about themselves, their company, and their products. Then they will be good consumers. This is normally done through your occasional personal contacts with them and through your team newsletter. This group of people will not build your empire; you can't afford to spend a lot of personal time with them.

THE FORMULA FOR MANAGEMENT SUCCESS

Yes, you will need to pay some attention to the 90 percent of your team who won't build a business. This time is called management time:

- It includes taking an occasional call from a nonbuilder to answer a question or two. Always be helpful and encouraging and always let them know that you appreciate them and their efforts.
- Publish a monthly newsletter that is available on the Internet and through fax-on-demand. This way everyone has access to it. In the newsletter highlight a product, praise a leader of the month, and publish a top recruiters list and any other top 10 list you think will help drive your business. Where performance is measured, performance improves. Also publish the schedule of upcoming events and conference calls. Your newsletter helps everyone to feel included, and it saves time in communication with the team.
- Hold a regularly scheduled monthly welcome conference call for newcomers (e.g., first Saturday of every month at 10 A.M. Pacific time).
- Hold a regularly scheduled monthly product training conference call for everyone. You do not have to be the product expert on your team, nor do you have to hold this call personally.
- Hold a regularly scheduled weekly leadership conference call for your leaders (leaders must qualify at a certain level to participate).

- Hold a regional rally every quarter.
- Attend and promote the national conventions each year.

That is your entire management agenda. Spend 80 percent of your time building your business, training in the field, and leading the troops. Spend only 20 percent of your time in management mode. This is how you lead an all-volunteer network marketing army. Remember at all times you are in the people business. The better you understand human nature, the more powerful you will have the opportunity to be.

Leadership is and always has been about people following their passions. Leaders who have large network marketing organizations have just made those passions available to like-minded people and helped them to blaze the trails.

Greg Arnold has been a leader in the network marketing industry for over 30 years. Greg's networking career began when he was still a young man. While he was stationed in Savannah, Georgia, he was earning more from his network marketing efforts than from his military career. His network marketing earnings were so high that the military even launched an investigation until they discovered he was earning his money legitimately through network marketing.

In less than a year, Greg built an organization of more than 11,000 members. Wanting to share his network marketing expertise, he wrote and published *The Multi-Level Mangler in King Arthur's Court*. The popularity of this book has been nothing less than phenomenal. Network marketing industry leaders often use Greg's book to train their distributor teams.

Now living in his small hometown in southern Washington State, Greg remains active in the network marketing industry as an author, distributor, trainer, and consultant. He can be contacted at greg@greg-arnold.com. His free generic network marketing training newsletter is available at www.mlm-training-online.com.

Chapter 24

Free, Fun, and Creative Ways
to Find an Endless Flow of
Hot New Prospects for Your Business

Nick Hetcher

Network marketing can be the greatest business in the world if you have enough prospects to tell about your business. Without a constant flow of good prospects, your business will not grow. This chapter contains more than 100 ways to reach new prospects so you will never again have a problem finding people for your business and products or services. Prospecting your family and friends can sometimes be hard to do, especially if you have done so before with other moneymaking opportunities. If you have a solid business opportunity, then your warm market representing people you know is the best place to start. I understand that you won't go to all of them for various reasons. But if you go after the positive, outgoing, and friendly ones, there are definitely diamonds on your personal list.

The key to building a large residual monthly income with the any home-based business opportunity is to introduce the products and income opportunity to as many people as you can. You'll then teach the ones who join your business to do the same as they, in turn, teach their new distributors the same things. Teach people to teach people to be successful. The first 90 days in the business are probably the most critical since this sets your pace and establishes a pace for your group. To follow are several ways to build your business. Most are proven methods that I learned from others, and some I made up myself. You will want to keep your business extremely simple so virtually anybody who joins you can do it successfully by following a basic system. You do this by becoming a master inviter and let the automated systems (24-hour messages, web sites, three-way calls, live opportunity calls, local meetings, etc.) do the presentation for you. You do not do the presentation—let the systems do it for you! That way most people can see themselves able to do it, too, and are more likely to join you in business. Commit to working this business for at least a year during which you expose hundreds of people to your business opportunity and products or services. The more people you expose your company to, the richer you will become.

Your success is really a mathematical equation, or as some say, a numbers game. Whoever hands out the most company information packs and samples makes the most money. So pick one or two methods that work for you of reaching new prospects and give them all you have. Always remember, you are the messenger and these systems present the message. Let them do the presenting for you. After the system does the presentation, it is extremely important that you follow up with every one of your prospects to see what they think. Is this something they could see doing themselves? On a scale of 1 to 10, where do they rate their interest? You'll want to find the people who are interested in joining at that time or have questions for you and your sponsor or upline. Look for desire and a commitment to do what is necessary to achieve success.

Building a large and successful long-term business is all about building good relationships with people. The following are ways to find new prospects after you first go to the people you know. Now have fun, stay focused, and build strongly for your early retirement. Massive, focused, and consistent action results in massive residual income.

YOUR WARM MARKET

Always start your prospecting efforts by making a list of everybody you can think of. Start contacting those you would like to work with and think will be receptive to considering your opportunity. Contact them first by e-mail, letter, postcard, and/or phone. The phone is your greatest asset in this business, so learn how to use it well. Even if you don't think any of these people would be interested, your circle of influence should be the first group of people you contact. Even if they're not interested, they probably know somebody who would be. Ask them for referrals, too. If you're afraid to tell them about your business, then just focus on the incredible gift of fun, finances, and freedom you are offering them. Be proud of this industry and your company and offer it as you would any valuable gift.

MY SEVEN-SECOND PRESENTATION

Anybody can make some calls to notify others about their products and income opportunity. After making a few calls, it will get much easier and you won't be as nervous. Here's what you say: "Hey, Bob, I'd like you to listen to a two-minute recorded message about an opportunity I'm excited about." Then give them your company's recorded sizzle-call phone number and say, "Call me back and let me know what you think." If they ask you what it's all about, just say something like, "That takes all the fun out of it. Just take a couple of minutes, make the call, and let me know what you think." This approach works for people you know, not cold calls.

TAPES AND CDS

Use professional recruiting tapes or CDs that make your business simple and duplicable for virtually anyone who can hand out or mail one to someone. The great thing about tapes and CDs is that people can listen to them while driving in their cars to or from work. This is when they are most susceptible to the idea of eventually breaking away from their jobs and maybe working from home full-time someday.

THREE-FOOT RULE

Wherever you go, make sure you carry business cards and a sample if your company supplies those. Give a card and sample to everybody who comes within three feet of you. Make sure to have the company's (24/7) two-minute recorded message and web site information with it. Try to get people's contact information for follow-up; then always follow up with a phone call and ask them what they think. They'll tell you if they are interested or if they need any questions answered.

HOME PARTIES

If your company does not have a home party plan, you may want to start one yourself. Invite a bunch of people over for a product and business party. Serve your products (if they are edible, of course) and coffee or tea. You can make up your own presentation or play the company DVD. These meetings can build into weekly hotel meetings. To invite prospects, send out invitation letters or postcards and then call them to follow up. This can be a super way to grow your business, one that others can easily duplicate since people love parties. Just make sure they know it's a home business opportunity party so there will be no unpleasant surprises.

LOCAL HOTEL GATHERINGS

These can be a lot of fun, create a bond among local people, and serve as a great way to build your business fast. All local distributors need to do is to invite prospects to the meeting and let the presenter do the work for them. If you are organizing it, you may have to be the first presenter, or find someone who can do an adequate job. You may also want to offer training meetings on a monthly basis. Meetings are in vogue again and working very well for many companies. The personal touch of local gatherings is something that long-distance sponsoring will never be able to accomplish.

CHAT ROOMS

Chat rooms can supply a free and endless supply of targeted prospects day or night. Go to the bigger ones like Yahoo!, MSN, and AOL and head to the health or small business rooms. You'll need to abide by their rules. Usually you can send an instant message to any of the people in the room privately. This is the best way to work the rooms, one person at a time. Stay focused and start by breaking the ice. Ask, "How are you doing today?" After they respond, you might say something like, "Are you open to checking out a cool and lucrative part-time home business?" Then gently and quickly lead them to your company web site and brief company overview recorded phone message. Give them your contact information if they are interested and try to get their contact information for follow-up later. You could prospect all day and night, offering your income opportunity to hundreds of new people weekly with this method. With consistent daily action, you are sure to find some interested people, many of whom will become lifelong friends and business partners. The more you work this method, the better you will get at creating value for people to explore the possibility of working with you.

BUSINESS CARDS FROM
BULLETIN BOARDS

Go to the stores where you see all those business cards that business owners, salespeople, and network marketers post. Put yours there, too, but better than that, write down in a notebook the names and contact information of the entrepreneurs who put their cards there. These are the kind of people you want in your business. Go home and start contacting them.

GET TO KNOW SOME TOP DOGS

In most cases, these successful leaders are not going to join you, especially at first. They are probably doing well in another program and are not looking to make a move to another company. If you are able to get through to them, simply start a friendship. I've called many of the writers with featured articles and leaders who ran ads in network marketing publications. I just introduce myself and commend them for their leadership or inspiration. Over the years, I have made many good friends this way, and some of those top dogs have in fact joined me later in business. Remember, this business is all about building friendships, and these people, like all of us, started out at the bottom, too.

THE VOICE MAIL HIT

All professionals have voice mail, right? Go to the yellow pages and find the people you want to target—like chiropractors, real estate agents, message therapists, and others. Next, start calling after hours so you get their voice mails. Leave a powerful, brief message asking them to call your 800 number voice mail to hear a brief recorded overview and then to contact you for more details. You can even purchase a national toll-free phone book of businesses. Work this method diligently, and these professionals will be calling you to join your business after your company 24/7 recorded message or web site does the business presentation for you.

VIRAL E-MAIL

Do you ever get a funny joke e-mailed to you and then pass it on to your friends to enjoy, too? Start to send regular e-mails to your list of contacts. Do *not* spam. Build your list by meeting people and making friends. Once you've established a bit of a relationship, send a joke, funny photo, inspirational message, or other different or interesting message. Make sure your company web site information or your signature file is at the top or bottom of every e-mail. Along with the interesting message, your recipients get to see a brief ad for your business. If people like the e-mail, they will pass it on to their friends. Imagine one funny photo being forwarded to thousands or even millions of people across the world, each seeing your marketing information. And it's free!

TALKING OR VIDEO E-MAIL

Send e-mail with your own or a professionally voiced audio message promoting your business. Make sure to tell the people (in text) to have their speakers turned up. Then hit them hard with a short, powerful audio advertisement. Text with audio has much more punch than text alone. You can find audio services by doing a Google search.

Also, there are a few services that offer an inexpensive way for you to record and send quality video clips to your prospects. It's a great way to develop new distributors. This will work better if you are among the few now marketing in this way. Later on, it won't have the same punch as others discover this technique.

BATHROOM ADS

These ads are usually placed in nicer restaurants to reach a captive audience all day and night, day after day. Make sure your ad is powerful and can be read in 30 seconds. Also, offer easy-to-remember information, like my "Marketing Tools That Work for Network Marketers" web site, www.Freedom2u2.com.

THE LEAVE BEHIND

Leave a business card or mini-flyer on the shelf by the business and network marketing books and magazines in bookstores, doctor's offices, and libraries. Slip a few cards inside the publications, too. Remember to always carry your business cards wherever you go and leave them anywhere you feel people will see them. Your business cards will make you money.

FLEA MARKETS

This idea could make you a fortune and build a large organization fast. You can either set up a booth or attend flea markets as a customer and talk to the people running the booths. There are hundreds of prospects at flea markets, and many of these people are entrepreneurs, perfect for your business. Introduce them to your business and products or services. Explain the power of building a residual income (see Barry Friedman's chapter on this topic) so eventually they do not have to be spending all their weekends at the flea market working hard for little return compared to the money they can make with a successful business that can be built nationally or even internationally. They also probably know other sellers at the flea market who might well be interested in joining them in a lucrative network marketing business.

HIRE YOUR KIDS

Pay your kids (or any kids) to pass out your flyers, brochures, CDs, or cassette tapes. For a nominal cost, you can get thousands distributed to targeted prospects within hours.

REPS WHO ALREADY CALL ON BUSINESSES

Find people who are already selling to businesses. If they are working independently, like your products or services, and can find a fit for their current clients or customers, you'll have an instant cash flow. Target salespeople who interact with customers or prospects likely to be attracted to what you have to offer.

PROFESSIONAL SPORTING EVENTS

Stand outside these events and pass out your information to the sharpest people you see. Many of these people are professionals who just may be perfect for your business. Remember, the more people you expose your business to, the richer you can become.

ASK FOR REFERRALS

Always ask the people you're prospecting if they can refer their friends who may be interesting in making more money. You can come up with some excellent leaders this way. Say something like, "Jane, would you be willing to give me the names of three people you know who are either entrepreneurial or who may need some extra money?"

CELEBRITY ENDORSEMENT

Be it local or national, if a known celebrity joined your efforts to promote your company, it could be the ticket that shoots you into network marketing stardom. Ask everyone you know if they know of anyone who knows a celebrity of some kind. Many television or movie personalities and sports figures are willing to endorse quality products that meet people's needs.

WRITE ARTICLES

Write good and useful articles that business and network marketing publications and online e-zines can publish. They always give you credit at the end of the article where you can list your contact information. Say, maybe you can even write a chapter in somebody's book, like this!

GOOGLE AD WORDS

Ever notice those ads on web pages when you do a Google search? Google allows you the opportunity to advertise your products, services, or income opportunity by bidding as low as 5 cents for every visitor they generate to your web site. This is targeted advertising, and you only pay for the people who actually go to your web site. Say you are selling a hot new wonder juice. When people search for the word *juice*, your ad pops up for them to see. You can have several words trigger your ad to pop up. Make sure you use ad words that are narrow enough in scope to provide you with sufficiently qualified leads.

COLLEGE STUDENTS

Many of these students are very sharp and need extra money. They also have heard about network marketing from their parents and may be eager to get involved. They represent a growing, ambitious group who know many others who share their entrepreneurial nature and desire to earn extra income.

SIZZLE CARDS OR DROP CARDS

This is a method of prospecting that virtually anybody can do. You put a basic advertising message along with your contact information on business cards that act like miniature billboards. Leave thousands of these cards each month everywhere you go, as you go about your day. Place some on ATM machines, in phone booths, at gas pumps, at video stores, in magazines, in restrooms, on newspaper machines, in convenience stores (pay them to set up a little counter stand), in apartment buildings, at the post office, and everywhere else you can think of. If you put out a lot of cards consistently, like 500 to 1,000 a week, you will get a lot of prospects.

PLEASE HELP ME OUT

Send friends and business associates several of your business cards and ask them to help you by passing out your cards. This way they won't feel like you're trying to recruit them, and some may even join you without you needing to prospect them directly.

TIP WELL AND LEAVE YOUR CARD

With the outgoing waitress or waiter at the restaurant, develop rapport and leave your business card or flyer. If you want a better response, talk to them briefly about the business first. Share with them how you are looking for outgoing, hardworking people just like them to expand your business. Ask if they would be willing to listen to a CD (you just happen to have in the car) that explains all the details. Set up a time to follow up to answer their questions before you go.

PHONE CALL LISTS OF NETWORK MARKETERS OR OPPORTUNITY SEEKERS

If you have a better mousetrap, many of these people will join you in business. They already know about the benefits of network marketing and could be a great asset to your business. Create a compelling reason for calling them and pledge your support to their success should they choose to join you in partnership.

MATCHBOOKS

Have your ad printed on matchbooks and distribute them for free to bars and restaurants to give to their customers.

CLASSIFIED AND DISPLAY ADS

Place ads in local, regional, and national papers and magazines. Unless you're using a generic ad that does not mention your company name, make sure to get company approval or use your company's approved ads.

Make sure you have a marketing professional create your display ad. As with all forms of advertising, always test your ad before spending a lot of money. If the results are poor, try rewriting the ad or placing it in a different publication that better targets your ideal prospects.

ONLINE BUSINESS OPPORTUNITY FORUMS

Use a search engine to locate these forums. Look around and see to whom you can present your income opportunity. Many of these people are open to evaluating a good opportunity. Remember that many people are on the lookout for a good sponsor even more than a quality company or product line, so let your personality shine.

NONPROFIT GROUPS

Maybe your company has a fantastic way for nonprofit organizations to raise much-needed funds. Network marketing product-based fund-raisers are residual ongoing money machines that can grow year after year. This method of marketing your opportunity and products could meet the financial needs of schools, churches, clubs, and other nonprofit groups and result in an exciting pathway to build your business.

RADIO ADS AND RADIO SHOWS

Create compelling 30-second, 60-second, or 2-minute ads or 30-minute infomercials to introduce your products or services to radio listeners. Always make sure you get company approval on all ads. Conduct your own 30- or 60-minute radio show at a local radio station. Create a work-at-home-business show where you interview successful guests and promote your business opportunity during commercial breaks. Offer free products to radio personalities and DJs to give away to listeners. This is a low-cost way to advertise while getting a local celebrity's endorsement.

LEAD LISTS

Find a good, targeted source for network marketers and opportunity seekers who want to work from home. This can be a fast way to build your income because it can provide an unending source of prospects to whom you'll introduce your income opportunity. I once owned a lead-generation company and know how well this method can work. Live leads are even available so you can contact an interested prospect immediately after they request to get more information on a home-based business. When evaluating a lead-generation company, ask for at least five references of satisfied customers who have built their businesses successfully by calling their leads. Not all leads are of equal quality, so test a small batch before making a large monetary investment.

If you truly want success and the time and financial freedom to work where you want, when you want, with whom you want, and if you want, you must make a commitment to work hard and continue to sponsor new prospects every month and help them to do the same. It's not easy, but it is simple if you follow a proven, duplicable system and consistently pass out samples and information on your company and income opportunity. For more information on a detailed system that will support your success, I recommend *The 7-Step System to Building a $1,000,000 Network Marketing Dynasty* by Dr. Joe Rubino.

Remember, just one or two strong leaders in your organization can make you rich. Focused and consistent action can mean a large residual income for years to come. Commit to your success, make prospecting a way of life, and decide to never quit!

Nick Hetcher has an extensive and successful 25-year career in the sales and network marketing industries. The past owner of a successful network marketing lead generation company in the 1990s, he has been one of the top three distributors in a well-respected network marketing company, is the past owner of the trademark "Cheese Head" (working closely with football legends Reggie White and Jerry Kramer), wrote and voiced thousands of radio and TV ads and hosted his own radio show, and currently owns Freedom2u2.com (a generic web site created to help any network marketer achieve greater success fast) and the real-time leads web site MLMLeadCenter.com offering free leads of interested prospects. Hetcher has a passion to empower others and help them reach their personal and financial dreams through the time and financial freedom earned in this amazing industry we call network marketing.

Contact Nick Hetcher at nhetcher@new.rr.com. To get your free real-time prospects, visit www.MLMLeadCenter.com. Enter code "MLMC75" to get 75 free real-time leads with any order.

Nick also pioneered the massive growth of Green Zap, a company that pays affiliates $25 to sign up for their online payment transfer services. Visit www.greenzap.com/zappercash to get your free $25 reward and begin to receive payments from your online customers.

CHAPTER
25

Prospecting and Creating High Visibility to Attract Business Builders

Dr. Tony Alessandra

There are two ways to attract and develop potential network marketing business builders—getting people to come to you, or you going after them. Prospecting is going after them, while promoting high visibility is getting them to come to you.

One of the first things you can do in prospecting is be sure you're doing something in addition to working your current leads or sitting at your desk waiting for the phone to ring as a result of seeds you previously planted. Successful networkers do not wait for interested prospects to contact them—they are proactive! They develop an endless stream of business and social contacts. They ask their friends if they know of any people who might be interested in working from home or developing a secondary income stream. They give seminars and lectures to groups of targeted prospects regarding how to work from home, achieve financial security, plan for early retirement, or fund the educational needs for children. They send benefit-driven direct mail to the owners of businesses or target-market prospects who already possess a success mentality such as doctors or CPAs. They find out what kinds of business and social activities their profile prospect is likely to engage in, whether it is golf or chamber of commerce meetings, and they join and participate as well. They get involved in civic and professional groups to become known as people who support others to create lucrative second incomes, thus building a reputation. They know that the more visible they are with their prospects, the more likely they are to be credible with prospects, who will be more inclined to want to do business with them.

Another great source of prospects for your network marketing business is current or former customers who have already experienced the benefits of your company's products. Perhaps they are currently enjoying the products without fully understanding the business opportunity the products represent. One reason why former customers may no longer currently be active product users may simply be that they haven't been called on in a while and asked if they might be interested in placing an order. Or, if the customers were introduced to a distributor who is no longer actively building a business, they may not know how to order additional products. These former customers represent a gold mine right under your nose. When approached courteously and professionally, many will reorder products or services, while others will be open to learning how you and your company might enhance their lives through your income opportunity.

Remember, prospects are everywhere. Casually talk to other parents at your child's after-school baseball game. A customer or potential business builder could be sitting right next to you! What interests do you share with your prospects? Do they play golf? Consider joining them for an afternoon round. Always be thinking, "How could I create value for this particular prospect that would allow him or her to experience the value of working in partnership with me and my company?" If you make sure it's not threatening and it is easy for them to explore the possibilities of working with you to develop a second income, your prospecting efforts can be much more successful.

Your goal is to make sales and identify prospective business builders as you go about your daily efforts. Proper research, preparation, and legwork will lead to dramatically enhanced results, in contrast to a more haphazard approach in which you just hope to run into people who may need your company's products or have an interest in your income opportunity. Look at it this way. Imagine that you're in the plant business. You grow houseplants and carry 12 varieties, each of which blooms in a different month of the year, so you have a different plant available each month of the year. Each of these plants, however, requires 12 months to grow from seedling to full bloom. In addition, each plant requires attention once a month. This attention includes feeding, watering, pruning, and rotation. So you set up a schedule in which you plant the seeds a year in advance and then every month do what is required to continue or start the growth of each plant. The payoff doesn't come until a year after you've started, but each month thereafter a new plant will be ready to sell. You're all set—unless you forget a step some month, in which case you probably won't discover your oversight until many months down the line. By then it will be too late. In the plant business, you can't plant the seeds on the thirteenth of the month and expect to have a sale on the first.

The development of your network marketing business also requires investing in a future payoff. The time lag between planting your seeds and reaping the rewards varies. Each month, however, you must do what is necessary to ensure a future yield. The maintenance and growth of your business requires that you: (1) continually replenish your source of prospective customers and potential business partners; (2) qualify prospects to determine if they possess the sort of commitment necessary to achieve success in network marketing; (3) study the needs, wants, and dreams of each prospect;

and (4) propose solutions to these areas of what's important to them or currently missing in their lives that you might contribute to with your company's offerings or income opportunity.

Let's talk for a minute about sources of prospects. The first one I'll cover is called tip clubs. The purpose of these groups is to make each member aware of the resources available from the other members. This type of give-and-take results in a group synergism. Each person is able to bring to the group his or her area of expertise, centers of influence, social networks, and business contacts. With everyone bouncing ideas off one another, a kind of professional kinetic energy develops in which everyone can gain information, cross-sell, obtain referrals, and increase the drive to achieve. Most groups meet on a regular basis over breakfast or lunch. They often have a short program during which a member can describe his or her product or service.

Canvassing can be another excellent source of prospects if you follow some simple guidelines. This involves methodically contacting people or firms in your area who fit the model of the type of person you are most looking for. Perhaps they are members of a particular group or profession that has a natural link to your company's products or services. Or maybe they are centers of influence in the community or have a history of business success. Because they are unsolicited prospects, study their situation to discover any obvious need for your products and services. Determine when seems to be a good time/quiet time to contact them. If done with sincerity, interest, and research, canvassing can expand your prospect reservoir significantly.

Satisfied existing customers represent an excellent source of prospects for you. They'll talk to their friends and associates about their purchases, and they may mention your name. Occasionally a customer will tell you the name of an associate, but this is rare. So it's up to you to probe your customers tactfully for referrals. You might say something like, "John, who do you know who might benefit from a product like this?" Another approach might be to say, "John, I'm currently looking for a few new business partners. These might be people you'd consider entrepreneurial. They might be tired of their current jobs or worried about downsizing. They might be hardworking people who could really use an additional income. Could you think of three people I might speak with about our income opportunity?" This is a habit you could cultivate after each sale or prospecting call. I suggest having three intentions every time you approach a potential prospect: (1) explore interest in evaluating your income opportunity, (2) ask them to become a customer, and (3) request some referrals. If you're always tactfully asking customers and those you prospect with your income opportunity for referrals, perhaps they'll think of some for you even when you're not there. If nothing else, they'll be impressed with your enthusiasm and stick-to-itiveness.

An effective method to obtain referrals is to ask specific leading questions. One way of doing this is to review your list of qualifying criteria for prospects. Choose one criterion and base your question on it. For example, let's say one of your qualifying criteria is that the prospect is already successful in some arena. You would then ask your client, "Who do you know who has a track record of success in business?" Or ask, "Who do you know who is well respected in the community?" You should then remain silent, giving your customer or prospect time to think. When a customer is giving you referrals, especially if there's more than one, jot the names down without analyzing them. After he's finished, you can go back and question him on qualifying details.

Your customers are some of the most valuable resources for referrals that you have. They know other businesspeople in their field and are in the best position to recommend you to them. For this reason, you should ask any customers or prospects if you can mention their names when contacting people to whom they referred you. Through your current customers, you'll find new branches to follow to tap prospective new customers and potential business builders.

Professional groups are another excellent source for prospects. Consider joining organizations comprised of prospects within your target markets. As an individual, become involved with your family, friends, and different community groups. You'll lead a more fulfilled life if you're active and interested in the world around you. And there's certainly nothing wrong with letting people know what you do and speaking of your willingness to be of service to them. In the natural course of conversation we're always asked, "What do you do?" However, be aware that one of the fastest ways to turn people off is to launch into a sales pitch. Simply tell them what you do and leave it at that. Later, if you see that you may be of some service to them, you can approach them and discuss it in a relaxed and helpful way.

Once you get to meet everyone in the organization (if it's small enough for you to do so), you can try to obtain a membership list or directory. You are then in a position to systematically contact each one in an informative, casual way. It's not advisable to send blanket direct mailings; instead, seek to contact each person, developing rapport and creating value on an individual basis.

Now let's talk about directories. In addition to the yellow pages, your local library has directories on everything imaginable. Directories will save you time and energy. Some list specific people to contact, such as corporate officers or department heads. R. L. Polk & Company publishes a directory called the Polk City Directory that lists everyone living in every city in the United States with their occupation. This puts you in a position to send an introductory letter to as many people as you wish. There are also specialized directories for industries such as the hotel and travel industry as well as many other vertical markets.

Prospects themselves can also be great sources for other prospects. Many new network marketers assume that if a prospect isn't interested in your opportunity, then there is no potential left in the relationship. Not so. A prospect can be asked for referrals in the same way that established clients or customers are asked. With a prospect, however, it is paramount that you create a professional business relationship before asking for referrals. If you're perceived as being credible, trustworthy, and ethical, your prospects will have no qualms about referring you to others. In fact, the better your relationships with prospects, the harder they'll work to think of referrals for you. When they can, people like to help those they like.

Also, consider centers of influence. A center of influence is someone in a position to steer you to prospects or steer prospects to you. An athletic trainer may be the perfect person to recommend people interested in weight loss or nutritional supplements. A pet care professional might recommend others who breed, groom, or otherwise work with pets. An accountant, attorney, or banker may be able to recommend entrepreneurial individuals. Whenever possible, focus on building a trusting relationship with them *before* asking for referrals. Be sure they know the benefits you offer so they are confident that you would be providing a valuable service for their referral. Let them know your goals of contributing to others so they can be aware of the kind of prospects you're looking for. Make sure they know that you sincerely want their help. Give them a formal presentation describing your services or products. Provide them with an extensive list of testimonials, personal and business references, and professional materials to support the integrity and value your company and products provide. Centers of influence are very concerned about referring only those people who will not undermine their reputations. Be sure you report back to the center of influence after you contact the person referred. And finally, find a professional way to reciprocate or to say thank you.

Of course, when prospecting, don't overlook your friends and social contacts. This group makes up the typical first source of prospects for your product and income opportunity. They can provide a rich source of prospects. It's not uncommon to learn that your friends and relatives have only a vague idea of what you do. Whether you can sell to them is secondary. Like any prospects, they may be able to refer you to others. After the initial contact, for those you want to continue networking with, devise a method of maintaining contact. Start a traditional mailing or e-mail list and send them something periodically to keep them up-to-date on you. Newsletters, brochures, direct mail correspondence, e-zines, and birthday cards will all serve you well. Just keep in mind that when you approach a friend or relative, it's best to do it in a way so that they understand that there is absolutely no pressure or expectation on your part that they must do anything. Create value and allow them to have the choice about joining your team or purchasing your products or services.

Chambers of commerce are also excellent places to prospect—especially for the small business market. It is their job to keep up-to-date on local businesses and to aid in their development. For example, if your targeted market was nonprofit organizations that may be interested in utilizing your products for a fund-raiser, the local chamber would very likely have a listing. The information is relatively easy to get and is usually free.

You also might consider starting or joining a local study group. Study groups have become a very effective tool for strengthening networkers in their careers. A study group can be composed of networkers from the same or different network marketing companies. They form close, business-related friendships in order to help each other grow and develop as network marketing professionals. At each meeting, they bring one another up-to-date by comparing notes on recent events, types of strategies planned, obstacles encountered and overcome, and other insights on how to build a business effectively. Each member strengthens the others by offering observations, assessments, feedback, and support. Just make sure the group is kept noncompetitive. For this sort of group to work, it is never appropriate to attempt to enroll members from other companies into your organization. This rule must be made clear to all new members while asking any violators to leave the group.

Let's look now at trade associations. If your target market consists of a very specific type of business, there is a good chance that most firms in this business belong to a trade association. The association could be very helpful in providing you with information on its membership. Most trade associations publish a monthly or quarterly magazine or journal for their membership. This could keep you current on trends and issues in your target market industry. The trade association might also have for sale a mailing list of its membership. This could be helpful when you are doing your direct mail prospecting.

Another area of prospecting to consider is producing your own newsletter. The rate of technical advancement in practically every field is so great that few individuals can keep abreast of it. If you are targeting one of these fields and you have a thorough understanding of the changes as well as a knack for writing, you're in a prime position to produce a newsletter. As an enterprising networker, you could develop a monthly or quarterly newsletter in which you call attention to new products, services, and technological improvements. This would provide a service to your customers and prospects, and save them time. It would also keep you in their mind as someone with whom to do business.

Now let's look at some general ideas to keep in mind when prospecting. First of all, no matter what source of prospecting you utilize, *always* have a prospecting plan. The basic elements include (1) setting objectives, (2) classifying prospects, and (3) evaluating your results. The objectives set for your prospecting plan should be very similar in nature to any other type of marketing objective you would develop. All objectives should be quantifiable. This means they must be measurable for purposes of evaluation. Measurement criteria should also be specified, such as identifying and contacting so many new prospects per month. Objectives should also be realistically grounded, while at the same time motivating you. They should not be so grand that there would be little probability of achieving them. They should be time specific. Without a beginning and an end the objectives will be of little value. And they should be put in hierarchical order. If more than one objective is needed, rank them in terms of importance so you will be clear about how you will set your priorities.

Once you've identified prospects you want to contact, classify and record them according to categories that are meaningful to you. For professionals, you could divide them by doctors, lawyers, architects, and so on. For centers of influence, there would be accountants, attorneys, and bankers. For niche market business prospects, there would be subdivisions for each target market that your products, services, or opportunity might appeal to.

To assist you with implementing this, design what I call a "Prospect Data Sheet." It will include pertinent data, such as the prospect's name, company name, address, phone and fax numbers, e-mail address, type of prospect, and a record of the actions you have taken, with dates, and the actions you intend to take. Moving forward in your business requires creative prospecting and a comprehensive prospecting plan. If you have a plan and you work the plan, you'll have an unending flow of qualified prospects and a consistently growing organization.

Dr. Tony Alessandra, PhD, CSP, CPAE, helps companies build customers, relationships, and the bottom line. Companies learn how to achieve market dominance through specific strategies designed to outmarket, outsell, and outservice the competition by applying his marketing, sales, service, and relationship-building skills. He offers practical ideas that produce profitable bottom-line results.

Tony has a street-wise, college-smart perspective on business, having fought his way out of New York City to eventually realize success as a graduate professor of marketing, an entrepreneur, a business author, and a keynote speaker. He earned his MBA in 1970 from the University of Connecticut, and his PhD in marketing in 1976 from Georgia State University.

He is the founder and president of Online Assessments, a company that offers numerous online multirater assessments on a powerful technology platform; chairman of the board of BrainX, a company that offers digital accelerated learning programs; and co-founder of MentorU, an online e-learning company.

Dr. Alessandra is a widely published author with 14 books translated into 17 foreign languages, including *Charisma* (Warner Books, 1998); *The Platinum Rule* (Warner Books, 1996); *Collaborative Selling* (John Wiley & Sons, 1993); and *Communicating at Work* (Fireside/Simon & Schuster, 1993). He is featured in more than 50 audio/video programs and films, including *Relationship Strategies* (American Media); *The Dynamics of Effective Listening* (Nightingale-Conant); and *Non-Manipulative Selling* (Walt Disney).

What is it about Tony Alessandra that gets people so excited? It's really very simple. He reaches people—from the board of directors to the frontline folks in the trenches. He gets across important information so people can grasp it, remember it, and use it.

Recognized by *Meetings & Conventions* magazine as "one of America's most electrifying speakers," Dr. Alessandra was inducted into the Speakers Hall of Fame in 1985—and is a member of the Speakers Roundtable, a group of 20 of the world's top professional speakers. For more information about Dr. Alessandra, contact him at: (702) 567-9965, fax (702) 567-9964, Tony@Alessandra.com, www.alessandra.com, or www.OnlineAC.com.

CHAPTER
26

Octopus Networking: Stretch Your Tentacles and Inspire Others to Help

Romanus Wolter

Yesterday as I sat down to get a haircut, I noticed for the first time that I was the only customer in the shop. My barber anxiously asked, "How do I bring in new clients? I've never had to network before but I think I have to now. Over 40 percent of my clients have moved out of the city in the past year."

Reality has hit his business, and as a small business owner, he doesn't have the advertising budget of a large company to lure customers back with special deals or direct customers to his doorstep. How can he reach and excite these customers to buy his service?

The way for any traditional business or any network marketing business to grow and prosper is much the same. With some imagination, willpower, and a technique I call octopus networking, anyone can create new opportunities to increase sales. The key is to create a marketing message that inspires other people to help you succeed.

Octopus networking is the ability to make one networking effort produce multiple results—increasing returns without increasing effort. When you hit an octopus on the head, its tentacles stretch out and reach in different directions. Network marketing business owners can do the same thing. By leveraging their own value and targeting other businesses or successful people, a single networking effort continuously pays off.

In addition to prospecting typical individuals, we can grow our network marketing businesses with velocity by targeting centers of influence. The head of the octopus is any person or place that reaches a large number of your potential customers or prospects. This includes nonprofit organizations, famous people, small store owners who sell to your target market, or companies that offer complementary products. You want to inspire these entities to deliver your message to your potential customers and future partners, helping you network even when you are not physically present.

While trying to expand your network, there will be moments when you will think, "I am going nowhere fast." Relax. To become a successful network marketer, first realize that there is nowhere you must go in order to meet the right people. That's right. You do not have to go to a chamber of commerce event, an industry meeting, or a financial workshop to succeed. Instead of traveling to networking events, save time, money, and frustration by encouraging others to bring the right people to you!

SUCCESSFUL NETWORKING

To stay energized and moving your network marketing business forward as you create your message and learn the rules of networking, I ask people to follow what I call the "three rules to live by." These three rules act as a reminder to continually focus your message and let others help you achieve the success you deserve.

The three rules to live by for network marketing success are:

1. Speak from your passion.
2. Listen to others.
3. Write down their ideas.

Surveys have shown that 99 percent of working people dislike their jobs. Speaking from your passion is a great technique to grab people's attention. Tell everyone what you truly love about the product or service you are selling. Just by revealing your passion, you entice people to listen to you. The best way to communicate your passion is to focus on your intent. What are you truly trying to accomplish? Write down how your business will benefit other people. People cannot argue with benefits. Instead, they will begin to share your vision and goals and then try to figure out a way to help you.

This action also energizes you to keep going when times get rough. Passion establishes a foundation of believability and possibility. Any questions people have about your ability to deliver on your promises become diminished.

Listen to other people; they have the contacts, strategies, and information that can help you move forward faster. By listening, you make them part of your sales team. People love it when their ideas are recognized and appreciated. This does not mean you have to act on all the ideas presented. People want to be heard, but they also understand that you are the one who determines the right action to take.

Write down all the ideas presented to you. Get into the habit of asking for referrals. Ask others for ideas on how you can best build your network marketing business. The first four letters of *listen* are LIST. Circumstances change and we can't predict the future, so take note of all the ideas and referrals people present so you don't lose them. A special note: Use the back of the person's business card to record their ideas and contacts. It helps you keep track of who gave you the contact, resource, or strategy you needed to succeed.

Octopus networking works like this:

DREAM LIKE A CHILD, DECIDE AS AN ADULT

The secret to success in life and business is to dream like a child, decide as an adult. When you wake up in the morning or start a new sales or prospecting task, look at the world through a child's eyes and see the possibilities. Just as a child does, ask for help when you need it. Frustration and nonaction set in when we continually try the same task and expect different results.

Then decide as an adult. Use your intuition, experience, and knowledge to decide on the next action step to take, and then take it! Tapping into the possibilities and taking action energizes you to move forward and accomplish your goals. And it shows people that you believe in yourself enough to actually act on suggestions and ideas presented to you.

DEVELOP AN EFFECTIVE MESSAGE
BASED ON BENEFIT

Octopus networking starts with your ability to inform people about the benefits your products or services provide. When people are looking to purchase something, for themselves, their families, or their businesses, they immediately ask themselves, "How will I or my company benefit from this product or service?" People analyze this question instantly—research has shown usually within 10 seconds. Therefore, you must be able to immediately and effectively explain how your products or services will help them achieve success, health, happiness, or some other benefit faster. Do not focus on describing what it is but rather how it benefits the person with whom you are speaking. Benefits move customers and opportunity prospects to action.

Ask yourself, "When a customer or prospect meets me or receives my brochure, do they understand how I can help them?" "Do I have a message about my product line or business that I can use to easily tell others about it?" If not, it is time for you to create a winning "instant impact message." An instant impact message is a brief, powerful statement based on benefits that begins every sales conversation. Benefits are simple to remember, making it much easier for people to become part of your sales force by referring new customers or prospects to your business. Plus, they become more confident in their referrals because they understand who you can benefit.

The goal of an instant impact message is to become known as someone so people remember you and the benefit you offer to your customers or income opportunity prospects. For instance, "I am known as the Kick Start Guy and I provide action steps that close the gap between goals and success" is the message I use to open conversations. I use it on all my marketing materials so people hear the same message repeatedly. This simple statement makes it easy for people to refer to me their friends who have a dream or organizations that help others achieve success.

Creating a winning instant impact message is really quite simple—just focus on benefits. Focusing on the unique contribution your product or business opportunity offers helps your business stand out from the competition, and more importantly, it helps your customers remember you. Develop your own winning message by:

- Defining your "external intent." How does your product, service, or income opportunity specifically benefit other people? Make a list of ideas by writing down anything that comes to mind. Do not edit. Some of my clients express this as, "My company helps our customers to . . ." or "Our income opportunity allows people to . . ."

- Looking over your list and circling any key descriptive words— words that resonate with the benefits you provide that jump out at you. These words create an emotional foundation for your message.

- Using only the circled key words to develop a shorter, stronger statement focusing on the key benefits your business provides. You can use connective words such as "a," "an," and "the," but put an effort toward using just the key words you circled. Keep your message to less than 10 words, creating a powerful statement that people will be able to remember and repeat to others.

- Saying the sentence aloud as though you were telling someone about your business at a cocktail party. Ask yourself, "Would they understand my business and the benefits I offer?" If not, rewrite your message until you can concisely state how your products, services, or income opportunity help other people succeed.

- Sharing your new instant impact message with friends, family members, and colleagues. Remember the three rules to live by? Your instant impact message provides you with the ability to speak from your passion. Now is the time to listen to others' input, write down the words they present, and revise your instant impact message as you deem appropriate.

- Using your instant impact message all the time—at business functions, at cocktail parties, on your business cards, on your stationery, in any marketing brochures you develop, and even in the line at the grocery store. The more that people hear about your business, the greater your credibility becomes, making your sales process easier.

STRETCH THE OCTOPUS' TENTACLES

Now is the time to break the rules! Instead of always going after sales or prospects with only your own resources, stretch the tentacles of the octopus even further by finding a way to partner with centers of influence, organizations, or other companies that communicate with large numbers of your customers. It is a perfect way to spread credible messages about your business.

For instance, is there a nonprofit organization that can use your products or services? If so, provide them at a discount and in exchange for a testimonial, announcements in the nonprofit's newsletters, or a link on its web site, creating a win-win for both of you. Nonprofits have boards of directors made up of high-profile decision makers. When you are introduced to them via an organization they have a personal interest in, making a network connection with them becomes easier.

Keep your network growing by approaching businesses with complementary products or services that also serve your customers. Is there a way you can partner with them to offer a more complete solution to your customers? If so, create networking possibilities by developing joint brochures or linking to each other's web site.

By uniting together, you strengthen a sense of community, deliver what customers need, plus create new opportunities to deliver your message. The result is that these "octopus tentacles" expand your reach further than you ever imagined. This is the foundation for saving time, money, and frustration to create successful sales channels.

CONTINUALLY BENEFIT YOUR CUSTOMERS

Do not stop networking once you have achieved a result. Continually deliver your instant impact message and discover new ways to benefit others. By helping them achieve greater success, you keep your products or services "top-of-mind." As new people enter their circle of influence, they are more likely to refer you!

For instance, can you provide them with another product (maybe from one of your referral partners) that will save them time, money, or frustration? Do you have any additional contacts or information that can help them sell more effectively? Do you have any referrals for them? If so, share those names.

ENGAGE NAYSAYERS!

No matter how seasoned a network marketer you are, when someone says something negative about your business or your abilities, it stings. Conventional wisdom says that you should just ignore any naysayers. After all, won't they just hold you back from your goals?

The opposite is actually true when you are trying to discover unique methods for successfully networking. Some of the best strategies and contacts are born from unwelcome criticism. Negative comments often contain kernels of truth—the people offering them just do not do a great job delivering them. Your goal in networking is to engage these naysayers, determine what experiences and ideas they have to share, and then ask them for help to achieve your goals.

Ask naysayers for help? Yes! These individuals are used to being ignored by others but have numerous experiences and contacts to share. By simply listening to them rather than dismissing them, you can make them an important part of your networking circle.

Perhaps they may have had a negative experience with a network marketing company, distributor, or product. Engage naysayers by requesting that they tell you all about their horrible experience. Show you are listening by repeating back statements they make to you. If they say you will never be able to get past people's objections about the network marketing industry, you say, "You may be right. Getting past prior traumatic experiences can be difficult. What would you suggest to make it possible?"

Your goal is to find the truth, anger, or pain in what they are saying and discover new strategies they have to offer. As you hear them out and listen to their ideas, their defenses fall, and they will share their years of experience. And if they don't have an interest themselves, they may just provide you with the name of someone who can help you achieve your goal. Now that is successful networking!

The foundation to achieving network marketing success faster is to realize that it is okay to ask for help. The most common notion people have is that in order to succeed, you must go it alone. But getting help is not a sign of weakness. It is just smart business. When someone else introduces you, it instantly increases your credibility and encourages people to trust you, making your sales process easier and your networking efforts more exciting.

Remember that the key to achieving success in the field of network marketing is right there in its name—networking! Welcome to the world where successful networking is really just building a circle of continual referrals rather than a straight-line effort to create your own success.

Reaching more than 2.4 million entrepreneurs monthly, Romanus Wolter is the "Kick Start Guy." As the author of the best-selling *Kick Start Your Dream Business* (Ten Speed Press), co-founder of www.KickStartSuccess.com, and *Entrepreneur* magazine's Success Coach columnist, he provides practical, proven action steps that close the gap between goals and success.

As a radio host and speaker, Romanus leaves audiences energized and with enough creative ideas to last two lifetimes. His programs are tied together with passion and action! As more than one person has said, "Romanus does not view the cup as half-full or half-empty—it's overflowing!" Romanus' best-selling small business guidebook, *Kick Start Your Dream Business*, provides the information and inspiration people need to succeed. The action steps in the book apply to both a person's life and career, giving them the ability to make powerful choices. It helps change "I can't" into "I can!"

Romanus obtained a master's degree in international marketing. As an entrepreneurial consultant in London and Hong Kong, he learned what it takes for small businesses to expand. The practical steps captured in *Kick Start Your Dream Business* leverage this rare experience. His new small business web site at www.KickStartSuccess.com, provides the action steps, expert advice, community, and resources people need to succeed.

Romanus is a columnist for *Be Your Own Boss, The Magazine for Working Women* and has a monthly "The Kick Start Guy" segment on Entrepreneur Radio. His observations on what it takes to succeed have been reported in respected publications such as *BusinessWeek*, Bloomberg Television, the *Chicago Tribune*, Quicken.com, *Money & Profits*, the *Korea Times*, the *San Francisco Chronicle*, and numerous other media.

CHAPTER 27

Heating Up Your Cold Market

Amy Posner

B uilding a network marketing business is about talking to people. Naturally, it follows that you are always going to need people to talk to, and how to go about finding enough of those people is an especially important part of the larger success puzzle. Reaching Out Methods (ROMs) are simply ways of marketing in order to find people interested in building a business. Depending on your personality and style, as well as available time and budget, there are various methods from which to choose.

Having a few different ROMs working in parallel is generally a sound marketing approach for your network marketing business. Some strategies will be more long-term, while others will work more quickly; some will require a larger financial commitment, some will be low-cost, and some will be no-cost. Some ROMs will be in your warm market, some in the cold. Each has its merits; the point is not to rely on one alone, but to always have at least a few different methods working for you at any given time.

Let's take a look at several ROMs in detail, including working with Internet-generated leads; advertising through newspaper, radio, and magazine; and working in affinity groups.

Remember, you are running a business, and it makes sense to approach it in a businesslike manner. That includes having a marketing plan, consistently working that plan, and evaluating it on a weekly, monthly, and quarterly basis. Doing so will enable you to see what's working and what's not, which in turn will allow you to invest more of your time and resources in those methods that yield the greatest results.

Many of us started our businesses in the warm market, talking to people we know. This has been the classic staple of network marketing training—who hasn't heard of the idea of starting out by making a list of family and friends?

However, that doesn't necessarily mean the warm market is the preferable way to go for everyone. Some people distinctly prefer to get started in the cold market first. This can be more difficult in some ways (for example, you may have less credibility with people you don't know than with those you do), but some of us are simply more comfortable there—and that's okay! In fact, sometimes cutting your teeth in the cold market and getting some success under your belt is exactly what will then enable you to feel more secure approaching the people you know and doing so with more conviction.

I've always been a phone prospector. Put me on the phone and I can talk to anyone I've never spoken to before without fear or intimidation. But drop me off at the mall and ask me to meet people—and at the end of an hour I'll be wanting to quit the business. Don't get me wrong; it's not that I'm unfriendly or a recluse. I just know what I like and what I'm good at.

I had an eye-opening experience years ago when I recruited a dynamic woman who was keen to build her business. I trained her to do what I do: call people on the phone. A week into her business, she called and told me she realized that she had made a mistake; this wasn't going to work for her.

We got together to talk about it. In conversation, I learned that she felt opposite from the way I felt: The thought of having to pick up the phone and talk to people was more than she could bear. In fact, she was someone who wanted to go to the mall and just see who turned up!

We discussed how to do that and what else she could do to get her out and meeting more people face-to-face. Her business started growing almost immediately—and I learned a huge lesson that has served me very well ever since: We're all better getting started in those areas and using those methods with which we already feel comfortable. What works best for you may not work best for your new distributor!

Ask your new distributors (and for that matter, ask yourself this, too), what kinds of things can you see yourself doing to start talking to people about your business? Listen carefully to their answers and help them make a plan based on those responses. Eventually you'll want to get out of your comfort zone, but starting there can be very helpful. For many people, just starting a business is enough out of the comfort zone, so it's good to have a way to start it that's not so scary or intimidating.

There are only two choices: talking to people you know, or talking to strangers. From there, the question is how to go about contacting people in either group. Being somewhat of a cold market expert, I'm going to focus on mostly on cold marketing methods. For talking to people you know, I'll refer you back to your sponsor or upline to help you come up with your top 10 list and work on how to best approach them.

INTERNET-GENERATED LEADS

Although the prospects may not be as targeted as ones you might find by advertising in a trade journal, business magazine, or newspaper, working with leads generated over the Internet is very cost-effective.

With the Internet, unlike more traditional media, you can buy a specified number of prospects, which enables you to schedule and plan your work more efficiently. Again, it's a good idea to be using at least two or three ROMs, but by incorporating this method, you know you'll at least be sure to connect with a certain number of people each week—guaranteed. (As long as you make your calls!)

Working in the cold market, and particularly with Internet-generated leads, there are two key elements that make the process work: (1) making a personal connection with your prospects and then (2) qualifying them to the next stage, which may consist of getting them information to review on a web site, through a conference (by phone or online), or by snail mail (sending a brochure, CD, or personal letter), or a combination of these things.

Remember, with the people you're calling you have *no* credibility going in. They don't know you and in many cases have never heard of the company you represent. Many people have had some sort of experience or contact with other network marketing businesses, often less than successful, so you may have to overcome their skepticism.

The majority of people are actually quite friendly and personable, though . . . with the occasional curmudgeon thrown into the mix just to keep you on your toes.

Your initial call to a cold-market Internet prospect should contain certain basic elements.

Brief Script

You should have a concise script that gives an overview of the company and the business you are presenting. Keep this part very brief—one to two minutes maximum! Longer than that, and you're likely to wear out your welcome.

There are two critical reasons you want to keep this first call brief: first, you need to qualify them and move on to your next prospect; and second, from the moment they pick up the phone, you are also training them. You want to plant the seed in the prospect's mind that this first call is simple, straightforward, and uncomplicated—in other words, that it's something they could imagine doing easily themselves.

Benefits

In your script, make sure to include a clear statement of what's in it for them. Think about what got you excited and write that into your script.

First, Connect

Before you even begin with your script or tell them about the company, you want to connect with them. This is best done by asking questions and getting to know them a bit. If you're not a natural schmoozer, prepare some basic questions that will break the ice and help you establish a bit of rapport. You don't need their life story. Remember, you're keeping this call brief.

My partner and I have worked with all sorts of connecting questions over the years. The very best, most effective question we've found is this:

"John, if I might ask—tell me where you are in the process of looking for a business: are you casually browsing, or seriously looking?"

This question is very simple and nonthreatening, and it will often get the other person talking and cutting right to the chase. More often than not, people will respond by telling you not just whether they're casually browsing or seriously looking but *why*. This allows you to step directly into how your opportunity can work for them.

If they give you a simple, short answer (for example, "casually browsing"), you can follow up with, "Well, tell me, what are you doing now? Are you looking for something to supplement a current income?" Engage them in a little conversation and you'll be able to get a sense of what they're like.

Remember, you are the interviewer—the CEO for your own company talking to a potential candidate for a very important position building your future and theirs. So be bold. Be polite and respectful, but don't be afraid to ask some serious questions. You'll be surprised at how forthcoming people will be if you give them the opportunity. It gives you a chance to size them up, and it also gives you the chance to connect on a personal level, which opens them up to hear your message. When they can sense you're for real, they attach that credibility to the company you are presenting.

Next, tell them you want to give them the nutshell version of your business, and if there's a fit you'll get them more information. This is where your short one- to two-minute overview comes in.

Have Them Grade Themselves

After you've finished with your brief presentation, say:

"John, from the little bit you've heard, where do you see yourself on a scale of 1 to 10, 1 being 'no interest' and 10 being 'excited to learn more'?"

If they're under a 5, tell them that's really not enough interest to pursue this any further, thank them for their time, and dial another number.

If they are a 5 or 6, ask them if they have any questions that might raise their interest level a point or two.

If they are a 7 or above, take the next step.

The Next Step

Don't go any further into your business at this point; instead, ask them when they would like you to call them back. This way you get their personal commitment to set a time with you.

If you're using a web site or e-mail delivery for your follow-up information, then this appointment should be within the next 48 hours. If you use snail mail for your information package, you'll have to allow a few more days.

Set the appointment and confirm it by reading it back to them. Ask for alternative phone numbers, such as a cell phone.

Be Impeccable in Your Follow-Up

Impeccable follow-up is key to recruiting in the cold market, so keep track of your appointments and follow up exactly when you say you will. This is one of the most critical aspects of cold-market prospects; it is also exactly where a lot of people drop the ball. Remember, when you first speak with a cold-market prospect, you start out with a credibility level of zero. Your follow-up is their first opportunity to judge your reliability. Doing what you say you will do will make an impression on your prospect. Even if your follow-up call results in having to reschedule, your keeping your commitment on a consistent basis will impress them (even if they are not overtly aware of it) and it consistently sends the message that you will be a supportive, reliable business partner.

Sometimes it may take as many as 10 calls before your prospect makes a decision, and that's not a bad thing. During that time, a lot of bonding and connection take place. By that final phone call, they have come to feel as if they know you. (They do!) And if you've done what you said you would each and every time, they've come to know you as someone they can count on.

Some of these aspects of communication can seem very subtle. Don't be fooled. In a business of duplication, they are powerful—and critical. Other methods you use will follow a similar process once you get the person on the phone.

ADVERTISING

Although they are expensive in some markets, working with newspaper, magazine, and radio ads can be a very effective way to build your business. Generally, the larger the city, the costlier the ad will be. There are some ways to get prime space for less money, and I'll cover those briefly. Most network marketers who use print ads run classified newspaper ads, since they are less expensive than display (larger boxed) ads. Think of your classified ad as a headline—and as with your telephone presentation, always make that headline about what's in it for them. If you are at a loss for ideas, pick up a local newspaper or business magazine, go to the classifieds, and see what catches your eye. Use or adapt some of that language in your ad.

Most magazines have a deadline two to three months in advance of issue date, so these purchases need to be planned in advance. Here's a little-known advantage this schedule creates: When they are getting close to deadline and still have unsold space, you may be able to purchase some of that space at a discounted rate. Simply call the magazine and ask them, "Do you ever sell remnant space?" Find out when their deadlines are and call back at that time of the month to see what is available.

Radio stations will also sell time for less as it gets closer to airtime for various programs. If you have a recorded ad prepared that they can listen to right away, they may sell you space very inexpensively. After all, once the time slot has passed on a certain show, it's gone forever. Some revenue is better than none at all. Sometimes the more popular shows are booked months in advance and in certain markets remnant space just doesn't exist—but call around. We've had some great success running ads during drive time (commute time) in both the United States and Canada.

One of the great things about radio ads is that you gain instant credibility when your ad runs on a show people listen to regularly. It's almost as if the host is endorsing you, especially if you get the host to read your copy. This can works wonders for the response you'll get.

THE LONG HAUL

The thing to remember about these types of more traditional advertising is that it often takes multiple placements, while you test and retest and retest yet again, before you find something that pulls well for you. Also, most people need to see something multiple times before they take action. Multiple placements establish credibility in their minds. If they see an ad over and over, they start to gain the sense that you wouldn't continue paying for it unless it was working and that what you're offering is legitimate and viable.

This takes commitment of both time and money. You need to be clear going in that this ad campaign is probably not going to be a rapid process.

Can it be worth it? Absolutely.

Once you have taken that time and care and have found the copy and formula that works for you, you can leverage it by running it in multiple markets at once. If you have the budget for it, this strategy can produce great results.

When working with ads, unlike buying Internet-generated leads, you won't really know how many responses you're going to have to work with in any given week. This is a good reason to include buying a certain number of leads in your ROMs. That way you'll know that whatever else you have going, you'll always have some people to call and talk to. After all, the only thing that moves your business forward is talking to more people and doing it on a regular basis!

AFFINITY GROUPS

Yet another great way to find more people to talk with is to look for strangers with whom you already have something in common. Are you an engineer? A quilter? A pilot, nurse, teacher, lawyer, graphic artist, video game designer, classical guitarist, yoga practitioner, fly fisherman, finish carpenter? Whatever profession or avocation you have, there are groups of people with similar interests or professions who will be more open to hearing what you have to say simply because you already have something in common.

Look for mailing lists, local community organizations, and online chat rooms. Some cities sell their voter registration books, which tell you the names, professions, and ages of the people residing at a particular address. There are lots of creative ways to use that information to let people in your community know what you are doing.

Maybe you're an accountant. You can find other accountants through the yellow pages or an online search engine and send out a postcard mailing.

Perhaps you're a stay-at-home parent. Many communities have newspapers geared toward families with children. Find some local events and make a point of meeting new people. Listen when they talk. When you hear a problem that might be fixed by more money flowing into the family bank account, offer to get them some information that could help their situation.

MAKING IT WORK FOR YOU

In network marketing, as in any business you want to build, it's essential to create your game plan, execute that plan, analyze your success, and then adapt your actions based on that analysis. Don't be afraid to change course if something isn't working. Don't stick with something that isn't working because it's familiar or because it has worked for other people. Your business takes a long-term commitment and laser-sharp focus on the activities that make you money.

At the end of the day, talking to people is what builds our business. There are so many ways to connect with new people if you keep your mind open and actively pursue these new connections. Each of the different approaches I've outlined here requires different personality strengths and styles, as well as different time and financial budgets. Find a few things that you can easily see yourself doing, and maybe one that seems like a stretch. Then test them all to see which work best for you considering the resources available to you. Be flexible, be creative, be methodical, and be persistent—and you'll be successful!

***

Amy Posner is the CEO of Leads Lab. Born with an entrepreneurial spirit, she was a partner in three traditional businesses before the age of 35. Introduced to network marketing in 1994, she became a top income earner and created online training systems and audio and print marketing and training materials. Posner has traveled throughout the United States and Canada teaching others how to recruit, train, and inspire network marketing teams and showing people how to achieve their goals.

Network marketing has given her the time, flexibility, and freedom to do the things she enjoys most and has had a positive impact on her life in so many ways. Work is now a more natural part of her life that fits in with everything else she does. Posner now spends her time doing the things that matter most to her: helping other people live their lives this same way is her work. It doesn't get any better than that!

To learn more about Amy Posner and her leads company, visit www.leadslab.com.

CHAPTER
28

The 7 Best (and Most Profitable) Internet Prospecting Tools

Chris Zavadowski

"When all else fails, fresh tactics!"

—John Travolta as Sean Archer in *Face/Off* (1997)

Let's face it. Prospecting stinks! Sure, you might be one of those unique bulletproof super-distributors out there, making six figures a month, oblivious to any "no" you hear, and addicted to talking to strangers. If that's you, congratulations! Skip to the next chapter—because you don't need my advice.

But if you're the regular, everyday, hates-to-hear-"no" distributor, just trying to make a few extra grand each month, keep reading. I know there are many more of you in the network marketing world than there are Mr. Top Producer. So these killer methods are for you.

However, two words of caution before we begin:

1. Each network marketing company has its own set of marketing rules and regulations. Make sure you check with your company before going down any marketing avenue that is new for you.

2. Some of these marketing methods might be a little controversial. I can promise you, they all work like gangbusters, but they might not click for *you*. That's okay. While each system and method builds on the previous one, you can still use this chapter à la carte. Pick and choose the tactics that work for you and your team.

Let's begin . . .

THE MODERN MIRACLE:
PAY-PER-CLICK ADVERTISING

If you've never heard of pay-per-click (PPC) advertising, hold onto your seat! This is probably one of the greatest tools you can add to your online marketing arsenal to instantly see results. In the past few years, this has become the best way to quickly drive online visitor traffic to your web site for as little as $0.01 per visitor. Imagine, in under 10 minutes, you have laser-targeted prospects and customers pouring into your web site (and buying).

Sound too good to be true? It's not. If you've ever searched at Yahoo.com and seen the sponsored links up top, or used Google.com and noticed the classified ad–looking links on the right-hand side of the screen, you've seen pay-per-click advertising in action.

I'm sure you've noticed that the Internet has slowly been moving away from "free" and more toward a "paid" model, right? So why should search engine results be any different? Instead of having to hire a search engine expert to get you ranked high in the results for whatever search terms you want, you can now buy those top rankings.

Here's how it works: When you set up your account with a PPC search engine, you'll first pick the keywords you want to bid on. A keyword is the word or phrase you want your ad to appear under when people are typing that word or phrase into the search engine.

Notice, I said *bid*. The person bidding the most gets the highest ranking. Yes, there will most likely be others online who are aiming for the same keywords as you. But, as long as you're not targeting broad, generic terms like "MLM," "home business," or "network marketing," and are getting very specific with the terms you choose, you'll be in much better shape.

You want to use the most laser-targeted, specific keywords you can find. The broad terms will only waste your money. The key is to think of what your ideal prospect is typing into the search engines. What is he searching for? What is the problem she is looking to solve? Those are the keywords you should be bidding on. I recommend www.KeywordMillions.com for brainstorming your massive list of keywords. The site also has a free version you can try out.

Now that you have your keywords chosen, you'll then give the PPC company the copy or text to use for your ad. Think of this as a highly targeted classified advertisement—you've got to say a lot in a small amount of space. Load as many benefits into your ad as you can. For a crash course in writing sales copy, I highly recommend John Caples' *Tested Advertising Methods* (Prentice Hall, 1998). You'll find plenty of helpful examples you can adapt for your PPC efforts.

Next, you'll fill in the web site you want people to end up visiting. Be sure to use a tracking link so you can make sure your keywords are actually paying off. (You can use a service like www.PPCAdvertisingManager.com to easily manage this.) That's what makes this form of advertising so great. If you are not getting a return on your investment, then you can quickly kill off the nonperforming keywords and keep the ones that are making you money or bringing you prospects.

And the last step? Set your daily or monthly spending budget, and set the maximum bids for your keywords. Voilà! You've now put your first classified ads online in front of millions of targeted prospects. Keep in mind, depending on which PPC service you're using, you may have to wait a few days for your ads to be approved and appear. But the wait can be well worth it. And with some services, your ads will appear within just minutes and you will get visitors to your web site within an hour. Exciting! Now that you've had a true crash course in this method, here are the top three pay-per-click search engines to start testing, in order of priority:

1. Google's Adwords (www.Google.com/adwords)
2. Overture (www.Overture.com)
3. FindWhat (www.FindWhat.com)

With literally hundreds of PPC search engines out there, the opportunity to get fresh eyes on your web site is endless (check out www.Pay PerClickSearchEngines.com for a comprehensive listing). If you want to become an overnight expert in pay-per-click advertising, I recommend Perry Marshall's web site www.DiscoverAdwords.com. It's an excellent how-to resource that will give you advanced strategies to help you succeed.

By the way, most network marketing companies provide you with a web site. But unfortunately, it's not always designed to sell. It's strange how most companies fall down in this department. If that's so for your company, then you may want to set up a new web site with your own sales materials, getting people to respond in whatever way you prefer—phone, e-mail, fax, online, mail, and so on.

Here's a bonus tip: If you are tired of telling people to go to your company web site with a long domain, like www.mygreatcompany.com/assoc /554523 and would prefer to send them to a short domain name like www.sallyswealth4u.com, then check out www.GoDaddy.com. You can buy a new domain name for about nine bucks, and then have it forwarded to your long company web site address.

SET IT AND FORGET IT: AUTORESPONDERS

How would you like to have 100 percent automatic marketing? While a truly 100 percent hands-off system is a fantasy, I can tell you that achieving a 98 percent automated marketing system is not, when you use something called autoresponders. An autoresponder is the Internet's equivalent of a fax-back system on steroids...lots and lots of steroids. All your prospects do is fill out a form on your web site or send a blank e-mail to a special address, and presto, your autoresponder system will send an e-mail out to them on autopilot. The system is completely hands-off for you once you program the autoresponder with your e-mail messages. (For an example of a down and dirty autoresponder sign-up form in action, visit www.InstantMLMSalesLetters.com and go about three-quarters of the way down the page. You'll see how I give away samples of my site for free when people simply enter a name and e-mail address.)

Now here's where it gets exciting and why I consider autoresponders one of my secret weapons. You can have the same autoresponder system set up to send your prospects a series of e-mails and messages, completely on autopilot and on a schedule you determine. You can send them e-mails for a week, or one a day for a year, or one a month, whatever you want to happen. This sequencing feature is what makes autoresponders extremely powerful. You only have to do the work once to set up the autoresponder messages and then they'll go out forever, until you pull the plug. I've tested many third-party autoresponder systems and highly recommend www.AutoresponderProspecting.com to get you started. It's very inexpensive and very easy to set up.

So exactly how should you add autoresponders into your network marketing business? I recommend you build three main autoresponder lists:

1. *Prospects and leads.* With this autoresponder, you can constantly communicate with your prospects and educate them about network marketing and your opportunity.

2. *Customers.* You should use this list to keep in touch with your existing customers and build a relationship on autopilot. Educate them on how to best use your product or service. Ask them for testimonials and questions. Encourage referrals. And even let them know about other things they can purchase from you.

3. *Downline.* Do you have a certain amount of training and education you want everyone in your team to get? Then use an autoresponder to help out. Not only can you make sure important information gets to each new team member, but you can also send out broadcast e-mails on a regular basis to remind your downline of conference calls, announcements, and other important events.

Over time, I have received many questions about e-mail prospecting, how to get past the spam filters, how to use autoresponders, and more. So if you want answers to any of those questions and step-by-step training on how to use autoresponders, plus a sequence of letters completely written for you, visit www.InstantMLMEmails.com for more details.

I've made tens of thousands of dollars using autoresponders in my business. Not a week goes by where I don't make money from something loaded into my autoresponder. It's a beautiful thing! All of the sorting, prospecting, and selling is done by my autoresponder, not me. Thanks to technology, the e-mails look like they are coming directly from me and are even personalized with the first name of the recipient.

With that having been said, do not be overwhelmed by the idea of creating a massive amount of messages. Even though some of my autoresponder sequences send messages for over a year, I certainly didn't start that way. I added a new message every week, or once a month. If you do the same, before you know it you'll have a great autoresponder making you sales and appointments month in, month out.

Here's an important tip: Most people ask for only a name and e-mail address when creating autoresponder sign-up forms for their web site. This is a huge mistake—and one I used to make. With spam filters proliferating and the government slowly getting more and more involved in regulating e-mail, you should be capturing your prospect's complete contact information. That includes address, phone number, fax number, and the like. If you're putting all your eggs into one basket, you're going to be in big trouble with e-mail delivery problems down the road. I'm slowly collecting full contact information for all of my prospects now, and you should, too.

THE INTERNET GOES OFF-LINE:
POSTCARD PROSPECTING

Okay, so in a chapter about Internet methods, why am I talking about using postcards in your business? Simple. Thanks to the Internet you can now use inexpensive, effective direct mail in your business and never have to touch a postcard or lick a stamp. Using the United Status Postal Service, you can now send dirt-cheap postcards right from your home computer (visit www.USPS.com/netpost for details). The only catch is that the recipient has to be in the United States, although I predict that will change in the future. With e-mail not being as reliable as it used to be and with spam on the rise, your mailbox is less overflowing than it ever has been. In fact, I just read a study showing direct-mail response rates at an all-time high. So what are you waiting for?

You should use postcards for the same three groups of people I mentioned in the preceding section. In addition to those groups, here are a few more ideas to get your mind going.

- Send a thank-you to new customers.
- Send a postcard for Thanksgiving, Christmas, Hanukkah, Halloween, and so forth.
- Promote a special discount your company might be running on joining your business or buying products.
- Announce a new product.
- Ask for testimonials.
- Wish people a happy birthday.
- Send out a monthly postcard newsletter.
- Remind your downline of their goals with pictures of cars, exotic locations, and so on.

Use your imagination and you can come up with many different postcard ideas. Simply decide what the end result is (phone call, visit to web site, e-mail to your autoresponder, or others), and then work backwards. The more creative you get, the more fun you and your recipients will have. And if you're using these postcards with a cold list of prospects, this is a wonderful way to have them raise their hands and contact you once you get them interested.

If you're serious about cutting through your prospects' clutter and really catching their attention, I highly recommend adding postcards to your business. I invite you to stop by my www.PostcardProspecting.com web site to get more details on using postcards in your network marketing business.

YOU'RE THE EXPERT: WRITING YOUR OWN PRODUCT

This method—writing your own information product—is one that many of the network marketing gurus use to build their downline on the back end. They'll sell you generic training tapes, books, or CDs on the front end, and then on the back end, they'll invite you to join their team.

It works. Why? Because you look up to them as the expert since they made themselves published authors. And people are always attracted to the leaders and experts. So how can you leverage being The Expert? Easy. Create your own information product. Although you can make CDs, tapes, books, binders, manuals, and more, the easiest, quickest way to publish your own product is by creating an e-book. Simply put, it's just like a regular book, except when people buy it or pick up a free copy, they download it and read it on their computers.

But what should you write about? That depends on your goal. If you want your e-book to bring you new prospects, I would pick a niche and write an e-book about how to earn extra money for that niche. For example, my background is as a professional theater performer and director. So if I wanted to recruit other theater professionals, I could easily write an e-book called *Attention Actors! 5 Proven Ways You Can Earn a Second Paycheck—Without Waiting Tables or Even Leaving Your House!*

Or, if I wanted to sell a health product that would help people avoid cancer (or any other ailment your product or service helps to relieve), then I could write an e-book on *The #1 Way to Live a Cancer-Free Life!* For a long-distance service: *How to Save 36% on Your Long-Distance Bill Every Single Month—100% Legally!*

Got the idea? Your goal should be to write to one specific group of people—a certain niche or occupation. Provide them with useful information that speaks to them. And throughout your e-book, gradually make the case for why your product or opportunity is the only one that solves their problems.

Relax, this is a lot easier than it sounds. In fact, even if you can't write, can't type, or flunked high school English class, you can quickly and easily write your own e-book in as little time as seven days. A friend of mine, Jim Edwards, has an excellent web site that helps you create your new e-book in just one week. If you want to be considered an expert on a topic, I highly recommend www.OneWeekeBook.com. Or, if you want someone to ghostwrite your e-book, visit www.eLance.com to hire a writer for a few hundred bucks.

Regardless of which method you choose, the moment you publish your own e-book, you almost instantly become an expert on whatever topic you write about. And that newfound celebrity can create a flood of profits for your business.

THAT TIME OF THE MONTH: PUBLISH A NEWSLETTER OR E-ZINE

The next few Internet methods are going to be short and sweet, but don't discount them. They are just as potent and profit-producing as anything else I've taught you so far! And this method—publishing your own newsletter—is no exception.

You can publish either via direct mail or online. You can use the same USPS service I recommended earlier to send full newsletters, in addition to just postcards, or you can publish online. If you go the online route, I highly recommend you still collect full contact information when people sign up for your e-zine. If you want more help with your online newsletter, check out www.StartYourOwnEzine.com for free resources and tips.

Of course, you can also make sure people get your newsletter by sending one out monthly to your existing customers, prospects, and downline members. That way, you aren't selling your newsletter on the front end, but are using it to regularly keep in touch with your contacts once you establish an initial relationship.

Newsletters are a powerful way to bond with your customers. Be sure to pick a format and topic, then stick to it. And also be sure to mix in a dose of your personal life and current events. It's a lot more entertaining to read that way. If you are consistent in your publishing cycle, people will come to rely on you.

But beware! The number one crime you can commit is to be boring in your marketing. I publish a free newsletter, "Instant MLM Profit Secrets" (available at www.InstantMLMProfitSecrets.com), full of articles, tips, resources, and other fun things you can use to grow your business and get more enjoyment out of it. I found that when I injected a lot more personality into it, the results were much more successful. Now, not only do I talk about business, but I discuss holidays and trips, host contests, and even talk about my personal life. When you start your newsletter, make sure it's informative and fun for the reader!

CAN YOU HEAR ME NOW?: ONLINE AUDIO

Let's face it. Not every prospect or customer responds to the same means of communication. Some like e-mail, some prefer to receive letters in the regular mail, and still others like to actually hear your voice before responding. My friend and a brilliant marketer, Stephen Pierce, refers to this as "multidimensional marketing." You should be contacting your prospects, customers, and downline every way you can.

In the past two years, multimedia has been hitting the Internet in a big way. It has been around for a while, but the technology has gotten to a point where even people on dial-up modems can hear and understand multimedia presentations on web sites. That means you can now quickly and easily publish your own voice on a web site or send it in an e-mail.

For the last year, I've been adding audio into my online marketing and I've seen great results. For example, go to my main web site, www.Instant MLMSalesLetters.com, and look at the testimonials. You'll see that not only do I include a picture of the person, but I also have a button you can click to hear their testimonial. It's a lot more believable when you can listen to the person you're reading and seeing. Plus, they didn't have to do anything special to record the testimonial. I use an awesome service at www.InstantOnlineAudio.com that allows me to give anyone a special toll-free number they can call and record their comments. Instantly, that recording becomes available for me to use online. Pretty neat, huh? That same service allows me to send online "audio postcards" and do a number of other impressive things with audio. Be sure to check it out and think of ways you can be using audio to communicate with people.

LIGHTS, CAMERA, ACTION: ONLINE VIDEO

Yes, the time has come when you can easily put video on your web site.

You know how effective infomercials are, right? Well, imagine having your own little mini-infomercial posted on your web site. Not only can your prospects and customers hear you, but they can actually see you talking to them.

Up until very, very recently, you'd have to spend thousands of dollars on equipment and software that would post video to your web site. But a new service has just been launched that is changing all the rules. Check it out at www.InstantOnlineVideo.com. Instead of spending thousands of dollars on equipment that takes you months to figure out, all you need to do is buy a $40 webcam and you're set. Pretty amazing what technology can do for your business now!

So there you have them—the seven best Internet prospecting tools. Each one allows you to leverage your time once and benefit forever. Pick the one you're most interested in and get started. Once you have it figured out and working, move on to another and another. If you want to share your successes or have additional questions, I encourage you to contact me at www.InstantMLMSalesLetters.com. To your success!

Chris Zavadowski has gained top recognition online and in the network marketing community for his unique ways of helping others grow their Internet businesses and downlines. Through his training tools and speaking engagements, he has taught thousands his successful ways of working with the Internet. Unlike many other business-building tools available, all of Chris' marketing resources are grounded in solid direct-marketing principles.

Having been online since 1987, Chris is best known for his breakthrough web site, www.InstantMLMSalesLetters.com. The Internet's first-ever collection of generic fill-in-the-blank sales letter templates for those in network marketing, The "Instant MLM Sales Letters" collection provides you with all of the sales letters you need for prospecting, downline training, and product/service sales.

It's been called "truly brilliant" and "the most user-friendly, no-nonsense down-line-building tool around."

Chris is also the creator of www.InstantMLMEmails.com, a multimedia course that shows you step-by-step exactly how to get your prospecting e-mails past the spam filters and how to put your e-mail prospecting on 100 percent autopilot. He also developed www.InstantMLMScripts.com, a best-of-the-best collection of proven scripts to use when prospecting, calling leads, setting up appointments, and more, and www.PostcardProspecting.com, an audio-video course teaching you how to use low-cost direct-mail postcards and your computer to build your business without touching a single stamp.

A Phi Beta Kappa Virginia Tech alumnus, Chris holds degrees in both music and theater. Also a professional director, actor, and musical director, he has performed and directed in venues ranging from the Kennedy Center to his own solo shows to Signature Theatre.

Chris currently lives in Centreville, Virginia, and he welcomes your feedback. You can contact him and sign up for his free seven-part "Insiders Secrets from MLM Millionaires" mini-course at www.InstantMLMSalesLetters.com.

CHAPTER
29

The Internet Can Replace
Your Warm Market

Max Steingart

The first thing a person is usually asked to do when joining a network marketing company is to make a list of the people they know. The list includes your family members, friends, neighbors, and people with whom you work. The list is called your warm market. After the list is made, you're supposed to tell everyone on it about your new business venture or products. This has been the standard method for starting since network marketing began.

If you're not comfortable going to your warm market, don't feel alone. Most people don't like going to their warm market for one of several reasons. Whether these reasons are valid or not, you may feel this way because:

- Your spouse won't let you.
- You're not going to recommend something you're not sure about.
- You don't have any credibility with the people you know.
- You've been in so many networking companies that you don't have friends.
- You don't feel comfortable trying to make money off your friends.
- You don't want to sell to your friends.

If you can't or won't talk about your business to the people you know, your only other option is to talk to strangers. Talking to strangers about your business exposes you to rejection. The sales cliché "You have to go through 100 no's to get a yes" is familiar to almost everyone in sales.

The Internet changes everything because it gives you access to an unlimited number of people. It also makes it easy to identify the best people to contact. It's not uncommon for you to get 8 out of the 10 people you connect with on the Internet to look at your business. The Internet can replace your warm market as the place to go to tell people about your business or products.

Cindy is one of my favorite online success stories. Her organization increased by more than a thousand people in three months as a result of someone whom she met on the Internet. Here's how it happened and how it can happen to you, too.

Cindy was a 32-year-old postal worker who lived in a small town. She really didn't like working at the post office. Her goal was to make enough money in her part-time networking business so she could quit her full-time post office job. She wanted to spend more time riding her horse. Having recently moved from New Jersey to Florida, Cindy didn't know anyone in town. She didn't have a warm market. In fact, the only people she knew in Florida were her fellow co-workers at the post office. And no one there wanted to hear about her new business.

She'd heard from other people in her company that people were using instant messaging on the Internet to meet other people. A few of the people she talked to about business networking on a computer said they were using it to find dates, too. Cindy knew that if other people could find someone online to talk to about their business, she could, too. So she purchased a computer with the sole purpose of using it to meet people.

The first thing everyone is required to do when signing up for any of the free instant messaging systems (Yahoo!, ICQ, MSN, AOL) is to create a screen name. Most people use a variation of their birth name when they initially sign up. Cindy learned very quickly that her choice of screen name would influence the content of her instant message conversations. A good screen name makes people curious about who you are and what you do.

Cindy chose CS33407 as her first screen name because her initials were CS and her zip code was 33407. Whenever she had an instant message conversation, the person always asked about her screen name. Why CS33407? What did CS33407 represent? What was the significance of the number 33407? These questions became a predictable part of every instant message conversation she had.

When Cindy changed her screen name to TheCynergist2005, people still asked questions about her name. Why TheCynergist2005? What did TheCynergist mean? What was going to happen in 2005? Cindy's answers to these questions made people interested in learning more about what she did. "Synergy is a combined action or operation between people that is mutually advantageous to all the parties involved. I enjoy connecting successful people together in an enterprise that changes their lives. I really like what I do" was her answer every time someone inquired about her choice of screen name.

"I'm working with a company that is creating a growing stream of residual income for me. By the year 2005, I expect my income to be large enough so I don't have a single worry about finances and I can be living on a large horse ranch in Ocala, Florida" was her answer when people asked about the number 2005 in her screen name.

It's possible to create and use more than one screen name. A screen name like MentorForHealth would encourage people to talk about health issues. The screen name MentorForWealth would invite conversations of an economic nature. The screen name you create acts like a magnet and attracts targeted people to you.

When Cindy created another screen name, SuccessGal2005, the nature of her instant message conversations changed. What do you do? What made you successful? Could you help me become successful? These were questions she routinely received when she sent an instant message to anyone. People still wanted to know the significance of the number 2005. But they were also curious and interested in knowing what she did to become successful.

One of Cindy's friends, Donna, created the screen name The-LifestyleChanger. Within five seconds of signing on to Yahoo! Messenger she received an instant message from a man in her area. His opening instant message to her was, "Hello, you've got an interesting screen name. What do you do?" This was a question she would be asked over and over again.

Donna responded with an answer that she would use repeatedly. "Hello. I work with other women. I show them how to create an additional income stream working from home that dramatically changes their lifestyle. Would you know any women who might be interested in something like this?"

The man answered, "As a matter of fact I do. Would you have some time later today to speak to my wife? She is looking for something to do from home." Twenty minutes later, Donna was on the phone with the couple talking about her business.

The Internet opened doors for Cindy and gave her access to more people than she could ever meet on her own. The more people Cindy met online who became involved in her business, the more she realized how valuable a resource it was. Cindy explained how the Internet gave her an advantage:

"If I walked into a room full of strangers for some networking, I would talk to a lot of people who just wouldn't be interested in what I had to say. It's unavoidable. I'd live the sales cliché you have to go through 100 no's for every yes. The Internet changes everything. Imagine walking into a room full of strangers. And I'm not talking about Internet chat rooms. This room has millions of people in it—and everyone in the room is walking around with a sign on their back that tells you all about them. I can pick out the best people to talk to based on the information they provide me with. It's as easy to send an instant message to someone who shares my interests and values as it is to pick a green M&M out of a bowl of mixed candy."

Cindy liked instant messaging people who shared her passion for horses. It was easy for her to talk to them. She could start a conversation with anyone by sending the instant message, "Hello, my name is Cindy. I have a four-year-old appaloosa stallion. What kind of horse do you have?"

Cindy was making friends online with horse lovers who were teachers, school principals, and successful business owners. Many of her new friends were interested in what Cindy was doing and signed up in her business.

Cindy always looked for people to instant message who knew a lot of other people. Her sponsor had told her, "Your success in business is going to be based on the number of people you can talk to, and the caliber of the people you talk to. People who know a lot of other people are your best choices."

The best example of Cindy's online success occurred when she met Roger. Roger was a very successful networker who was as passionate about horses as Cindy was. Roger was living the networking dream. His four-year-old business was generating $2,000 a month in commissions. The extra income made a big difference in his lifestyle.

Cindy liked instant messaging Roger. He recommended the names of books to read about networking and other resources that would help her. They put each other on their buddy list so they could each see when the other was online.

Roger looked forward to talking to Cindy. She had a great sense of humor and appreciated all of his jokes. He found it refreshing to talk to someone who was as enthusiastic about her networking business as he was about his. He enjoyed passing along business tips to her because she always acted on what he said.

Roger's company changed its commission structure three weeks after he met Cindy. He calculated that his income would be reduced from $2,000 to $700 a month, and he wasn't happy. The day he received his adjusted commission check, Roger saw Cindy on his buddy list and sent her an instant message: "Hi, do you have time to talk on the phone?"

Roger was interested in learning more about Cindy's business. He needed to find something to replace his lost income, and he wanted to act quickly. He knew in the short time of their online friendship that he would enjoy working with her. Roger knew there were numerous people who were unhappy with his company's restructured commission and were looking to make a change. He contacted Terry, one of the most successful people in his company, and told him about Cindy's business.

Terry's mid-six-figure annual income had been reduced, too. He had an organization of more than 150,000 people who had been negatively affected by the commission changes.

Terry always liked Roger and saw an opportunity to replace his missing income by getting involved with Cindy's company. In the following four months, Terry and Roger added a thousand people to Cindy's business.

Cindy watched in amazement as her business and income grew as a result of their activity.

Cindy had connected with someone who knew a lot of people. She became known as the "Internet Queen" in her company. She was able to quit her job at the post office and spend more time riding her horse. Cindy's lack of a warm market did not prevent her from achieving success in her business. Instant messaging provided her with an alternative way to meet new people. The Internet replaced her warm market.

Today, there are hundreds of millions of people using instant messaging. Yahoo! claims to have 237 million people using its instant messaging system. ICQ and MSN both claim to have 180 million users on theirs. AOL follows with over 90 million users.

For some people, it's easier to start an instant message conversation and make a new friend than it is to go to their current friends. The Internet can replace your warm market as the best place to go when you're ready to build your networking business. The new three-foot rule in network marketing is: When you're sitting in front of your computer, you're within three feet of the online world when you know where to find people and how to use instant messaging.

Warning: Instant messaging is a valuable tool when used properly. Sending out mass instant messages with a blatant sales pitch to someone—or spimming, as it's called on the Internet—is the same as e-mail spamming. It's not the smart thing to do—it will get you into trouble and not produce the results you want. In many states, it's against the law. Sending singular sales messages via instant messaging is also considered spimming.

Max Steingart used instant messaging to build a network marketing organization of more than 7,000 people in two years. One of his students put 1,000 people into her business in four months as a result of using his system.

Max is no stranger to introducing new computer applications to people. He has owned several successful businesses, including an *Inc.* 500 publishing company. He's a highly quoted author, a professional speaker, and an accomplished sailboat racer. AT&T called him a visionary of the computer industry.

Max has helped people use computers to connect with other people since 1975 when he introduced an innovative computer system to the yacht brokerage industry. *Money* magazine called him "The Match Maker" because his computer-generated lists made it easy for boat owners to connect with people interested in buying a boat. Today, every major yacht brokerage firm in the world uses elements of his system to conduct their business.

In 1989, Max was named "The Success Story of the Year" by *Inc.* magazine. Since 1996, Max has shown network marketers how to use instant messaging to connect with other people on the Internet. Max has been a keynote speaker at many network marketing conventions. His Internet presentations have been described as entertaining, eye-opening, educational, and visually dazzling. His interactive training CD "Shaking Hands on the Internet" and training course "Success Online: Relationship Marketing in the New Millennium" are an essential part of any networker's Internet toolbox. To download your free ebook, "Prospecting on the Internet with Instant Messaging," visit his web site, www.successway.com/bonus.

CHAPTER
30

Building Your Network Marketing Business with Trade Shows, Booths, and Fairs

Dr. Don and Mary Lou Vollmer

There are many places throughout North America and internationally where one can set up a booth to sell network marketing products and generate interested prospect leads. These events also provide your company, your products, and/or your services with greater visibility and offer distributors the opportunity to generate income. In this chapter, the different types of shows are covered individually.

There are several factors to consider when deciding whether to participate in a show or booth. The first consideration is location. Do you have to travel by air or train to the show? This adds to the expense and must be accounted for in the budget. Can you stay at home in the evening, or do you need to pay extra for lodging and meals? What are the other costs involved in the city you will be in? New York City is going to be more expensive than Denver, for example.

The second consideration is the cost of the show itself. Some of the trade shows can charge several thousand dollars for a 10-by-10-foot space. Other shows, such as a local fair, may be only $100. Some small events may have booths or tabletop space available for little or no investment. Evaluation of the end result is critical when making this type of financial commitment. It boils down to this: What will be the final cost of each lead or sale generated?

The next consideration would be attendance. How many people are projected to attend the show you are considering, and what are the exhibit hours? Note that $1,000 for a one-day show with four hours of legitimate busy time and eight hours of scheduled time may actually be less cost-effective than a show that costs $3,000 for three and a half days and four times as much contact with attendees. What types of products will appeal to this audience? How will the staff dress? Will a show special or a drawing for a prize be helpful? These are all questions to answer in the planning stages for the show.

How many people will be participating in the show booth expenses is another consideration. If you share a booth with four people and split the costs, it can be more cost-effective for everyone. When this is done there must be specific guidelines to have harmony among all participants.

Does the show you are considering allow products to be sold on the exhibit floor? Selling products directly from the booth helps to defray some of the expenses. Depending on the location, a tax license may be required for the days of the show.

What will be the measure of success for the show? Are you looking for total sales or lead generation? Set up the parameters for the goals you want to achieve at the show before you go. Another decision is the show message. What message do you want your exhibit to portray? Are you going to focus on one product line or have several, and how will these be displayed?

To recap, consider the following decisions when deciding on participating in a particular show:

- Location
- Type of show
- Budget
- Attendance
- Probability of sales
- Probability of leads

PROPER PLANNING

Create a budget for the show and set up a plan for preparation. One suggestion is to set up deadlines on a year-at-a-glance calendar. If deadlines are missed, the cost increases. Most shows have one deadline for registration, then another for renting carpet, and so forth. There is also a deadline for electrical and for drayage if you use shipping and setup by the exhibit hall. We have found that it is more economical to set up ourselves. When possible, we take our own display, along with everything we need to create a functional meeting. In many cities, the union requirements must be honored. You can do many things yourself , but two-wheelers are usually banned. Exhibit halls charge for everything—wastebaskets, vacuuming, chairs, and the like. We usually rent two tall draped tables, carpet, and one stool (if the show is local, we take our own stool). We take everything else, including a wastebasket and equipment for cleaning the carpet. This is a list of things we find helpful to bring with us to a show:

Change.	Scissors.
Clipboards.	Scotch tape.
Cover for tables when exhibit hall is closed.	Shimmery fabric for tabletop (gold and metallic blue are good).
Lead-generation information cards.	Stapler.
Lights with extra lightbulb.	Staple remover.
Pens.	Vacuum for cleaning carpet.
Pins.	Velcro.
Posters for display.	Wastebasket.
Products for display.	Wastebasket liners.
Receipt book.	

LOCATION, LOCATION, LOCATION

It is very important to have a good location in the exhibit hall. Study the traffic plan and decide what the flow of attendees will be. We have found a highly visible location close to the entrance and toward the center of the hall usually has a good flow of people. We also like corner booths if the cost is not prohibitive, as this location gives you traffic from several directions at once. We try to not be next to a direct competitor. And if you know someone who has a great deal of traffic to their area, locating next to them is fabulous.

Part of the success for any show is getting people to your booth. Some statistics suggest that between 50 and 80 percent of the attendees know which booths they will see before they arrive at the show. Creating ideas to make your booth a stop on their exhibit hall rounds will increase your traffic. Contact potential attendees at least three times prior to the show to generate traffic to your booth. We always do two mailings; we offer a show special and a free gift for stopping by our booth. We mail this to leads we received from previous shows. Our first mailing is a letter about the show special, including our booth number. We enclose a business card, requesting they bring it to the booth for their free gift. Our second mailing is a postcard with our booth number and a reminder to stop by for their free gift.

DISPLAYS

There are many types of display setups available to fit almost everyone's needs. The factors to be considered are: the number of uses per year, local availability or need to transport on an airplane, the type of shows involved, and the overall cost.

- *Simple display.* This would be for a table booth used for a small show, such as a church booth or health club. This may be appropriate for a once or twice a year need. Office supply stores such as Office Depot, Office Max, or Staples have a variety of inexpensive displays. There are board displays that can be purchased for under $10 and could be a fit for limited use for those with a lower budget. There are also sturdier and more attractive three- to six-panel interlocking displays. We have this model for local use where space is limited. It can be used as a stand-alone model to stand on the floor behind the table, or it will also fit on a six-foot table. The fabric panels readily accept posters, signs, or anything that has Velcro tape added to the back. This allows flexibility of your display usage.

- *Higher-quality display.* Banner stands with graphics of your choice have become popular. They fold down like a window shade and are very compact for traveling. They come in various widths, and a halogen light can be added. The banner-style display can augment any other type of display or be used in multiples as your primary display. Their cost is somewhat higher and would be recommended for those people who do a considerable number of shows a year.

- *Collapsible displays.* This can be table-top height or taller for a freestanding display. There is a great advantage because it folds into a compact container. If you are traveling by air, a smaller container (without wheels) can possibly be checked as a piece of luggage. Larger display cases would require additional airline costs. It is a good idea to check the dimensions with the airline you travel with the most. The advantage of this type of display for multiple annual usages is that it looks professional and can save you considerable rental costs.

With the larger shows, you will need two draped tables, one for the display and one for materials, products, and the like. We place one table toward the back of the booth space and one table on the side. We want it to be open and inviting for people to come into the area. A tall stool can be used in an area that permits optimal flow of traffic. This allows everyone to take turns sitting when the traffic is slower. The tall stool is closer to eye level and you can readily stand up to be with someone who shows interest. If you are doing only one major trade show a year, you have an option of renting various types of displays that can save you the initial costs plus the handling and shipping of the display. Skyline Exhibits, a worldwide company (www.skyline-exhibits .com), has the largest variety of displays. You also may inquire about any used units from any of the display stores in your area. The display we purchased was a used and refurbished display, and we have been using it for over three years.

Once you arrive at the show, it's time to set up your display and make it as attractive as possible. We like the display to be eye-catching and not cluttered. A nice clean display is attractive and inviting. Design your graphics to be bold and easy to read. Large eye-catching signs in bold print across the display should outline benefits for the participants. This will draw people to your booth. Some statistics show that signs with a red border are read 26 percent faster than others. Who you are and what you have to offer should be the main components. An attractive display of the products you are selling always invites curiosity. We usually display products on different levels set off by a sparkly gold or metallic blue fabric. Mirrors and shelves are also good for eye-catching displays.

THE FUN BEGINS

The booth is set up and the exhibition opens. There are several keys for making this a success. Have fun! Make this the only place you want to be today and convey that to the prospects. Dress professionally. This will vary with the type of show. Some shows will be khakis and golf shirts and others will be suits; dress accordingly. Since you are on your feet most of the day, the choice of shoes can make a huge difference in how comfortable you are. In this case, choose comfort over fashion so you don't need to limp out of the exhibit hall at the end of the day. Overdressing or underdressing can be equally disastrous. Stand at the front of the booth with your clipboard and pen in hand and invite people in with a handshake and a greeting. You need to be outgoing and have a short sentence to invite people into the booth to show them what you have to offer. Greet them and ask questions—then listen to the answers. You have an average of 60 seconds in a show to hear what the prospect wants and show someone that you have what they are looking for. Three to five minutes is the maximum time you can hold their attention. People generally have a limited amount of time and an agenda. Success will be greater if you meet their needs rather than your own. Ask the questions that will get them to tell you about themselves and cannot be answered with a yes or a no. If you have a product that can be sampled on the spot, that is always a good opener. Tell stories; this increases the odds that they will remember you. Summarize frequently and talk about the benefits rather than the features of your products. Before they leave the booth have a solid commitment for a follow-up time and a contact person and be certain to fulfill that commitment.

We suggest using lead-generation cards that are printed on card stock so that people can fill them out anywhere if there is a rush. You want them to include the information that is specific to your product or service. It is also good to have the basics such as name, address, phone and fax numbers, e-mail, and best time to call, who to speak with, and so on. We also ask about special interests and if they have an interest in the financial opportunity.

Some of the larger professional shows have lead-generation machines. The participants have a card with their name on it that resembles a credit card. When this is scanned through the machine, it prints out their basic information, such as name, address, telephone, e-mail, and fax. These sheets can be stapled to your lead-generation cards where you will have more personal information. We highly recommend these machines. Using one avoids the possibility of getting home and not being able to read someone's handwriting. It also allows you more time to talk with each person as they aren't wasting time writing down mundane information.

We limit the amount of things we hand out. You'll quickly see that most of your handouts go right in the trash, or they hit that round receptacle when the participant gets home. We typically hand out one sheet of information and make certain that it contains our contact information. We mail the information we deem important immediately so prospects have something they will remember. We have business cards available, and also attach them to everything we sell. We print our business cards and have our picture on them. We also use these in every mailing in the belief that will jog their memory. Another person we work with uses very bright-colored cards that she has printed. They are attractive and she feels they are less likely to be thrown away.

THE FORTUNE IS IN THE FOLLOW-UP

After-the-show follow-up is an important element to ensure your success. We get a package of information to each individual immediately the week we return from the show. We enclose a letter thanking them for stopping by along with some of the information they requested at the show. If you consider your prospect to be a potential star for you and your company, consider mailing Priority Mail. This method of delivery is always opened. We send out a second mailing very soon after the first mailing. This is the time to send your four-color brochures and one or two information sheets. You can follow up a few days later with more information that fits the particular individual's interests. Mail only a few pieces at a time; otherwise everything goes into the read-later pile. At this time, a personal follow-up call is critical.

Reintroduce yourself and remind your prospect/customer of the company you represent. Then ask if this is a good time to talk for a few minutes. Ask what they liked best about the information you sent. If they haven't looked it over yet, set up a definite follow-up time. Ask if there are any questions and answer them. Then ask for the order. Follow-ups on this are similar to what your procedure is currently.

Some of the research on shows says that you need seven contacts in the next year. We have three immediately, two before the show the next year, and a drip campaign with information of interest throughout the year. We use traditional mail, phone, fax, and e-mail to communicate periodically with these prospects. For those people who use e-mail it is a simple and effective way to communicate. We send out newsletters with pertinent information to these leads, usually on a monthly basis if they have e-mail. We periodically mail pertinent information to leads, and also make occasional follow-up phone calls. We generally categorize the prospects into A, B, or C leads. We have less follow-up with the C leads.

We place our leads into a database manager in the computer. Very often we take our laptop to the show and enter the leads in the evening or on the plane home. By the time we get home, we are ready to do a mail merge and print letters and envelopes.

Occasionally, we will have others wishing to generate leads share in the cost of the booth, even though they have not attended the show. When that happens, we share the leads equally. Everyone gets the same number of A leads, B leads, and C leads. When we are working the show in this manner, we explain that our business partner, Jane Doe, may be calling them to follow up. In those cases, we have follow-up stationery and business cards with all of our names on them. This avoids confusion for the prospect. For shows that require air travel and hotel costs, this method of sharing expenses serves to control the budget.

Sharing a booth with people in another downline can present some challenges. Make certain that each individual gets their share of contacts and no one person takes over a space in the booth. For booths with multiple participants, set up a schedule that outlines each participant's scheduled times.

Niche market trade shows are a great way to develop a customer base in a specific market. All of the professional organizations have shows throughout the United States and often worldwide. We have found that many times the smaller meetings are much more profitable. If your product line fits into a niche market, these shows are usually very successful.

There are also regional shows such as county and state fairs. Often local chambers of commerce sponsor fairs for their members to tout their businesses. Many local areas have festivals or picnics. Other places to check out the possibility of a table would be at health clubs, schools, and churches.

CONCLUSION

There are some very significant advantages for participating with trade shows, booths, and fairs. You have the opportunity to have people coming to you for your product or service. This can save you a considerable amount of time and automatically make cold leads warm, possibly even hot. Book a show today, be prepared, have fun, and prosper.

Thanks to network marketing, Don Vollmer is a retired dentist and Mary Lou Vollmer is a retired dental hygienist. They were able to sell their dental practice and retire on the income generated from their network marketing opportunity.

They began their network marketing careers in the early 1980s and quickly moved to the top position in that company, winning two Cadillacs along the way. In 1989 they began with their present company, Oxyfresh Worldwide, where they are regional directors and members of the advisory board of directors. They speak nationally and internationally, championing others to achieve the same financial and personal freedom they enjoy through network marketing. When not supporting their ever-growing organization, the Vollmers now live a lifestyle of choice, traveling and spending time with their family. To learn more about the Vollmers, visit www.oxyfreshww.com/donaldv or e-mail mlvollmer@castlepines.net.

CHAPTER
31

Party Your Way to the Top
of Network Marketing!

Jan Ruhe

There are several ways to build a network marketing company. The way that made me a fortune was through home parties. Talking one-on-one, building relationships, and creating rapport is the slow road to success, as far as I am concerned. Relationships grow over time, when trust is built. Find a company that has great products. Fall in love with your products and share them! Fall in love with your opportunity and share it! And then, the critical part is to help others do the same!

Here's a strategy that has worked well for me: Spend the first two weeks of the month selling your company's products and spend the last two weeks heavily recruiting those who express an interest in your income opportunity. Focus on getting 52 or more home parties scheduled every year. Put the word out that you have eight openings a month, two a week. Book backwards—that is, start booking way out, asking for hosts to pick a date in December, and book up December, then November, then October, and so on. When you get to your parties, announce that you are booked for the rest of the year and have a waiting list for hosts to have parties for you, should you get a cancellation. By creating this posture, you will be looked upon as a very serious network marketer. People want what they can't have. It takes focus and desire. Do what others won't so you will have what others don't have! At your parties, make sure to rebook the host for another party later in the year or for the following year, whenever you have availability.

The more home parties you hold, the more you will realize that, unfortunately, so few people are fired up about anything in life. The more successful you are, the more excited and fired up you will become and the more you will begin to magnetize others to you who want what you have. The excitement and happiness in your life will attract others who want these qualities in their lives! Become a perpetual student of our great profession. Book by book, seminar by seminar, CD by CD, begin to learn from different people about the joy of selling and the joy of empowering others to succeed. Realize how important personal growth and development is. Readers are leaders and leaders are readers. Plan to be a leader of thousands. Build your own dynasty and your own tribe of followers who will become leaders, too. After all, someone has to party for a living! Be eager to succeed.

Know that behind every sale, a reason or motive exists for your customer to buy. At a home party, motives vary from guest to guest. A specific product will usually appeal to only one or two of your customers' 10 most common buying motives. When you answer the question, "Which buying motives does my product or opportunity satisfy?" you can formulate a successful presentation around your product's benefits. Today's buyers all have a buying motive. There are 10 main motives why anyone buys anything. Structure your presentation around these and you will increase your sales at your parties. Here they are:

1. Desire for wealth.
2. Desire for health.
3. Desire for admiration from others.
4. Desire for gratification of some appetite.
5. Desire for amusement.
6. Desire for safety of self or dependents.
7. Desire for utility or use value.
8. Desire for self-improvement.
9. Desire for saving time, trouble, or worry.
10. Desire for comfort.

Knowing how to create value for your prospects and customers, why speak to them just one-on-one? That is certainly one way of doing the business. Although I do that, too, it's the slow way to build a network marketing business. Contrary to what some may say, you don't have to get rich slowly in network marketing! Sometimes, it can be a challenge to consistently give your presentations to at least one person a day. The benefit of having a home party is that you can give your presentations to 10 or more prospects at one time! Do the math! Prospecting one person a day equates to 365 prospects a year. With a home party, it's easy to speak with 10 or more prospects a week. Ten times 52 weeks equals 520 prospects, in addition to those whom you prospect daily! Doesn't that make a lot more sense? To increase that number, if you schedule and hold two home parties each week, you can see twice that many people, or more than 1,000 prospects in a year! To convert those suspects to prospects to recruits, you have to believe in what you are doing and present your products and opportunity enough times to find key leaders. Do enough home parties and you will succeed!

In the process of doing regular, weekly parties, some special sayings and stories have kept my spirit alive. Start collecting your own vitamins for your mind! Here are a few of my favorites:

- If you continue to do what you have always done, you will continue to get what you have always gotten.
- You can't heat an oven with snowballs.
- Network marketing is not a job. It's a way of life.
- There is a day that you get into network marketing, but nothing happens until the day network marketing gets into you.
- Don't let your convictions become your restrictions.
- Transfer regret into get, get, get.
- Be a go-giver as well as a go-getter.
- The 3 Ds of success are desire, dedication, determination.
- Go for a paycheck, not a playcheck.
- Don't be average. Be a champion.
- The top bananas get the most light.
- Normally a door does not slam open.
- "I will persist until I succeed."—Og Mandino
- "It's a funny thing about life; if you refuse to accept anything but the best, you very often get it."—Somerset Maugham

STEAM System. Get the fire of desire. To build your parties' attendance, ask for referrals using the STEAM System. To do this right, you will want to carry a special bag/purse/container with business cards, flyers, a pad and pen to capture names, and catalogs or any of your other team-building tools, including Scotch tape and pushpins. Always be prepared to put up a flyer on a bulletin board or tape a flyer onto a window or have your business tools to pass out into the world. One of the easiest words in network marketing to remember to use is the word *here* and just hand out your business tools along your daily path. Exit your house to prospect daily. While you are out and about prospecting every day and in every way, keep the word *steam* in your mind. When chatting at the store, in line with people, or in casual conversations during the day, always ask the STEAM System questions:

Ask: "Who do you know who is in *sales*? I am looking for some new distributors for a team I am building, and salespeople normally do really well on our team."

Ask: "Do you have children? Who is your child's favorite *teacher*? Or do you have a personal *trainer*? I am looking for some new distributors for a team I am building, and teachers and trainers normally do really well on our team."

Ask: "Who is the most *enthusiastic* person you know? Enthusiastic people normally succeed big time in what I do."

Ask: "Who do you know who has a positive attitude? Positive people generally do really well in what I do."

Ask: "Who do you know who needs some extra *money*? Boy, do I have a way for them to make it starting today!"

As you capture names, remember that the fortune is in the follow-up. Leads are hot for only 24 hours. Get right on them! You can't stroll to a goal. Get fired up to return calls, have conversations, set up meetings, e-mail your prospects, and in every way try to reach them within 24 hours of meeting them.

Use an easy, duplicable training system. The one I teach is the Go Diamond Training. How did you learn your multiplication facts? Most people were taught by memorization. Saying them over and over . . . 2×2 is 4, 2×3 is 6, and so on. Repetition is the mother of skill. Isn't that a relief that it doesn't fluctuate? It stays the same in every situation. No one changes it to reinvent the wheel. It's been around for years and still holds as true today as it did 100 years ago. There's no need to improve it or change it in any way. Some were taught multiplication tables by using flash cards. The Go Diamond Training is as simple as that! All you do is set up your 20 or so cards, using the template that I created. Plug in your own information and you have your training ready. It's always the same and always duplicable! The Go Diamond Training is put onto poster boards that you can pack in your suitcase. You can pass them out at meetings and expect that they will always get results. They are also available for a quick presentation on a table in a restaurant. Be smart. Do what works. You don't have to reinvent the wheel!

The way to the top in network marketing is to have thousands of distributors each doing a little bit. Keep your presentations at a home party to less than 20 minutes. Have your setup take less than five minutes. Watch your grammar and dress and use a word list to help you build a vocabulary that attracts people to join you. Here are some examples of words to make your own: absolute, abundance, accountable, accurate, admirable, affluent, ambitious, appreciate, attentive, awesome, believable, belong, bold, bountiful, brilliant, caring, certainty, cherish, clear, commitment, fantastic, gripping, and inspired.

Seek out those who are living the lifestyle and who have actually built a network marketing business from the ground up. They are a truly select group! Find mentors who will encourage you, who will lift you up and give you new ideas. Say over and over daily, "Abundance and prosperity are coming my way!" What your mind believes, you will achieve! Become the best upline you can be with a commitment to guide others to the top. When you promote leaders and make them successful, you will get everything you ever dreamed of attaining. Network marketing through party plans is the stuff that dreams are made of. Tell the host, "You get the people there, I'll do the rest!" And remember to always use the two words that everyone loves to hear: "you get"! These are the words that precede the benefits that your company offers.

People love to congregate, party, and entertain. Have your own home party and see how much fun it can be! The more you learn, the more you earn. Knowledge is not power; only action is power. So start taking massive action today. Plan ahead, work your plan, and go for greatness. Network marketing is not a job; it's a way of life. Live the lifestyle that network marketing promises for those who put their focus, energy, passion, love, determination, and desire to not be denied a fabulous future. If it's doable for one, it's doable for all. Jump into network marketing and get started. Make this the day you decide to make your life an incredible masterpiece through network marketing! Be the one who says, "I am so thankful I did!" instead of those who say, "I wish I had."

So, at your party, what will you serve? Do you know the sizzling soup recipe? In order to make a good soup, it is necessary to have the right ingredients. In network marketing, this means distributors who are excited about the business and who are also bringing in other excited distributors. Put them all into a huge pot with some water and assign each one a degree value. The values go like this: 5 degrees for those you sponsor, 10 degrees for those who you've sponsored sponsor, then 20 degrees for those who they sponsor, and 40 degrees for the ones that they, in turn, sponsor. Why do the degree levels increase with subsequent generations? Because if your third level is moving, they are heating up your soup and your second level is getting excited. This is firing up your first level and the team is sizzling! When you get all of these degrees of heat going, it won't be long before you have your own soup sizzling! Fill your soup pot with distributors who are excited about the business! Watch the temperature reach 300 degrees! As soon as possible, you'll want your distributors starting their own soup pots. Add some enthusiasm, empathy, understanding, and fun, and watch the soup continue to sizzle for years to come. Go for greatness! Take care of your future. After all, that is where you are going to spend the rest of your life! Happy networking!

Jan Ruhe is a living legend in the network marketing profession. In 2005, she celebrated 25 years in the same company. She has been the top-paid Discovery Toys Diamond distributor in the United States for many years. She has built a network marketing business by getting her first recruits, then building strong leaders direct to her. Her business has 22 legs wide, direct to her. In the 1990s, Jan was invited to speak at an Upline Masters Seminar. From that one 20-minute speech, she has been booked worldwide via word of mouth for years as a top trainer in network marketing. She has trained more than 75,000 distributors in the United States, Korea, South Africa, Hungary, Ireland, Scotland, England, and Canada. Jan has helped to create several millionaires in network marketing. She has been featured in magazines in Korea, Germany, the Netherlands, England, and the United States. She started with network marketing when she had two children, Sarah (age 4), Clayton (age 2), and baby Ashley was on the way! During her career, she was a single mother for four years and never let those years slow her down. Today, Sarah and Ashley are both leaders in her Discovery Toys business. Clayton holds three Colorado state football records, unbeaten for over a decade. All her children are champion young adults today! Jan became a millionaire in 1994, has taken the girls on a mother/daughter African safari, sent Sarah around the world to college on a cruise ship, built her dream home in Aspen, Colorado, and has college educated all three children from the income she has earned from her business. Today, Jan is considered the leading network marketing woman trainer in the world. She and her husband Bill travel to 11 countries a year teaching and training thousands of distributors how to succeed in network marketing.

For more information about network marketing by someone who has actually done the business from day one; who did not retire to become a trainer, but continues to run her own multimillion-dollar toy business with more than $300 million in sales, and who lights the path for millions of networkers worldwide through her seminars, books, and web page, please visit www.janruhe.com.

Jan has written eight books, some available in more than 10 languages. They include *The Master Presentation Guide*, *The Rhino Spirit*, *The Lady of the Rings*, *True Leadership* (with Art Burleigh), and *Go Diamond* (with Jayne Leach). Available as both book and CD are *Fire Up!*, *MLM Nuts $ Bolts*, and *Let's Party!*. *The Keys to Success* by Jan Ruhe and Jeff Roberti is on CD. All are available at www.janruhe.com.

CHAPTER 32

How to Use Direct Mail to Promote Your Network Marketing Program

Larry Chiappone

C an you build a successful network marketing business using direct mail? Why do you think that if you mail 10,000, 20,000, or even 100,000 brochures, you will be rich? Why do you think you should get even one reply? Do you respond to every piece of mail you receive? Do you even look at every piece of mail you receive? And if you do, if you were given a quiz 10 minutes after you looked at your mail, would you remember every piece you received?

Most people use direct mail in a haphazard manner. They just mail out their offer to some untargeted list of people they think are prospects and then sit back and wait for the responses to come pouring in. But, guess what? They don't!

Let's look at the reality of the situation for a moment. The Direct Mail Marketing Association studies have concluded that most direct mail fails to produce the initial results to earn back the cost of the promotion in the first place. So why do it?

My experience points to the fact that direct mail for the network marketing industry is the most cost-effective, time-saving, least-rejection method known to man today! It's the way you use direct mail that makes all the difference. Direct mail should be considered an ongoing, never-ending promotional method. Too many networkers use direct mail once or maybe once in a while, instead of employing an ongoing promotional system. Of course, when direct mail is used only once or just once in a while, the Direct Mail Marketing Association has concluded that most mailing campaigns will fail.

Too many network marketers do not use direct mail wisely, and consequently think it is too expensive or just doesn't work. So the question becomes, how can you use direct mail to promote your network marketing program effectively? You can start immediately by changing your philosophy on what direct mail can do and can't do, then develop a six-month mailing campaign to promote your program, with a firm commitment to stick to it!

Your campaign should start with creating your own promotion for the program you are endorsing. I recommended that you use postcards to generate leads. Instead of using the same promotions that hundreds of others in your company may be using, be different from the crowd. Keep it simple. Too many mistakenly think that success in direct mail is a function of simply presenting a glitzy offer that appears to come from a well-established company.

People like to deal with people. So, develop a totally separate postcard that you and only you are using to differentiate yourself from others promoting the same program. The headline for your postcard should say something about how a person can achieve financial success by joining this program now. Right under the headline should be a toll-free voice mail number that people can call to get more information. Your goal is to develop as many leads as you can. Too many want to make a quick sale without cultivating relationships with potential prospects first. Notice that you didn't just jump on board without first learning if this business or the people you'd be working with were right for you! So don't lose any potential sales or turn away any potential business partners by trying to sell them prematurely.

Let's look now at how to make the postcard most effective. After the toll-free voice mail number, list some bullet points outlining important information about the program. Give prospects several reasons why they should consider joining the program and spell out some of the benefits they can realize by doing so. Keep it brief and to the point. Remember, the job of your postcard is only to generate leads. Once you acquire the leads, you can effectively begin to build relationships while communicating value to your prospects.

Setting up a postcard and getting a toll-free number may sound expensive and difficult. It need not be! If you want to promote your offer effectively, make sure you work with experts who have experience in making this business-building modality work effectively for network marketers.

Let's recap. The intended result of mailing postcards is to generate prospects who actually are interested in what you have to offer. When prospects call your toll-free number, give them a description of what you are promoting and the choice of leaving their name, address, and phone number for more information. Here's where your real promotion comes into play. Once you have obtained your prospect's name, address, and phone number, put them on your main mailing list. You will now develop your own mailing list of interested prospects. These are your gold mine names. This list will make you money now and in the future!

Once you develop an interested prospect, send this person information on your program. Use your company's material to add the element of duplicability to your campaign, but add a personalized cover letter. Make it simple by typing one letter and just adding each prospect's name to personalize each communication. After you send your prospect an information package, place a phone call a week or two later. Your success will dramatically increase with a follow-up phone call. Even if you don't call, send out a second follow-up communication two to four weeks later and then a third or fourth follow-up a couple of weeks apart.

Think about this for a moment. Who do you think you have a better chance to enroll in your network marketing program, a person who has never heard of you or a person who requested your information and with whom you now are building a relationship? The answer should be obvious.

All the successful networkers I know use this strategy of generating leads and then following them up. It's pretty much a sure bet that if you are failing with your direct mail promotions, you are not using this strategy.

Here's the real magic of this system. As your career in network marketing develops, you will periodically have new products, benefits, or company developments that may interest many on your list. Since you are developing a constant list of qualified prospects, some may be ready to join you now while others may not, for whatever reason. As these prospects' situations change, many may later be ready to consider your offers. That's why you need to put these names into a database and keep following them up. You will be building a positive relationship with all of these prospects. Your ultimate success can really turn out to be a numbers game! The more prospects you can develop a positive relationship with, the more money you will make over the course of your network marketing career.

Try this test. Answer some mail you receive or reply to some ads you see. You don't have to actually do anything when you get the information. Just make note of who follows up with you and who doesn't. Make note of how they follow up and how many times they follow up. You will then be able to determine who is succeeding and who isn't.

Achieving success using direct mail starts with mailing out your promotion to a prospect. However, the way you mail out your offers and who you mail them to make a big difference in determining what results you will experience. Your budget probably will determine which of the two methods of mailing offers you'll use: solo mailings or cooperative mailings.

Obviously, a solo mailing implies that you are mailing your flyer or postcard directly to a prospect who receives only your offer. You will always get your best response with solo mailings! Unfortunately, this is the most expensive method of direct mail promotion.

A cooperative mailing is the cheaper alternative. Your flyer is mailed with other flyers to prospects, so each will be receiving a bunch of offers together in the same envelope. Your response will be much lower than if you had mailed your offer out by itself, but it also will be a lot less expensive. To determine which method is better for you, you'll likely need to try both and track your ratios to see which is more cost-effective. Many successful net-workers use cooperative mailings to generate leads and then send solo mail-ings to these leads on a regular basis. This is the strategy I suggest unless your budget allows for solo mailings exclusively. I regularly do both types of mail-ings at reasonable rates and am happy to speak with anyone to determine which method may be best for each individual.

There is an acronym that advertisers use—TINA, which stands for "There is no average." You will never know what average response you should be getting for your offer. Every offer is unique, and so is every mailing. Mailing your offers out to as many people as possible is the best way to gen-erate the maximum number of responses. This is called testing! Your prospects may find some offers more appealing than others. Stick with the of-fers that generate the highest interest and, by all means, keep testing! When you advertise, there are *no* guarantees in terms of responses you can expect. Advertising is *not* a science. It is a calculated risk. But by testing, you can keep your risks manageable!

Though you have little control over what response you may get, you do have control over one thing: your decision to continue to advertise. If you don't advertise, you'll certainly not get any response. This you know for sure. When you advertise consistently, at least you are giving yourself a chance to succeed. The better you grasp the lead-generating and follow-up system I've discussed, the better are your chances at succeeding.

Consider the awesome potential of building a successful network mar-keting business. That's why you should only get involved with a network marketing program you really believe in and can stick with and continue pro-moting for a minimum of six months. Don't forget to also show others the value of building such a successful program. The beauty of network market-ing is that when your new distributors promote, they are also promoting for you! You make money on whatever they do. Imagine having 10, 20, 100, or 1,000 distributors joining your business and then constantly generating leads and following them up. How big will your organization be then? Teach your distributors to duplicate what you are doing, and you will achieve an over-whelming level of success.

Let's now consider the type of prospects to whom you should mail your network marketing opportunity. I've found that the best prospects are those who either answered an ad for or otherwise decided to become involved with a direct-mail moneymaking opportunity. This type of person will always be your best prospect.

Allow me to offer one last gold mine suggestion. When you start build-ing a quality mailing list for your own use and keep mailing to it regularly for your network marketing program, don't you also think others would be inter-ested in renting your list, too? In network marketing, quality mailing lists are hard to come by. By generating leads, cultivating them, and following them up on a regular basis, you will not only be building strong organizations that will make you lots of money, but you will also be developing a high-quality mailing list. Many prospects who may not be a fit for your opportunity may have an interest in a different opportunity! Because of this fact, your list will be in great demand. This will also result in an additional residual income source that can be quite lucrative.

Advertising is not easy! It can be very frustrating. Be patient, work hard, be consistent and persistent, test your offers, and continue to learn about your business. Network marketing has the potential to be a great, life-changing business. Treat it as such and you will succeed beyond your wildest dreams.

If you need help in promoting your business through web site advertising, small print media advertising, mailing lists, having mailings done for you, getting 800 numbers, and creating postcards, Larry Chiappone, president of Chiappone Mail Enterprises, Inc., can help. With a 20-year record of supporting network marketers to be successful, Larry has been featured in most of the best money-making opportunity magazines, including *Six Figure Income, Opportunity World, Ben Franks,* and *Network Marketing Business Journal,* as well as in other top publications. To subscribe to all his informative free articles and learn more about his discounted services, send two self-stick first class stamps to Chiappone Mail Enterprises, Inc., P.O. Box 1300, West Babylon, NY 11704. With his services, Larry's sole purpose is to help your business grow. When you succeed, Larry succeeds. Send for his free 16-page catalog now! If you would like a subscription to his "Article of the Month" series, simply send $10 for a lifetime membership to the same address.

CHAPTER
33

Proper Follow-Up: The Hidden Gold Mine

Jeff Mack

O ther than the actual activity of prospecting, following up is perhaps the most important step in your quest to build a successful network marketing business. This is the activity that defines your results in that it's often the determining factor between success and failure or between wild success and mere mediocrity. In this chapter, we discuss some of the reasons, intricacies, and subtleties of how and why the follow-up process can enhance your overall success in building a team.

Obviously, you have to introduce someone to your business and/or products first. There are some great tips contained in this book that if followed will greatly increase the rate at which your team grows. However, even if you do prospect and do it with great proficiency, unless you follow up correctly, your work may very well be for naught. Please understand that no matter how exciting your product and business is, life often gets in the way of people calling you back, even if they have every intention of doing so. Therefore, unless you follow up on the material and information provided, or even follow up on a passing comment or conversation, the potential seeds you plant may never sprout, grow, or bear fruit.

I call the follow-up process the "hidden gold mine" because the benefits of following up correctly are abundant, and in many cases continue to bear fruit for years to come. Let's take a minute and discuss some of these benefits.

ACCOMPLISHING YOUR INTENDED OBJECTIVE

Whether your goal is to add a new member to your team, to create a new customer, or both, you're going to need to follow up with the individual with whom you initially spoke to help that process along. In some cases, your next conversations will be "textbook" and things will go as planned, and you will have your new consumer or partner. However, if you hadn't followed up, they likely would not have been proactive in seeking you out, even if they were interested. Thus, your initial time, energy, and resources would have been wasted. I've seen it happen time after time. So, preventing this from happening is one obvious benefit of following up. However, what if the conversation wasn't so perfect, as is normally the case?

What if your potential partner has questions, concerns, objections, or misconceptions? These things happen more often than not when that little negative voice inside all our heads begins to talk and we let it take over. Remember when it happened to you sometime in your life? How did you overcome it? I'll bet that somewhere there was a friend, a parent, a coach, or a mentor who helped you overcome those fears or concerns or, at the very least, provided accurate information and feedback to allay any misconceptions. This is another reason why your follow-up call or contact is so important. By answering questions your prospects may have or laying the factual framework over any incomplete or inaccurate information they have gathered, you are not only building your reputation and relationship with those individuals but are also ensuring that they make their decision based on the facts, all of which works in your favor.

GETTING A REFERRAL

Referrals can be one of your best sources of leads. While they can come from many sources, referrals from people who have said no to you about either your business or your product can be one of the most fruitful sources. All you have to do is ask. This is one of the ways to turn an unsuccessful encounter into something that pays lasting rewards. In fact, some of my best partners started out as referrals from someone else.

Since it's been proven that people, especially those with whom you have some rapport, have a difficult time telling you no three times in a row, the follow-up call or meeting provides a great opportunity to maximize your chances of getting referrals from that person. So if they ultimately decline your business, see if they would like to try some products, then ask for a referral. Your demeanor, professionalism, and likability will spell the difference in this and countless other facets of our business. If people like you, they will want to help you out, so be sure to ask for those referrals. If you ask for multiple referrals (three perhaps), you have an even better chance of getting at least one.

BRANDING YOURSELF

One of the best things you can do for your future is to be seen as a person who is a professional and one who can be counted on. How many times have you encountered people in your life who had the best of intentions but didn't actually follow through? Or, perhaps, they set appointments but were constantly late or, worse yet, didn't keep them. How did you feel about that person in terms of your ability to count on them? Now contrast that with how you felt about the person who was always on time, who kept appointments like clockwork. This is the person you want to be and the follow-up step gives you the opportunity to brand yourself in the eyes of your potential customers or partners as such.

At the end of each phone conversation or appointment, establish your next point of contact with your potential customer/partner, whether that is a follow-up phone call, a three-way phone call, or an additional meeting or event. Then, follow through like clockwork as you said you would, even if that means that you are to touch base with them in three to six months because the time is not right today. By doing so, you will brand yourself as a professional and as someone upon whom they can rely. This will leave a lasting impression that can live in their minds long after your contact with them is over. Therefore, if and when your prospect is ready to move to action in the future, with whom do you think they'll want to be involved, you or someone else? It's so rare to find people who fall into this category! Therefore, doing what I've mentioned here will automatically set you apart from the pack.

MAKE THE MOST EFFICIENT
USE OF YOUR TIME

An additional benefit of being clear on when your next point of contact is with your potential partner/customer is that you'll save yourself a great deal of time. You'll cut down on the annoying phone tag and the slowing down of the process by having to wait on them to return your call. You'll also save yourself time by getting a clear picture of whether the individual is truly interested. If they miss the agreed-upon time and don't call you back or make the scheduled appointment, thus not respecting you or your time, then you know that they may not be a good candidate and you can move on more readily. Of course, a quick reminder call 24 hours before any face-to-face appointment or event will remind them of the appointment and cut down on no-shows. It also serves to help you clarify their level of interest even further. I consider all of this an integral part of the follow-up process.

LEAD BY EXAMPLE

Here's one thing people rarely realize. From the minute you make the initial contact with a potential customer or partner, you're training them on how they should do the business. They are going to remember what you did when you called them, what steps you took, and how you reacted and responded. Providing the right example for your current team and those who decide to join you in the future is critical to growing and leading an organization that duplicates. To that end, being the professional you want your people to be provides the right example for them to follow and in turn gives you an edge. This is true not only in following up, but in every facet of this business. This may seem daunting, but when you really think about it, it actually makes this business very simple.

THE PROCESS

Now that we've discussed some of the benefits of following up, you can see not only how important this step is but also why it truly is a hidden gold mine. Now let's talk about how to "mine," that is, the precise steps and elements of following up properly. Being an engineer by training, it helps me to look at things in steps, so that's how I'll lay it out for you in order to be as clear as possible, starting with the initial contact.

Step One: The Initial Contact or Phone Call

Since we're not really talking about prospecting in this chapter, there's not much to say here other than this is where it all starts. Regardless of what presentation or information means you choose, be sure that when this call or conversation is over, you and your potential customer/partner have agreed on when to talk again. The best thing to do in this regard is to ask them what works for them, and then be sure to have a meeting of the minds in terms of when you should talk about this next. For example: "How much time do you feel you'll need to review this information?" Or "Let's plan a time to talk again to avoid phone tag. Is 10 A.M. or 8 P.M. tomorrow better for you?"

I especially like the second example because it gives them two options that work for you and helps to eliminate procrastination on their part. Of course, you want to gauge yourself here. If you're speaking to a customer or someone just casually interested, too much pressure will work against you. But if you are speaking with someone, particularly a potential partner, who you know has more than just a casual interest, creating a sense of urgency greatly works in your favor. As a general rule of thumb, your goal for the time interval between contacts is no more than 48 hours. I've found this time frame to be very important because within 48 hours, the information will still be fresh in their minds—but not for much longer than that! Also aiming for 48 hours helps you determine your potential partner/customer's level of interest while speeding this whole process up to an efficient pace. Of course, 48 hours isn't possible in every case, but it gives you something to shoot for. Two things are critical to remember here. One, your interests aren't nearly as important to your potential customers/partners as their interests are. Two, always treat them as you would want to be treated yourself, with dignity and respect.

Step Two: The Follow-up Contact

This actual activity is dictated mainly by whatever your prospecting system is, geography, and agreement with your potential customer/partner. It could be a face-to-face appointment, a meeting or event, or any number of possibilities. However, in most cases, and for the sake of this discussion, we'll assume it's a follow-up phone call. Your main goal for this call is merely to determine their level of interest. The best way to do this is of course to ask questions—the right kind of questions. For example: "Did you find the information as intriguing as I did?" Or "When I first looked at this, the possibility of working with a good consumable product and creating a residual customer base and income got me really excited [or insert what was the case for you]. What caught your attention about it?"

Either of these approaches works, but I really like the second one because it shares your ideas and points out another benefit that they may not have thought about. Plus, in both of these questions, you are assuming a positive response, which is very helpful.

As for the response you get, they're really are only three possibilities:

1. They aren't interested.
2. They haven't reviewed the information yet.
3. They are interested and want to learn more about your business and/or product.

Step Three: The Next Follow-up Step

Here are a few things to keep in mind for each of the preceding scenarios and what you should do when you encounter them. If, for whatever reason, you do not get a positive response, be sure to inquire more. Ask them why they feel the way they do, but do so in a respectful and genuinely curious manner. In no way do you want to seem confrontational or chastise them for having an opinion different than yours. However, you do want to try to get to the root of their feelings, because in many cases their opinions are based on a perception or comparison to things they've seen in the past and may not be completely accurate. After all, you don't want them to miss out on a fabulous opportunity just because they think they know all about it, right? So try to understand and clarify for them. See Dr. Joe Rubino's awesome book, *Secrets of Building a Million-Dollar Network Marketing Organization from a Guy Who's Been There Done That and Shows You How You Can Do It, Too* for some great material on overcoming objections. If for some reason they haven't been able to review your information yet (and this often happens), then repeat the process at the end of step one to set up another time; then observe what happens. If this continues to happen, it means that they have no interest, that they are not the right person for you, or that this is not the right time for them. If they have no interest or are not the right person, then you must move on, but do so in a way that strengthens your relationship rather than damaging it. If the time is not right, then get permission to contact them again in three to six months to update them on your progress and to see if the time is right to look again. Remember, people's personal timing does change, so this process is very important. I've actually had people decide to join me literally years after I first contacted them. I would just stay in touch with the ones I had the most respect for about every six months, building my relationship with them at each contact. As soon as their timing or their personal circumstances changed, we teamed up. You'll have the same experience if you follow what I suggest here and if you stay the course.

If you find during this call that there is a level of interest, then do not act surprised! That may sound funny but really, some people blow it right here. Be confident and advance the conversation further. Find out where their interest lies—in the business, the products, or both. If you ask one of the questions from step two, they may just let you know from the start where their interest lies. Then your job is easy. Just supply them with the appropriate information based on that interest.

It is important that you do not overwhelm them with too much information! Perhaps send them to a web site where they can access a limited amount of appropriate information, or even connect them to a conference call or other form of information. If you're new to this business, I believe your best option is to set up a three-way phone call with your upline partner. Your particular company, system, or upline training will guide you here as to what is appropriate, but just remember these four rules of thumb:

1. Ask questions to determine their specific interest.
2. Provide only information that meets those specific interests so you don't overwhelm them.
3. Use the system and your upline to build their confidence, your credibility, and their belief that they can do it.
4. Set up your next contact to be within 48 hours if possible.

This process is a simple one. Although the information I've shared here may seem to suggest otherwise, once you get used to it, you'll see this as a very simple and systematic approach to knowing when and with whom you should follow up. Your upline support team member will be there to share with you the benefit of their experience if you have any questions. The key thing to remember is that business is out there. You'll find some right away, but most of the gold you get will come about as a result of you digging consistently for it, or in this case, following up diligently and professionally. Therefore, you'll want to be sure to be diligent, be consistent, but also be sure to have fun! If you make it fun, people will be more likely to want to join you and you'll be more likely to do more of what you need to be doing.

In addition, you'll want to be sure you have a system that helps you keep track of your time and appointments. A critical part of this process is being professional and organized. If you show up when you said you would and call when you said you would and overall are seen as someone who can be counted on, you will leave a very positive impression in the minds of those you speak with about this business, regardless of their level of interest. As a result, people will come to respect you and feel comfortable referring others to you. That is where you ultimately want to get. Being diligent in this process will go a long way toward helping you become one of successful networkers who find that hidden gold.

Early in his adult years, Jeff Mack thought the traditional route—a college degree, hard work, staying the course—was the path to a great life. After a few years working as a civil engineer and project manager, he soon realized that his career, like most industries and careers, was driven principally by things beyond our control—such as interest rates, the economy, regulations, or investor favor. He began to see that this traditional route was simply going to let him get by, and Jeff wasn't satisfied with that future. About 14 years ago, Jeff changed his future by beginning to work part-time with Rexall Showcase, now known as Unicity. His efforts grew into a full-time enterprise that has transformed his life into an extraordinary one.

Jeff initially got started in his network marketing business part-time to generate some additional income and to learn what it means to be an entrepreneur. It wasn't long before his outlook and his life changed totally. Within a year, he was able to focus on his business full-time. Over the next year, his business income matched what he had earned as a civil engineer. The following year, his earnings exceeded $100,000. Since then, Jeff, who had never really traveled before, began to expand his business internationally. This took him to Hong Kong, Korea, Taiwan, Japan, Malaysia, Singapore, the United Kingdom,

Germany, and beyond—where he became a sought-after speaker and trainer at many international events.

Today, he runs his own growing international business from home that earns him a six-figure annual income without having the great risks and headaches that accompany most businesses. More important than the quantity, the quality of income has also allowed Jeff to diversify into other areas of business and investment. Jeff is among the top earners with his company, has been named to the U.S. advisory board for several terms, was named the Most Valuable Leader in his company in 2000, and has been featured in numerous publications including Richard Poe's best-seller *Wave 4*.

Jeff has had the privilege and opportunity to help thousands of other people all over the world improve their health and achieve their dreams, and he continues to work with and help those seeking a better way. You can learn more at www.JeffreyKMack.com.

CHAPTER
34

Visionary Leadership

Mike Melia

eading others can be a very complicated venture. In network marketing, successful leaders work hard to simplify the task. As a leader in this profession, you are leading masses of volunteers. Thus leaders have two very important results they must maintain in order to create massive success:

1. Create a compelling vision for your volunteers to buy into.
2. Keep your method of operation simple and easy to execute.

Creating a compelling vision is not a difficult task. Maintaining a true focus on that vision over time is essential to your success and a much greater challenge. It is when things get tough that true leaders rise to the occasion and show their inner character.

How do you create a compelling vision? First of all, demystify the process. A vision is simply a clear idea of what it is you want. Most people drift through life with a vague idea of what they would like their lives to look like, feel like, and taste like.

Your first step in becoming a leader with vision is to spend some time engaged in the soul-searching endeavor of defining and refining exactly what it is you want. Why do you want to be a successful network marketer?

If your answer is "To be rich," I recommend you take it further. What would riches do for you, your family, friends, and community? How would you feel if you achieved your goals? What would your life look like? How would things be different than they are today?

Once you flesh out your vision and know what it is that you want, then become fluent in speaking your vision. Keep your vision close to you at all times and stay focused on the positive results that holding that vision will bring.

A clear vision held over time is very likely to come into being. A crucial mistake many people make is to drop their visions when things get tough.

They spend time being emotionally down and feeling defeated. It is at these very times that focusing your vision on the most important results will strengthen your resolve and your inner fortitude. Focusing on what you want, especially when it doesn't seem to matter or appear to be achievable, is the mark of a great leader.

Winston Churchill said, "Success is moving from failure to failure without losing enthusiasm." Nowhere is this statement more applicable than in the arena of network marketing. Your enthusiasm is infectious. You have probably heard that "the speed of the leader determines the speed of the pack." Throughout history, great leaders have marched confidently in the direction of their dreams. I recommend reading biographies of historical figures who inspire you. My two favorites are *Let the Trumpets Sound*, a biography of Dr. Martin Luther King Jr. by Stephen Oates, and *Robert Kennedy and His Times*, by Arthur M. Schlesinger Jr..

As a leader, it is a great idea to study other leaders and books on leadership. Carry those books with you so your team members can see what you are reading and be inspired by your ongoing commitment to learning. Brian Tracy is fond of saying, "Leaders are readers." Ten years ago, I heard him say that if you spend a half hour each day reading in your chosen field, you will be counted among the top 5 percent of people in that field within a few short years.

Once your vision is clear, you can become more and more fluent in your vision by articulating it and sharing it with others. If you simply read these words but never write your vision and your goals down on paper, it is unlikely that this information will do you much good. Creating a vision is not a one-time activity, but rather an ongoing part of your life process. It is important to visit and revisit your vision—daily, weekly, monthly, quarterly, and annually. Over time, you will refine and tweak it and it will become a living force in your life.

BUILDING AND LEADING YOUR ORGANIZATION

Like the manifestation of true vision, building a massive, successful organization takes place over time. Without the factor of time, you cannot create anything that will last. What many people miss is that time is on your side. You need the passage of time to bring your vision into being and to grow your volunteer army. Therefore, create a good relationship with time.

Jim Rohn says, "It's not what you get, it's who you become. Then who you become determines what you get." Again this takes place over time, so be patient with yourself, your volunteer army, and the entire process. Who you become is vital because as you become the person you are capable of being, you also become an attractive force. It is through the power of attraction that your volunteer army will choose to follow you. And let's face it—if you think you're a leader but no one is following you, then you're only out for a walk.

No one signs on for a network marketing opportunity to have a new boss—someone telling them what to do. As a leader, it is essential to have your people buy into the process. As a visionary, you need to clearly articulate your vision and help your volunteers create, define, and refine their individual and collective visions. Learn how to create word pictures that elicit positive emotional feelings. Here are some examples of language that inspires:

"Imagine being able to sleep till you are done."

"How many people have ever wanted to fire their boss?"

"Now I can drop my son off at the bus stop in the morning and be back there at three o'clock to pick him up."

"Let's travel the beaches of the world together."

Continually express your vision for the future and continually ask your team members about what they want. Teach your folks how important it is to commit their goals to paper and to read over their stated vision every day.

As my brother Steve likes to say, "I should be able to wake you up at 3 A.M. and ask you what's most important, and you should be able to answer without missing a beat." The most successful leaders I know have one quality that stands out more than anything else—they are passionate about their commitment to helping others. Simply put, they care.

As Dale Carnegie put it in his classic personal growth best-seller, *How to Win Friends and Influence People*, it all boils down to two words—*genuine interest*. We are in the people business. Of course, your company markets goods and/or services, but as a network marketing leader, you are in the people business. Nobody cares how much you know until they know how much you care.

Don't be neutral or lukewarm in this area. Allow your natural curiosity to lead you in one of the greatest endeavors of all time. How can you help others to become more and thus achieve more? How can you help people connect with their dreams and their inner sense of purpose? How can you help people discover and rediscover their true passion and their inner power?

The greater your pursuit of true freedom, the greater your results will be. As a leader with vision, be clear about where you are going and be patient with yourself and others. Respect the notion that each of us is a work in progress. Reach for the highest in yourself and in others and always go the extra distance. To paraphrase the late President John F. Kennedy, "Ask not what others can do for you, but rather what you can do for others." Your business will grow and flourish as a result of your focus on contribution.

Mike Melia started out in the natural food industry in the mid-1970s. He resisted getting involved in the network marketing industry until he found a company that he could get passionate about. In 1994, he was introduced to Jeff Olson and The People's Network. He worked his way up through the ranks of this company, studying the industry and building a strong team in partnership with his brother Steve. In September 1998, The People's Network was acquired by Pre-Paid Legal Services. Mike and Steve applied the fundamental principles and practices they had learned from their mentor, Jeff Olson, and reached the top position within their first year. They were inducted into Pre-Paid Legal's prestigious Millionaire's Club after 39 months in the business. The Melias produced two audio programs telling their story and sharing the keys to success, entitled "Falling in Love with Your Future" and "After the Honeymoon's Over."

CHAPTER 35

Posture, Process, and Perspective Create Profits

Scotty Kufus

The three concepts that have shaped my thinking, communicating and peace of mind during my career are posture, process, and perspective. Posture is how you stand, think, and communicate in the face of uncertainty and how that makes other people feel at that moment. Process is the method or plan you intend to follow to accomplish your purpose despite the short-term distractions, obstacles, and shortcomings you may currently possess. Perspective is a point of view at a given period of time. To be a visionary and a powerful leader, you must be able to see short-term and long-term perspective at the same time. This will give you balance.

How do we nourish these skills and attitudes? How do we incorporate them into our daily action plans? How do we teach these skills to others? These are great questions to be more clearly understood in the coming pages.

POSTURING YOURSELF TO WIN IN NETWORK MARKETING

Let us start with posturing. It is a great deal like parenting. I have recently become a parent of a little boy. Aaron is now two. He is learning things every day—new words, ideas, hand signals, and attitudes. How I behave around him, how I choose my words, even the expression on my face has an impact on how he behaves. In other words, how I posture myself affects his choices. At a very fundamental level, that is what happens to us all every day when we communicate with anyone.

We are the main cause in the cause-and-effect equation. You can be a victim or take responsibility for your life and success. You can posture yourself more effectively by taking on the responsibility and belief that you can always alter, amend, or improve a circumstance based on your own communication. You are well on your way to success when you begin to prune, clip, and reshape your daily communication. If you are a victim of other people's attitudes, distractions, excuses, and body language, then you are destined to sacrifice your better future. So many people blame others for their circumstances. We have all done it. You can enter every circumstance and say, "I made that happen!" Good or bad, it will support your growth. You won't have to wallow in the mess. Just acknowledge it, clean it up, and try again.

In any partnership, the two people have a dynamic impact on each other's destiny. They modify behaviors, which modify actions, which cause different results. Any small change in behavior on one person's part affects the other. It is the yin and the yang of personal interaction, and you can impact your own destiny in a very simple manner.

If you wake up in the morning and you have a bad attitude or something happens during your day that changes your productive state of mind, you can change it very simply. If you are unhappy, distracted, or a little frustrated with your partner, child, or another employee or distributor, start singing or humming your favorite song. Only one of two things will happen—you will begin feeling great quickly or you will stop singing.

Posturing is your ability to take control of the direction. You are not always in control of the outcome, but you can modify the direction of a conversation over a day or in a business cycle or quarter. How you respond to each action is posturing. Do people know you are upset, interested, successful, talented, or broke? How do they know? Poker is a great example of a game where your posture is often dictated by your true vision. How powerful, emotional, important is your true vision? Does it drive you, guide you, and inspire you? If it doesn't, it's not your true vision for your life.

HOW LONG IS YOUR PERSPECTIVE?

The great Chinese warrior, leader, and philosopher, Sun Tzu believed that whoever has the longest-term perspective wins the battle. The battle is for your mind, your vision, your happiness, and your daily life. What is your true vision? How far away does it look to you? If your true vision is near, people tend to have momentum, excitement, productivity, and the ability to attract success. If it feels far away, people tend to be depressed, frustrated, angry, and resentful, and they repel any opportunity to make progress.

Most people's fundamental communication styles are forged by the age of 6. It takes a conscious and courageous effort to unlearn some often misunderstood comments or nonverbal mannerisms that communicate about what we think and believe. This powerful communication transcends the phone lines as well. People can hear your tone, your attitude, and your belief. This happens whether or not you are aware of it, like gravity. You must control and protect your vision, for it powers your posture. It is your battery, and only you can recharge you.

People say things, we interpret them, and this interpretation changes our own posture, which will affect our very next communication. Posture is controlling your next communication in spite of what you might interpret. We have all heard the commercial that says never let them see you sweat. Network marketing has many of those moments, especially in the first few weeks of getting started. If you have been involved for three to six months, people expect results. If you have been involved for two to three years, people expect great results or there is a diminished likelihood that they will join you. In those cases, they are looking at your attitude, what you have learned, and what other benefits you have gained. Friends, vacations, free time, education, and a great product experience all add to your posture.

NETWORK MARKETING SALES— THE ULTIMATE POSTURING

It is totally within your power to control the circumstances and the selling environment in which you operate. It all comes down to value. What is the value equation? What is a potential buyer's reason to take action? Why would someone want what you are selling? This may differ from why you think they want it. How effective are you at offering your products, services, or income opportunity without being attached to the outcome? You need to be completely isolated from the selling process while at the same time being in the middle of it.

Let's say you are offering cakes, pies, and brownies at a bake sale. Someone is thinking about buying something. They look over the goods and walk away. Are your feelings hurt? Probably not. But what if you baked everything and the money was going to pay for something important in your life? You might then put out quite an effort to sell them something. People would sense your desire to sell your goods. This pressure might work with baked goods but not with more costly items and certainly not with your network marketing opportunity.

People can feel your need to sell them if your posture is off. If they can feel your need to sell more than they can feel their desire for your product or service, you will have a difficult time. Conversely, if they feel the need for and value of your product and service and notice that you really don't need their sale because lots of people are buying, they'll want to be a part of the story. If everyone thinks an opportunity is fun, simple, and profitable, they will want to join. If they think that you will work your business and would succeed without them, they will be more likely to join the crusade. People usually don't want to be involved with something if they perceive that others have little interest in it.

This is where posture comes in. Knowing it is just a matter of time before people will buy, join, and sell your opportunity gives you better posture. Don't give people such an easy opportunity to reject you. One of the biggest reasons people do not join network marketing opportunities is because they fear rejection. If we can teach them to have a different perspective on rejection, attracting them to us will be that much easier.

PROCESS IS THE DIRTY WORK

Process is necessary in order to fully accomplish a desired goal. If you have a solid posture and perspective while you are waiting out the time line of process, you are well on your way. Process is a function of action and time. People hate process because they want instant gratification. If you learn to love it or at least embrace its power in your life, than success is just a series of actions away. This is often the toughest lesson for new network marketers to learn. Most quit before they reap the benefits of implementing the process.

Give yourself time to learn the process. No matter what the subject, it takes time to accomplish a result. Although you may get lucky from time to time in some pursuits, in building a network you will not fall far from your level of competency and enthusiasm when all is measured and rewarded. Consider the processes in your life. What does it take to make them successful? How many years must you learn, struggle, and relearn to master any of them? Success takes time.

- Education is a process.
- Friendship is a process.
- Rejection is a process.
- Communication is a process.
- Saving, spending, and investing are a process.
- Sales and recruiting are affected by process.
- Cash flow and momentum are effects of process.
- Happiness and sadness are effects of process.
- Success and failure are the effects of process.

Network marketing is also a process. You must understand that success results when those you introduce believe in the process long enough to do what it takes to introduce others who do likewise. The challenge with network marketing is that it usually involves working with a very under-trained sales force. The majority of successful people in network marketing did not have any sales background when they began. They treated it like a profession from the beginning and created a professional income. To be successful, you must learn the process, understand the posture, and have a solid perspective over time to develop a sizable and profitable organization.

SALES AS A PROFESSION

Sales is the process of providing value for a price. The more value that is created for the particular offering, the easier it will be to generate the sale. One of the keys to being a successful sales professional is to offer greater value than the cost. The more value you offer, the higher the likelihood people will want to buy. That is why the world is obsessed with the word *free*. The Internet is loaded with free promotions—free samples, free quotes, free food, and the like. People have been conditioned to bargain hunt, and there is no greater bargain than free!

Consider how you can use the value equation the next time you sell something in your network marketing organization. What extraordinary value can you offer—more training, more products, tickets to your company's next event, a free dinner? Look at how you can increase the value. A great idea that has worked for many of my successful network marketing friends is they agree to send 10 to 20 introduction packages out on their prospects' behalf if they agree to join at a certain level. Come in at the $500 level and I will do this. Come in for $200 and I will do that. Figure out the value equation and make your prospects a compelling offer.

ACTIVITY BEATS ATTITUDE

A bad attitude with good activity wins over a good attitude with no activity. I know a great number of nice, talented, and motivated people in network marketing who make absolutely no money! Why? No activity! This is simple stuff. I also have a few friends who are very grumpy, short with people on the phone, busy, and rarely return phone calls, and they make from $250,000 to $900,000 a year in this industry. Why? High levels of activity. They only focus on working with the willing. They don't talk long on the phone, but they talk with lots of people. Activity is the process, the dirty work in the network marketing business. It all comes down to repeating the right steps every day. If one commits to consistent daily action, success will follow. Imagine what combining a great attitude with massive action will accomplish!

ESTABLISH A DAILY METHOD OF OPERATION

Determine what types of actions result in success in your network marketing company. It could be getting people on conference calls. It might be going to training or opportunity meetings, or selling product at salons or to chiropractors. Whatever it is, do it and do it consistently, six days a week if you can. Prospecting is not something you do; it's a way of life! You have to stay committed to it. An athlete works out, a musician plays an instrument, a singer practices notes and octaves, an artist paints, a writer writes. What exactly do you do? Define it, write it on a piece of paper, put it on your wall, and commit to it for 90 days, and your life will change forever.

FUNDAMENTAL LAWS OF SUCCESSFUL NETWORKING

In sales, there are certain fundamental laws. Network marketing seems to amplify their importance because we are dealing with people's hopes and dreams and they guard them closely and rarely expose them for others to see. When they do reveal them or are at risk by investing some time or money, these laws become critical to understand and apply.

Law of Attraction

The law of attraction states that for things to be attracted, you must be attractive. That doesn't mean you have to wear a special suit or look a certain way. It means whatever you are selling, sharing, or giving away must have a value that is obvious to the other party. Sometimes network marketing companies' products and opportunities have weaknesses, flaws that may be obvious to some people and not to others. It may be the compensation plan, the product price, the competitive environment, the web site, company history, or lack of company longevity. The point is if you don't have a pretty face, then learn how to sing! Figure out what is attractive to others and talk about it with passion.

It is important that you can tell anyone what you like best about your company in 10 seconds or less.

The reason I like Company XYZ is _____. The products have done _____ for me and my family. We are on track to earn _____ dollars in the next few months, and it's fun, simple, and profitable. Do you know anyone who wants to have fun, make money, and experience _____?

Law of Familiarity

Asking someone their name is a simple task in itself. Most people don't have to think about the answer. They know their name, their age, where they were born, favorite foods, colors, movies, and more. No thought is needed. That is how familiar you need to be with answering objections, product questions, and marketing questions, and relaying your company's history. It takes only a few hours to learn these things and then 20 to 30 conversations to lock them in.

Law of Association: Books, Tapes, and People

Who do you spend time around? How are they affecting you, and is that okay? Surround yourself with quality people, ideas, and energy. Spend most of your time with people who support what you are all about in life; don't spend much time with negative people who wear you down. Do your friends think of ideas, concepts, service, and society or do they talk about gossip, celebrities, TV shows, and headaches? You have to love your family, because they are your family, but you do not need to drown yourself in pity, negative discussions, and arguments. Get plugged into a leadership tape series. Read books. Go to the library. Only 5 percent of Americans own a library card. The books are free, and all of the knowledge in the world awaits you, right down the street. Attend local mixers and Toastmaster meetings, and visit your upline in person or by phone as often as possible. Stay motivated by surrounding yourself with motivated people.

Law of the Farm: Planting and Reaping

The more people you talk to, the better your chances to succeed. Rejection is the process that paves the way of success. It is like the weather—it takes rain and sun to create a rainbow. The only way you are going to be massively successful is to take on a great number of conversations in a short period of time or do so for a long period of time. A parable teaches us that when we plant seeds in a garden, some fall on the hard soil, some seeds get eaten by the birds, and some seeds fall on fertile soil and grow. You never really know what seeds are ready to grow until after you water them. Farmers plant a great deal of seed and allow the law of the farm take root. In network marketing, you never know who is ready to take action. It often comes from unlikely sources and they do it for their reasons, not yours. It took me a great deal of time to realize that it isn't my fault if they don't join or take action. That is not to say that I shouldn't learn how to do a nice presentation and follow up properly. It just means that people show up with their own baggage, unspoken commitments and concerns, motivations and desires. Usually they do not share the real reason they are interested at the beginning. It often takes several weeks to find out. That is the law of the farm at work.

Law of Averages and the Funnel Concept

The law of averages is the single most powerful lesson to learn in terms of sales. There are three fundamental rules that apply to the law of averages:

1. Exposure is everything.
2. Fortune is in the follow-up.
3. Work with the willing.

Once you employ these concepts, you will be well on your way to success. You have to share the business, use the products, and talk to people. Expose your products to others in any way you can. It is best to have at least 100 conversations in 30 days to produce momentum in your business. (See Figure 35.1.) Commit to at least three conversations a day. Success results from follow-up. A third of the people are not interested, a third of the people will try the product, and a third of the people want to know more about the money. Work with the ones who are ready now. For now, forget about the ones who are not ready or don't want to be customers. We will go back to them later. Right now, you are looking for the willing—people who want to take action now. You will only need to spend a fraction of the time with a motivated, teachable person than you will with someone who needs to be convinced that you have a good opportunity. Working with the willing will make you more money in a shorter period of time (with fewer headaches) than anything else you do.

Law of Inertia

In network marketing, we somehow duplicate ourselves whether we like it or not. Once you begin to take action, the world around you changes. People need to see you active to believe that you are a leader. You can not talk about leadership—you can only demonstrate leadership. I have gone through periods of my life when I was a leader and times when I was a follower. People need to see you lead. Take action quickly, consistently, and passionately for three months. It will change your life forever when you realize that it's only 100 days to freedom and just 1,000 days to fortune.

Law of Increasing Returns

At the end of the day, success in network marketing is all about delivering value. The more conversations you have, the more lives you touch, the more

100 calls

60 prospects

30 customers

20 distributors

10 active ones

5 great leaders . . .

then, start 5 more profit tunnels.

Figure 35.1   The Funnel Concept

exponential growth you will have. The law of increasing returns is the opposite of "get rich quick." The key is to stay committed after picking a company that has systems in place, offers quality tools and events, and has leadership providing support.

You must be willing to change, knowing that you are a work in progress. You will be better tomorrow than you are today, wiser, more effective, kinder, and richer. You will have more knowledge and a better attitude through perspective and process. Your posture will improve. Your contact base will increase. Your sales volume will soar, and you will realize that you are on the path to greatness. It can be a rocky, dirty, and steep path, but many before you have climbed it. You can, too. Take action, set your course in motion, and be willing to grow and listen and learn. You have to believe that you are only a few months away from a tremendous growth spurt. Take action and your faith will be rewarded.

PERSPECTIVE IMPACTS EVERY THOUGHT YOU THINK AND ACTION YOU TAKE

William James said, "The real voyage to self-discovery is not in seeking new lands, but in seeing old lands with new eyes." Every process takes perspective to fully appreciate and learn from and requires a certain posture in order to improve your odds. Embrace the entire experience, good and bad, and then take responsibility for the current state of your business and skill sets, no matter the circumstances. The path to success is rarely easy or just given as a gift. It takes an exponential learning curve that makes the process much easier the more you do the necessary actions.

ATTITUDE: PERSPECTIVE WITH A SMILE

Passion is the key to attraction. People are inspired by those possessing passion. Passion is a form of perspective, an expectation that something wonderful is coming. When you are displaying passion in music, love, life, and in sales, people want to be a part of it. It's critical to find your own joy, march to your own drummer, follow your own path. If you know why you are doing something, you will eventually find out how and have the energy to see it through.

Silence is a demonstration of perspective. People who have the ability to hold a thought, consider an opportunity, and restrain themselves from impulses will likely make better choices. The unspoken word is often much louder than the spoken word. It has been said that it is better to remain silent and appear a fool than to open your mouth and remove all doubt.

Embrace the philosophy that suggests that whatever experiences you have always serve you in some way, if you are willing to adopt that perspective. Demand that your past serve your future and that your failures teach you successful ways *not* to do things. Demand that your victories provide strong emotions that remind you of joy, power, and unity with others. Remember that the journey is the destination; so don't miss the journey.

Feelings come and go like the sun and stars. If you rely on your feelings to dictate your daily actions, your commitments, your responsibilities, or your excuses, you are doomed to a dreary future. Don't blame how you feel or how someone else has made you feel because of their actions. Your attitude is always within your control. You are never a victim. Choose service, compassion, joy, and mercy when dealing with others. If you are upset, disappointed, or discouraged, find someone else to help as soon as you can. It's difficult to feel bad about something when you are helping someone else feel better. Manage your feelings. Have a perspective about them that allows them to float through the day like the clouds in the sky. Find them more fascinating than fearful.

Listening will create a sense of perspective. Listen to others with a degree of "at-stakeness." That means listening to them as if their opinion is better, wiser, and more experienced than your own. (Often, it is anyway.) Put your ego aside and listen to others as if they have something important to contribute to you. You may totally disagree with them but decide not to speak. Just sit with their perspective and exit that conversation knowing something new about them or how they think.

Initially, your success in network marketing will result only from getting in front of prospects. Time spent doing anything else is a distraction. How much time did you spend last week meeting new prospects and customers? Make a commitment to your upline to contact so many people a week, attend the next meeting with a prospect, or bring someone to a conference call. Distractions are expensive.

QUITTING IS NOT AN OPTION

In the end, your success in network marketing will result from your unshakable belief that you will be successful and from your firm resolve never to quit before you realize that success. By having a more powerful posture, employing a better process, and having a solid perspective on what is required to attain your network marketing goals, you will make success not only predictable, but inevitable.

> When I heard the learn'd astronomer,
> When the proofs, the figures, were ranged in columns before me,
> When I was shown the charts and diagrams, to add, divide, and
>   measure them,
> When I sitting heard the astronomer where he lectured with much
>   applause in the lecture-room,
> How soon unaccountable I became tired and sick,
> Till rising and gliding out I wander'd off by myself,
> In the mystical moist night-air, and from time to time,
> Look'd up in perfect silence at the stars.
> —Walt Whitman (1865)

Scotty Kufus began his journey in network marketing in high school at the age of 17. He was first invited to a friend's house under the pretense that a party was going on. Three people joined up that night out of 33, and Scotty began his pursuit to financial freedom.

Over the past 23 years, he has traveled all over the world building businesses in more than 20 countries and all told has had more than 500,000 people in his organizations. His groups have produced over $1 billion in sales. He has spoken in front of groups of 20 and more than 20,000.

He worked at Video Plus, the leading supplier to the MLM industry, for more than seven years helping to produce some of the most successful generic MLM videos of all time. He has helped consult on more than 50 different MLM projects in a sales and marketing capacity and has interviewed more than 2,000 people on camera. He has a thorough knowledge of operations, marketing, management, and the history of the industry.

Scotty launched his own MLM company in 1998 with two partners. Quantum Leap produced more than $13 million in retail sales in the first eight months. After selling that business to a publicly traded company in Dallas just 11 months after launch, he raised venture capital and started an Internet company to service seniors on the Internet. Within its first year Retired.com became the world's leading Internet company focused on the senior market. Within two years it attracted more than one million members.

He has become a part-time screenwriter in the past year, completing two scripts that are currently in different phases of production. The featured subject is about network marketing and the people involved. They are entitled "Get Rich Quick—The Movie," and "Living in Harmony."

Scott and Barbara Kufus and their 3-year-old son Aaron live in Olympia, Washington, where they enjoy fishing, hiking, and playing at the park.

Scott is currently the Director of Sales and Business Development at Oasis Life Sciences.

Oasis Life Sciences is the fastest growing natural products company in the world.

He can be reached at (360) 790-7100.

CHAPTER 36

What Are You Afraid Of?
Overcoming Challenges, Obstacles, and Fear

Ray Gebauer

The first step in overcoming challenges, obstacles, and problems is to accept the fact that they are inevitable. It is naive to expect that something great will be easy.

For most of my life, in my arrogance and shortsightedness, I'd quickly get irritated at problems, thinking, "It is not supposed to be this way" or "This should not be happening." Now, most of the time I remember that things are *not* supposed to be smooth and easy—except in my unrealistic expectation of how the world is supposed to be.

The second step in overcoming challenges and obstacles is to take a point of view that they are a necessary and useful part of life—that they are actually good and working ultimately to my benefit. Without challenges, obstacles, and problems, we would remain soft and weak, and it is only because of them that we can become strong, creative, resourceful, and victorious. Lifting small easy weights will not develop my muscles to be stronger or bigger; but the bigger the weights, the bigger the muscles. The bigger the problem, challenge, or obstacle, the bigger and stronger I become.

The third step in overcoming challenges and obstacles is to have a heartfelt appreciation for them as my teachers and my coach. I can choose to see them accompanied by an invisible purpose of making me better, wiser, and stronger, and for that I can be grateful. Rather than resenting, I can appreciate them. Just taking this point of view immediately empowers me. Plus, it positions me to get all the benefits from dealing with the inevitable challenges and obstacles that I have to deal with anyway (unless I succumb to resignation and give up).

But I will forfeit the not-so-obvious benefits if I go to my old way of thinking (paradigm) that "it is not supposed to be this way," that problems are bad and are simply deterrents to me getting what I want. Plus, there is little satisfaction in not having something to overcome, a battle to win, a giant to kill. The bigger the mountain, the greater the glory when I get to the top. There is a part of us that needs to conquer and overcome.

The other huge benefit of having a problem that is bigger than you is that you are then forced to enroll others into working with you in order to create a solution. You get a partner. You find a coach. You learn how to build a team that will be far more powerful than you ever would have been by yourself. You leverage your weakness and inadequacy to upgrade yourself from a small life of just you to a bigger life of working with others as a team.

If instead of appreciation I go into resistance and resentment, I create at least two new problems. The first one is stress—we already have too much of that! This can damage my health and shorten my life, as well as rob me of the enjoyment of life. The second problem I create by being in resistance and resentment is the very resistance that I think will combat the problem actually holds it more strongly in place. What I resist persists.

If instead I embrace the problem with appreciation, as an opportunity to grow and be creative, I will be empowered to deal with it more effectively and actually overcome it faster. Instead of unknowingly contributing to the problem's persistence by my resistance, I will also be creating a better me.

The fourth step in overcoming challenges and obstacles is discerning ahead of time what they are going to be. The most serious and dangerous ones are the ones we create ourselves. The external obstacles are actually easier to handle. The greatest enemy is within, which is fear or anticipation of pain.

WHAT ARE THEY THINKING OF ME?

Your biggest and most serious obstacle to manage is your concern (anticipation of pain) as to what people think about you. As you share yourself, your ideas, your perspective, your goals, and your dreams with others, some of them will not support what you are saying or doing. There is a possibility that you could even be put down or ridiculed. Two thousand years ago when the Apostle Peter gave his first presentation, some were amazed, some were confused, some mocked, and some believed. The pattern is still true today.

This concern (anticipation of emotional pain) of what people think of you manifests internally as anxiety. Externally, it shows up as procrastination or not taking any action at all. If you are not fully aware of this, you will be ambushed by it, and not really know what hit you! It knocks many out of the game, and they never return. To be forewarned is to be forearmed.

However, don't have an unrealistic expectation that you can eliminate this universal concern—I don't think we can totally, and we don't need to. The best most of us can do is manage it and not let it dominate us, and that is enough. Another challenge will be your disappointment that some people will not believe you when you share your thoughts about a dream or a project. It is almost inevitable that you will get discouraged, and that is okay as long as you are not surprised by it, and you don't stay stuck there. Just acknowledge it, feel it, and dismiss it as you move on.

Another obstacle will be your own unrealistic expectations. This can set you up for yielding to the temptation of quitting. Usually, things do not go as smoothly or as quickly as you expect. The answer is to not drop your expectations, because there is truth to the adage that you get what you expect. It just may take longer.

The way to be less affected is to not be emotionally attached to the results. You can be 100 percent committed to creating a certain result, but if it doesn't happen as you expected, it does not mean that you are not good enough or that you were wrong. If you are emotionally attached to your results, you will take your lack of results personally and judge yourself as inadequate, or even worse, as stupid or worthless. You will take yourself out of the game, and cheat yourself of the reward that comes from making a difference. And others will be hurt as well by your giving up and quitting. By default, you create a lose-lose instead of a win-win situation.

Set goals and have expectations that s t r e t c h you, but don't make up something negative about yourself (i.e., disempower yourself) if it doesn't happen as fast as you expect. If you don't get what you want, what does that mean? It means you didn't get what you want. Anything else beyond that is your interpretation, which you are then in danger of using against yourself to disempower yourself.

Another obstacle or challenge is the many distractions that dilute your focus and get you off track. You must be aware of this and get yourself back on track and refocused as soon as you realize you are off. Pay attention, adjust, and advance—correct and continue.

The greatest enemy of the best is the good. Do not settle for something that is good when there is something else that is better, or even the best. For example, doing paperwork, checking e-mail, reading, getting organized, and so on are all good and recommended activities. But if these good things displace more important things that actually move the action forward, then the better choice has lost out to the merely good, often as a way of avoidance.

Stay focused and remember this: The main thing is to keep the main thing the main thing! The main thing is the mission of making a difference.

Another major obstacle is one we create—our sense of inadequacy and lack of confidence. This can be the most disempowering and disabling challenge. It is the number one reason most people don't even get into the game and is the main reason most people will do far less than they could have.

The good thing about feeling inadequate is that it can keep us from falling into a worse trap of arrogance and pride. It keeps us from becoming too independent and overconfident. But that does not matter—you can still succeed. Just do not let your lack of confidence keep you out of the game. The best way to handle feeling inadequate is to accept it as normal, to commit to being teachable and getting trained, and then to play to win. Have a partner, be part of a team, get coaching, and ask for help and feedback.

REBUILDING CONFIDENCE AND BELIEF IN YOURSELF

There are three powerful ways to overcome lack of confidence. You harness the power of your past, your present, and your future by looking from a certain viewpoint. List 20 accomplishments or successes in your past, even if they seem small or unrelated to what you are doing now. If it even comes to mind as a possibility, it counts. Do it now.

1. _____   11. _____

2. _____   12. _____

3. _____   13. _____

4. _____   14. _____

5. _____   15. _____

6. _____   16. _____

7. _____   17. _____

8. _____   18. _____

9. _____   19. _____

10. _____   20. _____

This is a very effective way to empower yourself. When you remind yourself and remember what you have accomplished in the past, this gives you hard evidence that you are capable of achieving things. You create confidence for the current project, such as your business. This empowers you.

Now, circle the following qualities that you have now, in the present, even if they are not consistent or fully developed:

I love people; I'm positive and optimistic; I'm good at talking to people; I'm ambitious (vs. lazy); I'm self-motivated; I think big; I'm passionate; I'm goal oriented; I'm a hard worker; I'm self-disciplined; I'm determined; I'm honest; people like me; I'm trustworthy; I'm sincere; I have common sense; I'm committed to personal growth; I have integrity; I'm grateful; I have a powerful vision; I'm enthusiastic; I learn from my experiences; I'm resilient (I bounce back from disappointments); I'm cheerful; I have a pleasant smile; I'm confident; I'm teachable; I believe in myself; I believe in others; I have healthy self-esteem; I have humility (vs. arrogance); I'm creative; I'm loyal; I'm a good listener; I'm a clear thinker; I'm smart; I'm real and authentic; I'm focused; I have high ideals; I enjoy being around people; I enjoy helping others; I'm spiritual; I can explain things well; I have a lot of energy; I have good relational skills; people respect me; I'm organized; I work by my priorities; I'm intuitive; I'm a good reader; people take me seriously; I know how to have fun; I learn from my mistakes; I can influence people; I can solve problems; I handle stress and pressure; I'm on a mission; I'm a team player; I'm sensitive and empathetic; I respect others; I take responsibility; I care about people; I forgive others (vs. holding grudges); I'm willing to pay the price for success; I have a big dream; I see myself as a leader or becoming one; I am willing to change; I set a good example; I invest in myself; I see the big picture; I want to make an impact; I want to be somebody.

Count how many qualities you have marked. If you have more than a dozen, you have enough going for you to be successful. If you have considerably more than a dozen, you will just get there faster. The real question to ask yourself is not "Can I do this?" but rather "How long will it take?" A slow car can still get to the destination, and a fast car will get there sooner. But both can make it. It is just a matter of time—unless you give up.

The point of empowerment is this: When you see clearly what you have going for you right now, you create confidence for your life and for whatever you are working on. This gives you hard evidence that you have many things going for you to empower you to achieve. It is wise to review this often, even daily, because we so quickly forget.

Another powerful way to counter lack of confidence is to look at your current resources. Mark the ones that apply to you. You can probably even add a few:

All my current strengths, talents, and positive qualities; my future growth; my future experiences; people I know; people I have yet to meet; training and coaching; my health; books I'll read by successful people; tapes I'll hear by successful people; seminars and workshops I will attend; support from my partner, and if I ask, even from God; support and encouragement from family, friends, and anyone who believes in me.

Count how many resources you have marked. When you see clearly what resources you have working for you right now, you create confidence for your business.

Harness the power of the future by listing 10 future accomplishments to which you are committed:

1. _____   6. _____

2. _____   7. _____

3. _____   8. _____

4. _____   9. _____

5. _____   10. _____

Looking to the future (vision) in faith (rather than in fear) can increase your confidence dramatically and instantly, and make you unstoppable. For most people, the biggest challenge, what keeps their feet nailed to the floor, is fear. Your greatest threat to success is within you, not out there. It is fear that keeps people from even trying. It is fear that keeps people from taking risks or taking action. It is fear that causes people to quit and give up. So what do you do about fear?

The first thing is to understand exactly what fear is: Fear is simply an emotional response to anticipation of pain (physical or emotional). Most of the time this pain that we anticipate will never happen, and if it does, the fact is that you will be able to handle it anyway, if it does happen. You will not fall apart, you will not die, and you will become stronger for having handled it. Embrace this important truth: What does not kill me will make me stronger.

Fear is not a real thing—it is merely an emotion that we generate ourselves as a result of anticipating pain. Fear is an energy that we create that creates an illusion. And if you have the power to create fear, you have the power to un-create or delete the fear, especially when you realize what it really is (the absence of faith).

Second, it is imperative to understand and accept the principle that whatever you resist will persist! The more you resist fear and try to directly overcome it, the stronger it gets. The more attention you give it, the more it grows. It's like the alien Borg who assimilated other races, announcing in the *Star Trek* movies: "Resistance is futile!"

This is especially true of fear. If you resist fear, it has won, and you will be its prisoner. The way to deal with fear is, first of all, to accept it. Embrace it, and experience it fully. Just let it be there, and discover that fear cannot hurt or kill you. It is just there, like the sky is just there. In fact, fear is not even bad unless we allow it to limit and control us; then we rip ourselves off and live a small life. We can even miss our destiny.

Deal with fear by seeing it as a form of darkness. How do you rid yourself of darkness? Do you fight it? Resist it? Curse it? No, you just let it be there, and turn on the light. The light overcomes the darkness, as long as it is on.

Light is analogous to faith (belief). So, when you "turn on" the faith, the fear disappears, or at least the power of fear is diminished or disabled. So, how do you keep the faith (confidence) on? You create faith by harnessing the past, present, and future as described earlier. Also, since faith is contagious, if you deliberately associate with others who have greater faith than you, you catch it. It gets inside of you.

What do you do if fear (darkness) just keeps coming back? You just keep turning on the faith (light). Don't think that you need to get rid of fear. You don't need to. It can even be your teacher—just don't let it be your master. So, rather than taking a stand against fear (remember, what you resist will persist), take a stand of faith. Stand in confidence. Stand in belief. Associate with those who have strong faith, belief, and confidence. Attend meetings that build up your faith and confidence. The more people there are at a meeting, the more you will be impacted and empowered by being in the presence and energy of the collective faith of all the people. If you have access to conference calls, be on one a week. Talk with your partner every day, and if you don't have one, invite someone to be your partner for a certain project (e.g., business, marriage, being a good parent, achieving something, etc.). Listen to tapes every day that can build up your faith and confidence.

YOU HAVE THE POWER

Consider the source of fear and faith. Both have the same source: your imagination. You generate or create either one. We tend to think that fear or faith comes from the outside, but actually they do not even exist for you unless you create them. For example, consider the concept of fear of rejection. This is a huge obstacle for most people. This fear of rejection seems to be very real, and it paralyzes people. The real problem is not rejection. It is the fear of rejection. This fear of rejection is not something that happens to you—it is something you create. It is not real. Actually, all that is really happening is an anticipation of emotional pain, a belief that someone may judge you, which you interpret as painful.

Want to know how to overcome the fear of rejection? It's easy. Just face the truth. That's it. The truth is that there is very seldom any real rejection in life, even though there is a great deal of fear of rejection. Here's my evidence. If I'm sharing an idea with you and you tell me that you are not interested, or that you think that my idea is stupid or crazy, or whatever, I may tell myself that I was just rejected.

Here's what actually happened:

- I told you what I believed.
- You told me your opinion.
- Your opinion was different from my opinion.
- I concluded that you rejected me.

So where is the rejection? All that really happened was that there was a difference of opinion. There was no rejection! If you said to me, "Ray, I reject you," now I've been rejected. But how often does that happen? Unless I am told directly, "I reject you," there is no rejection going on. The only "rejection" is what I imagined. With this, I disempower myself.

Well, someone may say, maybe the guy just didn't say it, but he was actually rejecting me. So let's check it out. If I ask you, "Are you rejecting me?" you are going to say, "No, I'm not rejecting you—I'm just rejecting what you said." But it doesn't even matter whether or not I am rejected, because it is the fear that is the problem.

Even if you did reject me, so what? Am I damaged or injured? Will I die? But, if I can just see the truth that there is no rejection anyway, I have nothing to fear. I am anticipating pain that will never happen, like a little boy or girl who is anticipating the pain (getting hurt or killed) by the monster under the bed that does not even exist! The monster is merely an illusion (I recommend that you watch the movie *James and the Giant Peach*).

So, choose to create faith instead of creating fear. Like the angry mother said to her disobedient child—"I brought you into the world, and I can take you out!" Any fear that you have, you created. So, you can un-create it by creating faith that instantly displaces it. Choose an environment and people who are congruent with faith, who live by faith. We are all susceptible to fear, and we can all become people of great faith. It's your choice. Make the choice that best serves you and that empowers you to live life fully.

FEAR MAKES YOU SMALL, WHILE FAITH MAKES YOU BIG

More precisely, the fear that you create so disempowers you that you believe the lie that you are small and incapable, or that you will not survive some pain that might happen. Fear has a contracting effect, and creates a self-generated prison. Even though it is an illusion, at the time you do not realize that it is an illusion, because it seems so real. So you remain small and trapped. You feel like a helpless victim.

In contrast, faith and confidence empower you by helping you realize and accept the truth that you are, by design, powerful and capable, that you can survive any pain that might happen. Living by faith allows you to live life fully in an ever-expanding way. Isn't that what you want?

Whereas fear has a contracting effect and creates a prison, faith expands you and frees you to enjoy the freedom that you have. You are a powerful being with the power to create. God creates—He is the ultimate creator. Made in His image, you also create, automatically. You have been creating your entire life, even though most of the time we create unconsciously, thinking that things just happen, and that we are victims of circumstances.

So, as the creator you are, you can choose to create fear, or you can choose to create faith. So, since it is your choice, why not create faith that gives you life and freedom? Isn't that what you want? If you don't create faith, by default, you are probably creating fear that only rips you off, and ultimately it rips off others due to your inaction. Remember that just as darkness can exist only in the absence of light, fear can exist only in the absence of faith. Focus on creating faith, and fear will become a minor issue, as it is displaced by faith.

Think of what is at stake—your life, and the lives of others. Think of what it will cost you to allow yourself to be dominated by fear—the very fear you created. You can not afford to pay this ungodly price of living by fear! So, make a conscious choice and commitment to create faith and live by faith, and you will overcome all obstacles, challenges, and fear itself. You were created to be a winner—so be a winner! Think and live as one and you will create winning.

TRUE SELF VERSUS FALSE SELF (THE IMPOSTER)

The true you, the person you really are deep inside, is a person of faith and love, who believes in yourself and in the future. The real you is good, loving, and powerful. The real you lives in faith and confidence. The result of living from the true self is happiness and creating a big life with a big impact in the world.

The false you, the imposter, is the person who is run by fear. The false self is weak and insecure. The result is a small life with a small impact. The key to living life fully is to remember who you really are, underneath the artificial layers of fear that have been self-created: a person of love and faith. Be that person—be the real you! Who you are is important, and by living out of faith you make a meaningful difference! I challenge and invite you to live life fully, free of fear and full of faith!

Important Questions to Ask Myself

1. On a scale from 0 to 10, the number that best represents how well I handle my concern (fear) about how people may judge or disapprove of me is ____.

2. On the same scale, the number that best represents my level of confidence, based on the past, present, and future, is ____.

3. On the same scale, the number that best represents how well I handle the illusion of rejection is ____.

4. On the same scale, the number that best represents my commitment to create faith instead of creating fear is ____.

THE POWER OF ONE

One is a small number, but it can make a *big* difference. There is power in one. One makes a difference. The entire human population started with one. Oneness of mind (agreement and unity) makes a difference.

- How many points does it take to win or lose a game? One. What happens if you misdial a phone number by one digit? What happens if you are just one minute late for your plane departure? One makes a difference.

- The axis of the planet Earth is tilted at 23.45 degrees. A change of just one degree would be enough to flood large sections of the globe. One makes a difference.

- One apple seed properly planted and cared for can lead to an orchard of apple trees and thousands of apples, with multiple thousands of seeds. One spark in the wrong place can wipe out thousands of trees. One makes a difference.

- In 1923, one single vote gave one man the leadership role of his political party. It was the Nazi Party, and the man was Adolf Hitler. One makes a difference.

- For every historical event of significance there was one single person who made a difference (e.g., Abraham, Moses, Jesus, Martin Luther, Christopher Columbus, George Washington, Abraham Lincoln, and every mother!). One makes a difference.

- *You* are one person, and each person with whom you share the gift can make a profound difference, with a possibility of making a difference for hundreds and thousands of others. One makes a difference.

In the movie, *The Matrix*, Neo was "The One." In your life *you are the one! Be that one!*

Why?

Why are you doing this? Are you clear about it? If not, get clear now—just create it. Clarity is the absence of visual obstacles. Clarity is the natural state of things, and you must have it—otherwise you are driving in a fog. No one drives fast in a fog. So why are you doing this? What is at stake for you?

Why not?

Why not make your life into an adventure? Why not do all you can and help as many people as you can? Why not make a huge difference, and as a result make a huge income? Why not?

Why not you?

Others have done great things—why not you? Isn't it your turn now? Aren't you tired of waiting? Why not *you*? I say that you can create and do what you set your mind and heart to do! Probably not on your own, but as part of a team, combined with your commitment, you are unstoppable, and your success is inevitable!

Why not now?

The timing is not going to get any better. Now is the time, this is the year, and you are the one. Being in the right place at the right time is worthless and useless unless you take advantage of it. So why not now?

Just remember this: What is easy to do is also easy not to do!

Only those who dare to fail greatly can ever achieve greatly.

—Robert F. Kennedy

Most people go to their grave with their songs still unsung.

—Oliver Wendell Holmes

If you learn and live these priceless principles, you will be empowered and propelled into your better future, and you will be able to live life fully and find your treasure. Remember, not only is your future at stake, but people's very lives are at stake. And when you win, lots of others win, too! Who you are and what you do make a difference!

Ray Gebauer is a man on a mission to make a meaningful difference. His stated purpose in life is to empower people to live life fully, free of fear and full of faith. However, his first 19 years in this industry (1975–1993) were characterized more by frustration and failure, going through more than 40 network marketing companies without any success.

The past 10 years, he has developed an organization of more than 550,000 distributors with Mannatech. He went from living in a friend's unfinished basement, with no job, no income, and over $50,000 of debt in 1994, to earning more in a month than most people earn in a year. Instead of just chasing the dream, he is living it, and empowering others to believe in themselves and make their dreams a reality, too.

He is a popular international speaker and the author of the books *How to Cure and Prevent Any Disease* (www.CureanyDisease.com) and *The Treasure Map to Finding Your Treasure* (www.RayGebauer.net/treasuremap). For further articles on a range of subjects, visit his personal web site at www.RayGebauer.net.

CHAPTER 37

The Importance of High Self-Esteem to Your Network Marketing Success

Dr. Joe Rubino

In this book, the many brilliant contributors who were invited to share their wisdom were asked to write about any one aspect of building a business that they believed would most contribute to the success of our readers. We've learned from many of the most accomplished business builders, trainers, and leaders in network marketing about countless principles that are of critical importance in achieving top-level success in this profession. These insights range from how to craft a detailed business plan and set and accomplish goals to how to identify and enroll your prospects most effectively to how to best train and lead your growing organization—along with scores of other elements key to building a lasting networking dynasty. These are, of course, all extremely valuable distinctions whose mastery will dramatically support your business-building efforts. However, I'd guess that every leader who has contributed his or her wisdom to this book would agree that there is probably no other attribute more essential to your network marketing success and to the success of your organization than high self-esteem.

Lack of self-esteem is by far the most severe problem we face as a society today. Most children and adults suffer from feelings of diminished self-worth and manifest the results of these feelings in countless ways that adversely affect the quality of their lives and the lives of those around them. Low self-image is the source of disharmony among people everywhere. It is most often the underlying cause of scarcity, suffering, struggles of all kinds, conflicts, and even wars throughout the world. And, in network marketing, it is the biggest reason why people have little success to show for their efforts. It is at the core of why many fail to prospect and follow up others daily and are unable to powerfully enroll them into their opportunity. Low self-esteem is at the root of why so many can not handle the rejection, taking it personally when those they prospect are not interested, causing them to eventually give up and quit on their dreams to achieve a life-changing income. Low self-esteem most often leads to a return to a life of resignation, settling for a dimmed existence and trading in any possibility of a financially free life of choice, free of regrets.

Most of us did not receive the skillful parenting and early childhood experiences that were necessary to nurture our sense of self-worth. We failed to realize our inherent magnificence, and as a result, we often settled for less than we deserved. We may have worried about our futures, too often acted from the negative emotions of anger, sadness, or fear, or damaged our relationships with others. An inadequate self-image may have resulted in life pursuits that neither supported our happiness nor made the most of our special gifts.

As I see it, network marketing offers each of us the opportunity to take on the potentially life-changing gift of personal development, step into our personal magnificence, and offer this same blessing to those who decide to join us in this great profession. For this reason, I've chosen to write briefly about how we can each maximize our own levels of self-esteem and enhance our belief in our ability to bring about our ultimate success. At the same time, we have the power to champion all those we work in partnership with, sourcing their feelings of self-worth and thereby significantly increasing the probability that they will achieve success in this business as well.

Let's now examine some behaviors and attitudes that will contribute to a soaring self-image and to success in a network marketing business.

CREATE A VISION FOR YOUR LIFE THAT HONORS YOUR MOST IMPORTANT VALUES

Our minds can not tell the difference between actual reality and experiences that are vividly imagined. This is the reason that we laugh, cry, or scream at funny, sad, or scary movies. We get what we clearly envision and expect. We can take advantage of this ability to tap into what we want and expect to experience through our network marketing businesses by creating a vivid, written vision that inspires and empowers us and others to do what it takes to realize the vision.

I invite you to give up your right to invalidate yourself by keeping any of your negative expectations in place. Instead, create a vision that is filled with positive expectations for what your life will be like as a result of your network marketing success. This vision must honor your most important values. Perhaps these might include any of the following: freedom, adventure, belonging, creativity, contribution, love, excitement, happiness, peace, joy, recognition, security, and inspiration, just to name a few.

Include in your vision the answers to these questions:

- What will you be known for, what qualities will you embody, and what values will you honor as you live your life and work your business?
- What sort of activities will you typically do? What will a customary day at work look like? How will you spend your free time? What passions and hobbies will you pursue?
- What will you have as a result of who you are being and because of your successful efforts? Where will you live and with whom? Describe in detail your house, cars, and all toys and material possessions with which you'll surround yourself.
- Who are the people and special causes to which you'll contribute? How will you impact the lives of your family, friends, and network marketing partners? Remember, any vision that is about only you will not inspire others to join you in its accomplishment or inspire them to create visions of their own.
- Picture yourself building your business successfully. What will your organization look like? How will others see you? For what accomplishments will you be recognized? Picture yourself interacting with others in a way that reflects your high self-esteem and the rich relationships you have established.

Write out your vision in first person, present tense to describe every aspect of your life and business. Say, "I am experiencing material abundance and rich, rewarding friendships" rather than "I will experience" or "I hope to experience." Remember, we get what we expect. So, if you expect that you will (but are not now) experiencing or hope to achieve (but are not now achieving), your mind will manifest a reality consistent with these images of lacking what you want.

Read your vision at least twice daily. After doing so for at least 30 days, your subconscious will begin to create a physical and mental state consistent with what is needed to manifest your vision.

CREATE AN ACTION PLAN CONSISTENT WITH YOUR VISION

Network marketing has the potential to provide each of us with the level of income that can free us up to pursue our passions and honor our most critical values. Ask yourself, how much income will it take for me to realize all aspects of my vision? Who will I need to be and what will I need to do to make my vision come to pass?

Determine how many leaders you will need to develop and duplicate to achieve the income level you desire. From there, determine what your success ratios are: how many prospects will you need to speak with in order to identify and develop this many leaders? For example, if you know that you'll typically need to speak with 100 prospects to identify one do-whatever-it-takes leader, and your goal is to identify one new leader each month, you may need to speak with five prospects daily, five days per week in order to hit your desired number.

As part of your plan, you'll also need to determine where and how you'll find your prospects, what you'll say and give them, and to whom and how you'll introduce them as a next step. For a more detailed explanation involving all aspects of how to create an effective action plan, see my book, *The 7-Step System to Building a $1,000,000 Network Marketing Dynasty.*

MANAGE NEGATIVE SELF-TALK AND ACT FROM YOUR NEWLY INVENTED DECLARATION OF WHO YOU ARE

We all experience that nasty, negative, doubting voice of our negative self-talker whispering in our ear from time to time. The trouble begins when we forget that the voice is not speaking the truth and buy into those lies. This negative self-talk serves only to keep us from risking, preferring that we play small instead, in an effort to protect us from harm—otherwise known as rejection and what we interpret as failure. I suggest that you decide today to live by two new rules designed to support your belief in yourself and in your ultimate success as a network marketing leader. They are:

1. Give up your right to invalidate yourself or buy into any negative opinions you or others may have about you.
2. Decide today to act from a declaration of who you say you are. No evidence for this new, empowering declaration is required. In fact, you'll now be creating new positive evidence as you go.

Take all of the qualities you have decided to manifest in your life and business and craft a new declaration that speaks to who you are now deciding to be as a powerful leader. Use this as a statement from which to live. State your empowered declaration, like your vision, in the first person, present tense. For example, you might say, "I am a confident, charismatic, positive-minded leader committed to contributing to the lives of all I touch. I powerfully share the gift of my networking opportunity with a positive belief in its value to impact others' lives as well as my own."

Whenever you notice that you have fallen back into any old habits of questioning your ability or doubting your future success, simply remind yourself that this is not who you are. Give yourself a break; decide again to believe in yourself and step into a confident posture that will support your business success.

AFFIRM YOUR STRENGTHS AND ACKNOWLEDGE YOURSELF DAILY

We all have strengths and gifts that make us uniquely special and magnificent in our own ways. At times, we all temporarily lose belief in ourselves and in our ability to succeed in our businesses by impacting others' lives with our products and opportunity. We forget to focus on the awesome gift we can be in providing our opportunity to others and instead pay too much attention to our own fears and petty concerns. We become adept at recognizing all our weaknesses and identifying all the reasons why we fear we will not be successful in our quest to realize our dreams.

Instead of focusing on these challenges, get into the habit of recognizing the little things you do well. Catch yourself doing something right and acknowledge yourself for it. Ask yourself, "What did I do well today? What can I commend myself for this morning?" By looking for excuses to pat yourself on the back, you'll start to become more aware of all the things for which you really should be commended. Write yourself a daily brief paragraph outlining these worthy attributes and accomplishments. This can be as simple as congratulating yourself for speaking to a prospect whom you may not have ordinarily approached or asking questions to get to know someone better and build rapport.

Our conscious minds can entertain only one thought at a time. As the gatekeepers to our minds, it's up to us whether we allow that present thought to be a negative, fearful, or disempowering one, or a positive, affirming belief instead. We have the ability to manage our thoughts moment by moment. The more we get into the habit of substituting positive instead of negative thoughts, the easier this process will become.

Write out a series of positive affirmations that speak directly to any negative or disempowering beliefs that would influence your network marketing outcome. Again, write your affirmations out in first person, present tense. Write such statements as:

- I am a powerful enroller, able to contribute the gift of personal and financial freedom to others.
- I am a good listener, aware of what's important to others and missing in their lives.
- People like me, trust me, and want to learn about the benefits I share.
- I make friends easily.
- I act consistently and persistently, performing the massive action required to bring about my great success.
- I inspire others to make their lives work optimally because of my courage in sharing our opportunity.

Keep these affirmations by your phone, on your nightstand, on your mirror, in your car, and everywhere else to remind you of your power as you go about your day. For those wishing to take advantage of the power of subliminal and audible technology that was developed by Dr. Eldon Taylor, the world's foremost expert on the topic of impacting the subconscious through subliminal affirmations, I've produced a series of affirmations tapes containing 108 consciousness-impacting affirmations for network marketers called "Secrets of Building a Million-Dollar Network Marketing Organization, Secret #1: Self-Motivation."

TAKE ON A PERSONAL DEVELOPMENT PROGRAM

One of the best ways I know to take the rejection out of building a network marketing business while adding fun and fulfillment is to create a structure to develop those personal and leadership qualities you see as enhancing your life and business.

This can be as simple as selecting a quality to work on in your prospecting conversations and then rating yourself (1 to 10) as to how well you did after each conversation. When I began my business, due to excessive nervousness and a fear of being judged and rejected, I had a tendency to dump too much information on my prospects. I soon realized that just sharing a lot of details about my company, products, and income opportunity was not very effective in motivating them to join our team. Instead, I decided to work on the qualities of developing rapport, listening to what was important to my prospects or missing in their lives, and creating rich value for them in my conversations. I took on each of these areas of development for 30 to 60 days before adding another area. Eventually these intentions became habits and my enrollment success numbers shot up dramatically.

Another means of identifying what might be missing from your conversations to make them more effective is by taping your calls. Using an inexpensive cassette recorder and phone device, you can easily record your conversations. By listening to these later, you will often discover areas to improve upon to make your conversations more powerful. You can also ask your success-line partners to listen and give you suggestions regarding how to improve your calls.

Another powerful way to take on a personal development structure to enhance your confidence and effectiveness would be to follow along with a series such as my books, *The Power to Succeed, Book I: 30 Principles for Maximizing Your Personal Effectiveness* and *The Power to Succeed, Book II: More Principles for Powerful Living*. These books are designed as a yearlong self-study course to support network marketers and others to gain in confidence, enhance their self-image, and make the most of their ability to impact others with integrity.

CHAMPION YOUR TEAM

Our network marketing businesses not only provide us with an exciting opportunity to reinvent who we are as a possibility for achieving happy, fulfilling lives for ourselves but also offer us the chance to give this same gift to our partners. Our financial success in this business will be directly related to how effective we have been in championing our business partners (downline) to step into their self-confident personal power as they go about their business-building activities and support their leaders to do the same.

After experiencing 14 dynamic, life-changing years in the network marketing profession, transforming myself from a shy dentist who "couldn't lead three people in silent prayer" to a self-declared leader with a vision to impact the lives of 20 million people, I am convinced that anyone with a sincere desire can take on a courageous personal reinvention program to support their happiness, personal power, and success. Our networking businesses will grow in direct proportion to both our personal growth (as we increase our attractiveness as a business partner to others) and the level of massive, consistent action we engage in as we build our teams. As we take on more confidence and strengthen our belief in our ability to impact others' lives with our income opportunity, our prospects will become more attracted to us as they recognize our confident ability to support them in attaining their dreams.

Dr. Joe Rubino is an internationally acclaimed network marketing and personal development trainer, life-changing success coach, and best-selling author of eight books and two tape sets on topics ranging from how to achieve network marketing success, and personal and leadership development to restoring self-esteem and maximizing business productivity. An acclaimed speaker and course leader, he is known as a top network marketing trainer, and for his work in leadership development, listening and communication skills, life and business coaching, and team building. He can be reached at DrJRubino@email.com or by calling (888) 821-3135. Visit www.CenterforPersonalReinvention.com to sign up for his free newsletter or contact him to learn more about establishing a coaching relationship.

RECOMMENDEd RESOURCES

OTHER BOOKS BY DR. JOE RUBINO

1. *The 7-Step System to Building a $1,000,000 Network Marketing Dynasty: How to Achieve Financial Independence through Network Marketing*

This book is perhaps the most comprehensive step-by-step guide ever written on how to build a lasting, multimillion-dollar organization. *Success* magazine called master instructor, Dr. Joe Rubino a Millionaire Maker in its landmark "We Create Millionaires" cover story because of his ability to pass along to others the power to achieve top-level success. Now you can learn exactly how Dr. Joe built his own dynasty so that you can, too. Follow the seven detailed steps-to-success blueprint and join the ranks of network marketing's top income earners.

> Step 1: Visioning—Establish Your Reasons for Joining and Create a Compelling Vision
>
> Step 2: Planning—Create a Master Plan That Will Support You to Realize Your Vision
>
> Step 3: Prospecting—Effective Prospecting: Who, Where, and How and How Many?
>
> Step 4: Enrolling—The Power to Enroll: How to Become an Enrollment Machine
>
> Step 5: Training—Train like a Master Instructor: Structures for Successful Partnerships
>
> Step 6: Personal Development—Grow As Fast as Your Organization Does: Create Structures for Personal Excellence
>
> Step 7: Stepping Into Leadership—The Keys to Developing Other Self-Motivated Leaders

2. *Secrets of Building a Million-Dollar Network Marketing Organization from a Guy Who's Been There Done That and Shows You How You Can Do It, Too*

Learn the keys to success in building your network marketing business.

With this book you will:

- Get the six keys that unlock the door to success in network marketing.
- Learn how to build your business free from doubt and fear.
- Discover how the way you listen has limited your success.
- Accomplish your goals in record time by shifting your listening.
- Use the Zen of Prospecting to draw people to you like a magnet.
- Build rapport and find your prospect's hot buttons instantly.
- Pick the perfect prospecting approach for you.
- Turn any prospect's objection into the very reason they join.
- Identify your most productive prospecting sources.
- Win the numbers game of network marketing.
- Develop a step-by-step business plan that ensures your future.
- Design a Single Daily Action that increases your income 10 times.
- Rate yourself as a top sponsor and business partner.
- Create a passionate vision that guarantees your success.
- And more!

3. *The Magic Lantern: A Fable about Leadership, Personal Excellence and Empowerment*

Set in the magical world of Center Earth, inhabited by dwarves, elves, goblins, and wizards, *The Magic Lantern* is a tale of personal development that teaches the keys to success and happiness. This fable examines what it means to take on true leadership while learning to become maximally effective with everyone we meet.

Renowned personal development trainer, coach, and veteran author Dr. Joe Rubino tells the story of a group of dwarves and their young leader who go off in search of the secrets to a life that works, a life filled with harmony and endless possibilities and devoid of the regrets and upsets that characterize most people's existence. With a mission to restore peace and harmony to their village in turmoil, the characters overcome the many challenges they encounter along their eventful journey. Through self-discovery, they develop the principles necessary to be the best that they can be as they step into leadership and lives of contribution to others.

The Magic Lantern teaches us:

- The power of forgiveness.
- The meaning of responsibility and commitment.

- What leadership is really all about.
- The magic of belief and positive expectation.
- The value of listening as an art.
- The secret to mastering one's emotions and actions.
- And much more.

The tale combines the spellbinding storytelling reminiscent of J. R. R. Tolkien's *The Hobbit* with the personal development tools of the great masters.

4. *The Legend of the Light-Bearers: A Fable about Personal Reinvention and Global Transformation*

Is it ever too late for a person to take on personal reinvention and transform his or her life? Can our planet right itself and reverse centuries of struggle, hatred, and warfare? Are love, peace, and harmony achievable possibilities for the world's people? *The Legend of the Light-Bearers* is a tale about vision, courage, and commitment, set in the magical world of Center Earth. In this much-anticipated prequel to Dr. Joe Rubino's internationally best-selling book, *The Magic Lantern: A Fable about Leadership, Personal Excellence and Empowerment*, the process of personal and global transformation is explored within the guise of an enchanting fable. As the action unfolds in the world following the great Earth Changes, this personal development parable explores the nature of hatred and resignation, the secrets to transformation, and the power of anger and the means for overcoming it and replacing it with love. It shows what can happen when people live values-based lives and are guided by their life purposes instead of their destructive moods and their need to dominate others. If ever our world needed a road map to peace and cooperation and our people needed a guide to personal empowerment and happiness, they do now . . . and this is the book.

5. *10 Weeks to Network Marketing Success: The Secrets to Launching Your Very Own Million-Dollar Organization in a 10-Week Business-Building and Personal-Development Self-Study Course*

Learn the business-building and personal-development secrets that will put you squarely on the path to network marketing success. *10 Weeks to Network Marketing Success* is a powerful course that will grow your business with velocity and change your life!

With this course, you will:

- Learn exactly how to set up a powerful 10-week action plan that will propel your business growth.
- Learn how to prospect in your most productive niche markets.

- Discover your most effective pathways to success.
- Learn how to persuasively influence your prospects by listening to contribute value.
- Build your business rapidly by making powerful requests.
- Discover the secret to acting from your commitments.
- Create a powerful life-changing structure for personal development.
- See the growth that comes from evaluating your progress on a regular basis.
- Learn how listening in a new and powerful way will skyrocket your business.
- Uncover the secret to accepting complete responsibility for your business.
- Learn how to transform problems into breakthroughs.
- Develop the charisma that allows you to instantly connect with others on a heart-to-heart level.
- Identify the secrets to stepping into leadership and being the source of your success.
- And much more!

The *10 Weeks to Network Marketing Success* program contains 10 weekly exercises on 4 CDs or 6 audio cassettes plus a 37-page workbook.

6. *Restore Your Magnificence: A Life-Changing Guide to Reclaiming Your Self-Esteem*

> *"I have personally used this program's principles to support thousands of people to be self-confident, happy and prosperous. You owe it to yourself to read this book."*

Dr. Tom Ventullo
President, The Center for Personal Reinvention

With this book YOU will:

- Uncover the source of your lack of self-esteem.
- Complete the past and stop the downward spiral of self-sabotage.
- Replace negative messages with new core beliefs that support your happiness and excellence.

- See how you can be strong and authentic. Use your vulnerability as a source of power.
- Design a new self-image that supports your magnificence.
- Realize the power of forgiveness.
- Discover the secret to an upset-free life.
- Re-establish your worth and reinvent yourself to be your best.
- Create a vision of a life of no regrets.

7. *Secrets of Building a Million-Dollar Network Marketing Organization: SECRET #1—SELF MOTIVATION*

Utilize The Latest in *Whole Brain Inner Talk*™ Technology to take a trip to a deeper dimension of power within yourself and tap into The Most Important Secret To Success In Network Marketing . . . SELF-MOTIVATION!

Thought Modification Made Easy Audio Cassette Tape Series

Put to work for you the powerful combination of the latest in patented and scientifically proven audible and subliminal brain wave technology developed by Dr. Eldon Taylor, the world's foremost expert on offsetting negative information by inputting positive messages directly into the subconscious. This safe and highly effective proven technology has been independently researched at leading institutions such as Stanford University. For the first time ever, this technology has been combined with the 124 thought-altering positive self-talk affirmations developed by Dr. Joe Rubino, one of North America's foremost business trainers and coaches—the man *Success* magazine called a "Millionaire Maker." The result is a remarkable audio cassette tape series that will give you the power to alter any limiting thoughts . . . The power to maximize your personal effectiveness to rapidly build your MLM business on purpose and with confidence.

This revolutionary two tape set consists of one Positive Self-Talk Program, which combines audible affirmations with the shadowed subliminal Inner Talk® affirmations, and one Ozo self motivation program. Use the first tape at least once a day playing it in the background in your car or while you work or play. Use the second tape with headphones when you can take 20 minutes and close your eyes. The special frequencies will entrain brain wave activity and produce an optimal state for learning and conditioning new patterns, energizing you into action and filling your being with total confidence. It's like hiring Dr. Joe Rubino as your personal success coach!

NETWORK MARKETING RESOURCES

1. The Center for Personal Reinvention, www.CenterForPersonal Reinvention.com. Books, CDs, coaching, and courses by Dr. Joe Rubino and Dr. Tom Ventullo to champion your network-marketing business and your life. Free newsletter, articles, and success tips.

2. Mach2.org, www.mach2.org. Richard Brooke is one of network marketing's premier visionaries. This site contains articles and wisdom to build your business on a solid foundation.

3. *Networking Times*, www.NetworkingTimes.com. The premier publication in the network-marketing industry.

4. The Kick Start Guy, *Entrepreneur* magazine's Romanus Walter, www.kickstartguy.com, sound business and work at home advice.

5. Fortune Now, www.FortuneNow.com. Tom "Big Al" Schreiter's web site. Tom is one of the funniest speakers and an overall great guy with lots of knowledge about how to succeed in MLM.

6. PassionFire International, Industry Trainer, www.Passionfire.com. Doug Firebaugh's site, containing great resources to support business-building success.

7. Randy Gage, www.MLMTrainingCentral.com. Randy is one of the foremost trainers in the MLM industry. Great information.

8. *Network Marketing Business Journal*, www.NMBJ.com. A news publication owned by Keith Laggos. Timely news and training articles about the network marketing industry.

9. Brilliant Exchange, www.BrilliantExchange.com. Tim Sales of *Brilliant Compensation* fame's training and resource site.

10. MLM University, www.MLMU.com. Hilton Johnson's site. Articles, tools, and trainings by a top sales trainer.

11. Cutting Edge Media, www.MLMleadcenter.com. Lead generation, offering free introductory leads to test.

12. Online Automation, www.ResponsiveLeads.net. Lead generation.

13. *Home Business Magazine*, www.HomeBusinessMag.com. Working from home articles and resources.

14. No BS Marketing Help, www.nobsmarketinghelp.com. Lots of information about how to market on the Internet.

15. WTPowers, The most powerful Automated Prospecting, Lead Generation, Follow-Up & Training System available on the Internet. See what thousands of networkers in over 60 countries are raving

about! No-risk 30 days FREE trial (nominal $9.95 set up fee required) by visiting this link: www.wtpowers.com/bonus.

16. The NetMillionaire Training System. Entertain your way to success with this fun and exciting Network Marketing Board Game designed to train, sponsor, inspire and empower Network Marketers to achieve their dreams. For discounts and free offers, visit: http://www.netmillionairetraining.com/participant_bonus/.

17. Dr. Eldon Taylor's www.InnerTalk.com. Harness the power of the subconscious mind.

18. "Prospecting on the Internet with Instant Messaging" from Max Steingart's best-selling Internet course "Shaking Hands on the Internet," www.successway.com/bonus.

19. Art Jonak's www.MLMplayers.com. A great info-rich site featuring successful network marketers' insights.

20. Visual Talk Pro's Emails that sizzle plus Online Meeting Rooms. www.buildandshare.com/bonus.

21. Len Clements' "MarketWave—a full time MLM research and analysis firm serving the network marketing profession for over 15 years. If you want real facts about this industry, go to MarketWaveInc.com."

22. The Greatest Networker, www.GreatestNetworker.com. A great generic resource spearheaded by John Milton Fogg to support network-marketing success. Also, by Fogg, *The Network Marketing Magazine*, http://TheNetworkMarketingMagazine.com, an informative educational journal all about what it takes to be successful in network marketing.

Index

*The Ultimate Guide to Network Marketing:
37 Top Network Marketing Income-Earners
Share Their Most Preciously Guarded
Secrets to Building Extreme Wealth*

From the Best-selling Author of

*The 7-Step System to Building a
$1,000,000 Network Marketing Dynasty:
How to Achieve Financial Independence
through Network Marketing*

and

*Secrets of Building a Million-Dollar
Network Marketing Organization
from a Guy Who's Been There Done That
and Shows You How You Can Do It, Too*

Dr. Joe Rubino